International Kierkegaard
Commentary

International Kierkegaard
Commentary:
Two Ages

edited by
Robert L. Perkins

MERCER

IKC 14: Two Ages
Copyright ©1984 by
Mercer University Press
Macon GA 31207
All rights reserved

All books published by Mercer University Press are produced
on acid-free paper that exceeds the minimum standards set by
the National Historical Publications and Records Commission.

Library of Congress Cataloging in Publication Data

Main entry under title:

International Kierkegaard commentary.

    Includes bibliographical references and index.

    Contents: Passion, reflection, and particularity in Two ages/John E. Elrod—
Towards apocalypse/Michael Plekon—Kierkegaard's Two ages, an immediate
state on the way to religious life/Lee Barrett—[etc.]

    1. Kierkegaard, Søren, 1813-1855. Literair anmeldelse—Addresses, essays,
lectures. I. Perkins, Robert L., 1930-.

PT8131.G9T63434   1984   839.8'136   83-25106

ISBN 0-86554-081-0 (alk. paper)

Contents

Acknowledgements

All the contributors to this volume would desire to make acknowledgements, but it is a privilege reserved to the editor. Those whom the contributors would have named will be satisfied to have served their friends and colleagues. I am sure each would name persons who have the same functions as my friends and colleagues.

Here, every academic office of the University, from the President's Office to the Department has lent strong administrative support. Frederick P. Whiddon, President; Ralph Jones, Assistant to the President; James R. Bobo, Jr., Vice President for Academic Affairs; George R. Wilson, Jr., Assistant to the Vice President; Anthony C. Colson, Dean of the College of Arts and Sciences; Jeral R. Williams, Associate Dean; W. W. Kaempfer, former Dean of the College of Arts and Sciences; and H. W. Baldwin, Chairman of the Department of Philosophy, have to be mentioned.

This volume was also supported by a grant from the University of South Alabama Research Committee, Sheldon F. Gottlieb, Chairman.

Support staff in the Computer Center, Andy Lightbourne; in the Dean's Office, June Williams and Debbie White; in the Philosophy Department, Veronica Powell and Patti Gaubatz, have not just done their jobs, but have smoothed the way to this publication in innumerable ways with extra patience, understanding and labor.

The Advisory Board and the Volume Consultants read the volume, and their recommendations considerably improve it. The International Advisory Board has offered valuable advice on a number of matters.

The interest of Mercer University Press, Director Watson E. Mills, and Editor-in-Chief Edd Rowell, is appreciated.

Princeton University Press granted permission to quote from *Two Ages* and other copyrighted materials.

Last, but hardly least, the several contributors and the editor thank their families for the lost evenings and other scattered hours.

Robert L. Perkins

Sigla

CI   *The Concept of Irony*, tr. Lee Capel. New York: Harper and Row, 1966; Bloomington: Indiana University Press, 1968. (*Om Begrebet Ironi*, by S. A. Kierkegaard, 1841.)

EO   *Either/Or* I, tr. David F. Swenson and Lillian Marvin Swenson; II, tr. Walter Lowrie; 2nd ed. rev. Howard A. Johnson. Princeton: Princeton University Press, 1971. (*Enten-Eller* I-II, ed. Victor Eremita, 1843.)

JC   *Johannes Climacus or De omnibus dubitandum est*, and *A Sermon*, tr. T. H. Croxall. London: Adam and Charles Black, 1958. ("Johannes Climacus eller *De omnibus dubitandum est*," written 1842-1843, unpubl., *Papirer* IV B 1: "*Demis-Prædiken*", 1844, unpubl., *Papirer* IV C 1.)

ED   *Edifying Discourses* I-IV, tr. David F. Swenson and Lillian Marvin Swenson. Minneapolis: Augsburg Publishing House, 1943-1946. (*Opbyggelige Taler*, by S. Kierkegaard, 1843, 1844.)

FT   *Fear and Trembling* (with *The Sickness unto Death*), tr. Walter Lowrie. Princeton: Princeton University Press, 1968. (*Frygt og Bæven*, by Johannes De Silentio, 1843.)

R   *Repetition*, tr. Walter Lowrie. Princeton: Princeton University Press, 1941. (*Gjentagelsen*, by Constantin Constantius, 1843.)

PF   *Philosophical Fragments*, tr. David Swenson, 2nd ed. rev. Howard Hong. Princeton: Princeton University Press, 1980. (*Philosophiske Smuler*, by Johannes Climacus, ed. S. Kierkegaard, 1844.)

CA   *The Concept of Anxiety*, tr. Reidar Thomte in collaboration with Albert B. Anderson. Princeton: Princeton University Press, 1980. (*Begrebet Angest*, by Vigilius Haufniensis, ed. S. Kierkegaard, 1844.)

TCS   *Three Discourses on Imagined Occasions*, [Thoughts on Crucial Situations in Human Life], tr. David F. Swenson, ed. Lillian Marvin Swenson. Minneapolis: Augsburg Publishing House, 1941. (*Tre Taler vedtænkte Leiligheder*, by S. Kierkegaard, 1845.)

SLW   *Stages on Life's Way*, tr. Walter Lowrie. Princeton: Princeton University Press, 1940. (*Stadier paa Livets Vej*, ed. Hilarius Bogbinder, 1845.)

CUP   *Concluding Unscientific Postscript*, tr. David F. Swenson and Walter Lowrie. Princeton: Princeton University Press for the American-Scandinavian Foundation, 1941. (*Afsluttende uvidenskabelig Efterskrift*, by Johannes Climacus, ed. S. Kierkegaard, 1846.)

TA   *Two Ages: the Age of Revolution and the Present Age. A Literary Review*, tr. Howard V. and Edna H. Hong. Princeton: Princeton University Press, 1978. (*En literair Anmeldelse. To Tidsaldre*, by S. Kierkegaard, 1846.)

OAR   *On Authority and Revelation, The Book on Adler*, tr. Walter Lowrie. Princeton: Princeton University Press, 1955. ("Bogen om Adler," written 1846-1847, unpubl., *Papirer* VII 2 B 235; VIII 2 B 1-27.)

PH   *Edifying Discourses in Various Spirits*. (*Opbyggelige Taler i forskjellig Aand*, by S. Kierkegaard, 1847.) Part One, *Purity of Heart* ["En Leiligheds-Tale"], tr. Douglas Steere. New York: Harper, 2nd ed., 1948.

GS   Part Three and Part Two, *The Gospel of Suffering and The Lilies of the Field* ["Lidelsernes Evangelium" and "Lilierne paa Marken og Himlens Fugle"], tr. David F. Swenson and Lillian Marvin Swenson. Minneapolis: Augsburg Publishing House, 1948.

WL   *Works of Love*, tr. Howard and Edna Hong. New York: Harper and Row, 1962. (*Kjerlighedens Gjerninger*, by S. Kierkegaard, 1847.)

C   *The Crisis [and a Crisis] in the Life of an Actress*, tr. Stephen Crites. New York: Harper and Row, 1967. (*Krisen og en Krise i en Skuespillerindes Liv*, by Inter et Inter. *Fædrelandet*, 188-91, July 24-27, 1848.)

CD *Christian Discourses*, including "The Lily of the Field and the Bird of the Air" and "Three Discourses at the Communion on Fridays," tr. Walter Lowrie. London and New York: Oxford University Press, 1940. (*Christelige Taler*, by S. Kierkegaard, 1848; "Lilien paa Marken og Fuglen under Himlen," Kierkegaard, 1849; "Tre Taler ved Altergangen om Fredagen," by S. Kierkegaard, 1849.)

SUD *The Sickness unto Death*, tr. Howard V. and Edna Hong. Princeton: Princeton University Press, 1980. (*Sygdommen til Doden*, by Anti-Climacus, ed. S. Kierkegaard, 1849.)

TC *Training in Christianity*, including "The Woman Who was a Sinner," tr. Walter Lowrie. London and New York: Oxford University Press, 1941; repr. Princeton: Princeton University Press, 1944. (*Indøvelse i Christendom*, by Anti-Climacus, ed. S. Kierkegaard, 1850; *en opbyggelig Tale*, by S. Kierkegaard, 1850.)

AN *Armed Neutrality and An Open Letter*, tr. Howard V. Hong and Edna H. Hong. Bloomington and London: Indiana University Press, 1968. (*Den bevæbnede Neutralitet*, written 1848-1849, publ. 1965; "Foranledigt ved en Yttring af Dr. Rudelbach mig betræffende," *Fædrelandet* no. 26, January 31, 1851.)

PV *The Point of View for My Work as an Author*, including the appendix "The Single Individual, Two 'Notes,' Concerning My Work as an Author" and "On My Work as an Author," tr. Walter Lowrie. London and New York: Oxford University Press, 1939. (*Synspunktet for min Forfatter-Virksomhed*, by S. Kierkegaard, posthumously published 1859; *Om min Forfatter-Virksomhed*, by S. Kierkegaard, 1851.)

FSE *For Self-Examination*, tr. Edna and Howard Hong. Minneapolis: Augsburg Publishing House, 1940. (*Til Selvprøvelse*, by S. Kierkegaard, 1851.)

JFY *Judge for Yourselves!*, including "For Self-Examination, Two Discourses at the Communion on Fridays," and "The Unchangeableness of God" (tr. David Swenson), tr. Walter Lowrie. Princeton: Princeton University Press, 1944. (*Dommer Selv!* by S. Kierkegaard, 1852; *To Taler ved Altergangen om Fredagen*, by S. Kierkegaard, 1851; *Guds uforanderlighed*, by S. Kierkegaard, 1855.)

KAUC *Kierkegaard's Attack upon "Christendom," 1854-1855*, tr. Walter Lowrie. Princeton: Princeton University Press, 1944. *Bladartikler* I-XXI, by S. Kierkegaard, *Fædrelandet*, 1854-1855; *Dette skal siges; saa være det da sagt*, by S. Kierkegaard, 1855; *Øieblikket*, by S. Kierkegaard 1-9, 1855; 10, 1905; *Hvad Christus dømmer om officiel Christendom*, by S. Kierkegaard, 1855.

JSK *The Journals of Søren Kierkegaard*, tr. Alexander Dru. London and New York: Oxford University Press, 1938. (From *Søren Kierkegaards Papirer*, I-XI 1 in 18 volumes, 1909-1936.)

LY *The Last years*, tr. Ronald C. Smith. New York: Harper and Row, 1965. (From *Papirer* XI 1-XI 2, 1936-1948.)

JP *Søren Kierkegaard's Journals and Papers*, tr. Howard V. Hong and Edna H. Hong, assisted by Gregor Malantschuk. Bloomington and London: Indiana University Press, I, 1967; II, 1970; III-IV, 1975; V-VIII. (From *Papirer* I-XI 3 and XII-XIII, 2nd ed., and *Breve og Akstykker vedrørende Søren Kierkegaard*, ed. Niels Thulstrup, I-II, 1953-1954.)

LD *Letters and Documents*, tr. by Hendrik Rosenmeier. Princeton: Princeton University Press, 1978.

TCA *The Corsair Affair*, tr. Howard V. and Edna H. Hong. Princeton: Princeton University Press, 1982.

Introduction

Partly because everyone knows it,
no one wants to be made aware of it.

—Heiberg

Myths and Misunderstandings about
Kierkegaard's Concepts of the Individual and Society

With the publication of this volume of essays on Kierkegaard's *Two Ages* a myth should die. Whether the myth will die or not will depend upon the intellectual integrity of the academy, the professors, of whom Kierkegaard has a very low opinion.

The myth is to the effect that Kierkegaard presents his concept of the individual in a social and political vacuum, that Kierkegaardian inwardness and subjectivity is so pervasive and unqualified that for the Kierkegaardian individual (hiin Enkelte) there is no social and historical context, that society and history stop and cease to have effect on the individual who chooses himself before God. Consequently, since the individual is stripped of his social relations, is a bare particular, the Kierkegaardian analysis of the individual must fail. Such a view can be justified by a select reading of Kierkegaard's works, but it cannot be justified by a balanced and thorough reading of the whole authorship. A reading of *Two Ages* shows this select and partial reading to be humorous.

Three positions will be briefly presented to show how widespread and persistent such a reading of Kierkegaard's concept of the individual is.

The most recent, and the best argued, presentation of the view that Kierkegaard's concept of the individual is bound to fail (because of the lack of social and political content) is Mark Taylor's.[1] Taylor maintains, in a book that must challenge the students of Hegel as much as it challenges the students of Kierkegaard, that Kierkegaard's project is doomed to failure for all sorts of good Hegelian reasons. Taylor writes,

> By opposing essence to existence and eternity to time, Kierkegaard reduces historical process to inessentiality. Time no longer possesses intrinsic value, but is significant only to the extent that it points beyond itself to a transcendent eternity. In this situation, "consciousness of life, of its existence and activity is only the agonized suffering over this existence and activity, for therein it is conscious that its essence is only its opposite, is conscious only of its own nothingness." This awareness of one's inessentiality leads to a passionate self-negation through which the temporal subject seeks to regain essential being by means of reconciliation with the divine object. The project of faith, however, is destined to fail. Reified dualisms make reunification impossible and self-alienation inevitable. Subject and object, self and other, existence and essence, man and God, remain estranged. Hegel explains that in this form of experience, "there is on the one hand, a going out from my finitude to a Higher; on the other hand, I am determined as the negative of this Higher. The latter remains an Other, which cannot be determined by me, insofar as determination is to have an objective meaning. What is present is only this going out on my part, this aiming to reach what is remote; I remain on this side with a yearning after the beyond." For Kierkegaard, this "longing is the umbilical cord to the higher life"; for Hegel, it is the "ceaseless sigh of the self-estranged spirit."[2]

---

[1]Mark Taylor, *Journeys to Selfhood: Hegel and Kierkegaard* (Berkeley University of California, 1980).

[2]*Ibid.*, 269. The quotations from Hegel are from *Phenomenology of Spirit*, trans. A. V. Miller (New York: Oxford University Press, 1977) 127. Also *Lectures on the Philosophy of Religion*, trans. E .B. Speirs and J. B. Sanderson, 3 vols. (New York: Humanities Press, 1968) 1:177.

In this extended passage Taylor has not only focused the issues between Kierkegaard and Hegel in a precise way, but he has also shown his dexterity in subsuming Kierkegaard under Hegelian categories. Thus, Kierkegaard's efforts are no advance at all in the process of human thought; indeed his failure has already been overcome by Hegel's philosophy. This is more than remarkable because Hegel saw his own philosophy as a recapitulation of what has been, having denied philosophy the possibility of prophecy.

Still, one can apply Hegelian analysis to Kierkegaard if one wishes, and these tests do indeed suggest a view of Kierkegaard's individual as alienated, as outside a social and historical context. However, that is scarcely Kierkegaard's own view of the individual. We must let the complete concept of the individual develop through the successive volumes of the *International Kierkegaard Commentary* as Kierkegaard's various works are commented upon. Here, in commenting upon *Two Ages* it must be said that self-estrangement and "passionate self-negation" are false concerns.

Few, least of all Hegel, think that social conflict can subside or disappear in the historical process. Note Hegel's agony over the problem of poverty in the *Philosophy of Right*. There, the problem is not so much self-estrangement as it is class conflict and the problem of a classless class. Estrangement is simply a historical fact that provokes responses by persons and groups that philosophy will rationalize after the fact.

The same is true in *Two Ages*. The estrangement manifested there between the self and society is not simply an ideological construct. It is historical and social; it is actual. As with all such estrangement in Hegel, Kierkegaard argues that the resolution, if any, will occur in and through historical and social conflict. Philosophy will not, cannot resolve social and historical conflict. Philosophy, according to Hegel can only reflect on and rationalize the resolution. After the fact, philosophy can explain why things turned out the way they did, but it has no recommendations, imperatives or future oriented programs. This view of philosophy is precisely why Kierkegaard's thought escapes the molds of Hegelian philosophy. Kierkegaard has a sense of the future, the future of the individual who chooses his social and religious relations.

We note further that the conflicts upon which Kierkegaard ruminates in *Two Ages* are imbedded in social and political structures. *Two Ages* is not concerned with the self's relation to itself as, say, *Sickness unto Death* is. *Two Ages* is concerned with the self as up against and in conflict with social structures and other persons.[3]

The Kierkegaardian project of faith does not fail because the individual discovers himself as "nothingness." Rather, if *Two Ages* counts in the appraisal of Kierkegaard's thought, the individual's struggle is against the nothingness of characterlessness imposed by modern pressures of conformity. It is not Kierkegaard's thought that suffers over the nothingness of the self; it is rather the conformity and passionless complacency of the "Present Age" that discovers its own nothingness, and it is against this that Kierkegaard struggles.

Another issue Taylor's quotations from Hegel make clear is the vast difference between Hegel's and Kierkegaard's conceptions of the availability of "the Higher." For Hegel, the concept of "the Higher" that "cannot be determined by me" is "remote" and "beyond." For Hegel those words suggest a fault in a certain concept of the divine, for the divine is, for Hegel, entirely immanent within human thought, that is, ideality. If there were any sense to divine transcendence for Hegel, his system could not be complete, thought would not comprehend reality and the whole Hegelian project would fail.

For Kierkegaard, on the other hand, it makes perfectly good sense to talk of the divine as "beyond" or "not determined by me," for reality is not a system for finite intelligence (CUP, 107f). Neither is the divine "remote" for Kierkegaard. The divine is no further than how far a "leap" can take one.

> Look, everything is ready; look, the cruelty of abstraction exposes the vanity of the finite in itself; look, the abyss of the infinite is opening up; look, the sharp scythe of leveling permits all, every single one, to leap over the blade—look, God is waiting! Leap then into the embrace of God (TA, 108).

---

[3]Taylor discusses *Two Ages* at length, but does not perceive the social dynamics of the book. See *Journeys*, 55ff.

Taylor's construction of a Hegelian critique of Kierkegaard focuses two issues pertinent to *Two Ages*. First, Kierkegaard addresses an entirely different social situation than Hegel addressed
in the passages Taylor quoted from the *Phenomenology* and the *Philosophy of Religion*. To attempt to subsume Kierkegaard under those
particular Hegelian moves seems like attempting to classify giraffes
in the vegetable kingdom. But more important for philosophic clarity is the insight, missed by Taylor, that Kierkegaard addressed the
plight of the individual *within* the social and political situation. Second, the Hegelian concept of an immanent God is countered by
Kierkegaard by a concept of a transcendent God available and
reachable by persons from within the historic and social processes.
Kierkegaard, to be sure, breaks step with all purely immanentist
and projective views of God as he reflects in the above passage on
the paradox of the nearness and the transcendence of God. This joy
is very like those Augustine struggled to express in his *Confessions*.

If Taylor is the last of these critics who have great reservations
about the adequacy of Kierkegaard's views of the self in the world,
Hans Lassen Martensen, Kierkegaard's theology professor and
later primate of the Danish state church, was at least among the
very first.

Martensen discussed the inadequacies of Kierkegaard's
thought in what can only be considered a very loose and yet turgid
set of categories in his *Den Christlige Ethik*.

Briefly put, Martensen attempts to present his own position as
a synthesis of Hegelian and Kierkegaardian insights. He characterizes Kierkegaard's position as "nominalism" and Hegel's as "realism." Both positions must be maintained in his own higher view
of Christian ethics.[4]

How egocentrically he interprets Kierkegaard's most important
sentence, "The subjectivity is the truth," can easily be seen.

> I am the truth: that significant individual who has come in order
> to make himself universal, to communicate himself to all by found-
> ing the holy universal church. On that account every other human

---

[4]Hans Lassen Martensen, *Den Christlige Ethik, Den Almendlig Deel* (Kjøben-
havn: Gyldendalske Boghandel, 1871) 279.

subjectivity can be concerned with (can take part in) the truth, but can never *be* the truth.[5]

Martensen's interpretation is certainly a parody, and yet he means it seriously and as an accurate interpretation of Kierkegaard. Thus interpreted, Kierkegaard's mapping of the concept of the ethicoreligious truth does indeed lock him up within the most hopeless subjectivism and egocentrism. Again, as in the contrast between nominalism and realism, Kierkegaard's views appear to be extreme and one-sided.

Martensen also attempted to show that Kierkegaard's views of "the crowd" were extreme. The basis of Kierkegaard's antisocial pronouncements is, according to Martensen, of course, one-sided egotism.[6] Yet, strangely Martensen's interpretation of Kierkegaard's notion of the crowd is one-sided, for he discusses it only in the context of the church. His criticisms would have been stronger had he framed his criticism in a broader concept, society, for instance. For Martensen, Kierkegaard's view of edification does not require a church, for edification does not take place *en masse*. To be sure, Martensen asserts that Kierkegaard is correct to an extent, that edification comes only to individuals. Yet Martensen maintains that edification comes only in the meeting of the congregation. Again, it appears that the subtle point has slipped by Martensen: Is saying that edification cannot take place *en masse* the same as saying that it cannot take place in a congregation or that it never takes place in the congregation? "Never at any time will Christianity appear in individuals without first appearing in a society."[7]

Martensen thus appears to want to have his cake and eat it also. He accepts what he calls "a false socialism" in religion, but he rejects Kierkegaard's alternative, the individual.

It appears as if Martensen has missed the dialectical sharpness of Kierkegaard's concept of the individual, of subjectivity, the

---

[5]*Ibid.*, 282. Author's translation.

[6]*Ibid.*, 292.

[7]*Ibid.*, 297.

crowd, and his attack on Christendom. It is too easy to accuse Martensen of dishonesty because he was a bishop and had to defend the institutionalized church, for it overlooks Martensen's own philosophic pretensions. Still his insistence on the priority of the social to the individual prevented him from perceiving the sharpness of Kierkegaard's insights into the struggle of the individual against the pressures, peevishness and powers of society.

One can only conclude that Martensen did not understand the dialectical intensity of the struggle through which the form of life of the individual is conditioned by the society. He does not appreciate the conflictual basis of individuality. As *Two Ages* shows, the individual is such only in dialectical tension with his society. What Martensen cannot properly appreciate is that in the present age, the individual must to a great extent define himself against powerful social forces which will diminish if not destroy individuality. The irony is that though Martensen is very obviously interested in social relations, he, unlike Hegel, did not appreciate social conflict.

If Taylor and Martensen represent the latest and earliest poles of criticism of Kierkegaard's view of the individual, then the criticism of Martin Buber is certainly the most famous.

Buber's criticism is strung out over a large number of essays including even a passage in *I and Thou*. This is all the more remarkable for we know that he was a subscriber to *Der Brenner* and at least had the opportunity to have been exposed to Kierkegaard's social criticism as developed in *Two Ages*.[8]

Buber's criticisms of Kierkegaard come down to two basic issues. First, he thinks that Kierkegaard failed as a person when he did not marry Regina Olsen. This is indeed a personal attack on the reputation of a philosopher who suffered immensely over this matter. To write, "God wants us to come to him by means of the Reginas he has created and not by the renunciation of them,"[9] is to demean oneself by attacking another person rather than the per-

---

[8]Maurice Friedman, *Martin Buber's Life and Work: The Early Years, 1878-1923* (New York: E. P. Dutton, 1981) 301.

[9]Martin Buber, *Between Man and Man*, trans. Ronald Gregor Smith (Boston: Beacon Press, 1961) 52.

son's logic. Buber's marriage to Paula Winckler was happy and a remarkable match.[10] Add to this the high place given the married estate in the Jewish religion and one can sympathize with Buber's frustration at Kierkegaard's breaking of the engagement to Regina. Moreover, Kierkegaard gave all sorts of reasons, some good and some bad, at different times, for breaking the engagement. The multiplicity of reasons sounded inauthentic to Buber. Still, to suggest that the Reginas or the Paulas are "means" is scarcely to make a high ethical claim and is no evidence that Buber has a higher estimate of women than Kierkegaard. For all his criticism of Kierkegaard, Buber scarcely showed himself as occupying a loftier ethical plane than Kierkegaard, at least according to the quoted statement.

The second issue Buber brings against Kierkegaard is his treatment of "the other." Buber is offended by the text: "Everyone should be chary about having to do with 'the others,' and should essentially speak only with God and with himself." Buber writes, "Kierkegaard's meaning is evident that the Single One has to do essentially (is not 'chary') only with God."[11]

The most remarkable thing about such an interpretation is that it completely misses the Socratic in Kierkegaard's thought; to ignore the Socratic in Kierkegaard is to miss the heart of his philosophy. The importance of the dialogical principle for Kierkegaard can hardly be overstressed.

When one looks at the offending passage and Buber's comments we can understand Buber's deep revulsion. Kierkegaard's view of relation, according to Buber, is monological at worst, or dialogical only with God, at best. There appears to be a complete rejection of 'the others.' Buber did not notice the single quotes and so the whole sorry mess follows. Most of the time when Kierkegaard uses the expression, 'the others,' it has only the ordinary meaning and so he does not set it off with single quotes. However, there are three times when Kierkegaard did put single quotes

---

[10]Friedman, *Martin Buber's Life and Works*, chap. 18.

[11]Søren Kierkegaard, *The Point of View*, etc., *The Point of View for my Work as an Author, Two Notes About 'the Individual'* and *On My Work as an Author*, trans. Walter Lowrie (London: Oxford University Press,1939) 113.

around the words. From an examination of these three instances it appears that 'the others' refers to those who refused to act from cowardice, from fear of losing their dignity or position, or those who thought their calling placed them above criticizing *The Corsair* or defending the one man in Copenhagen who had the courage to defend 'the others' from *The Corsair*. 'The others' in this book then refers to persons lacking moral and social discernment regarding the abuses of the press and the moral courage to defend a man's reputation against slander, caricature, ridicule, and lies. This is a far cry from what Buber accuses Kierkegaard of asserting.[12]

Buber's widely believed assertion is based upon a careless reading of the text. One regrets to be so critical of one of the most esteemed thinkers of this century.

Buber's criticism is all the more inappropriate when one reads *Two Ages*, for then we see, again, that Kierkegaard is militating against those who constitute the public, whose envy causes them to level, to attempt to reduce every individual to a cipher, or to use Buber's language, to an It. It is more than unfortunate that Buber has misled two generations of his readers.

Our three critics have hard serious charges against Kierkegaard's concept of the individual in his social relations, and the essays in this volume, among other things, are offered to clarify this central notion of Kierkegaard's thought. After reading *Two Ages* one is at a loss to understand the critics' charge that Kierkegaard's view of the individual is simply one-sided, a passing phrase in the Hegelian dialectic or that the individual has to do only with God. These essays are offered to clarify Kierkegaard's thought in its historical context in the hope that a myth may die.

Historical Introduction

Søren Kierkegaard had painted himself into a corner. In the "First and Last Declaration" (CUP, unnumbered end pages) he

---

[12]Robert L. Perkins, "A Philosophic Encounter with Buber," *Bibliotheca Kierkegaardiana*, vol. 5, 243-73. The first analysis of this point is in Jacob L. Halevi, *A Critique of Martin Buber's Interpretation of Søren Kierkegaard* (Ph.D. dissertation, Hebrew Union College, 1959).

stated his firm determination not to write any more books. He even confided to his journal that he had determined to become a pastor (JP, 5:5873). The latter was a fantasy Kierkegaard had long entertained. But the ideas would not stop coming. What was he to do?

His resolution of this problem created for us one of the most remarkable books in his authorship: *A Literary Review. Two Ages, a Novel by the Author of "A Story of Everyday Life."* Kierkegaard worked his way out of the corner into which he had painted himself by writing a book-length review of someone else's book. This behavior must surely be the most humorous, contorted, and thankfully, last escapade to which Kierkegaard ever subjected himself and his readers. This long-winded title appears more simply, if less exactly, as *Two Ages* in the series "Kierkegaard's Writings."

There may be another reason why Kierkegaard wrote this book. His first book had been a review of Hans Christian Anderson's book *Only a Fiddler* entitled *From the Papers of One Still Living*. By concluding as he began with a long review of someone else's book he fed his own strong sense of symmetry. The review of *Two Ages* thus served to keep his pen busy, ironically to keep the promise not to publish more books and to satisfy some curious sense of symmetry.

Kierkegaard has a complex relation to each member of one of the most complex, productive and charming families in nineteenth-century Copenhagen, a family that was comprised by the author of "A Story of Everyday Life," her son and daughter-in-law.

Who was the author of "A Story of Everyday Life" referred to above? The author was an authoress, Thomasine Christine Gyllembourg, *née* Buntzen, the mother of J. L. Heiberg and the most important authoress of nineteenth-century Denmark. Her first marriage to P. A. Heiberg ended in a divorce triggered by his exile for radical political writing and her affair of the heart with Carl Frederick Ehrensvärd-Gyllembourg. The divorce was scandalous and was the best entertainment that season offered to the gossips of Copenhagen. The romantic fires (having a very Rousseauistic fervor) continued to burn until his death.

Fru Gyllembourg, her son J. L. Heiberg, and daughter-in-law Johanne Luise Heiberg, *née* Pägtes, lived together in a home that was at the same time a remarkable salon. Heiberg was the director of the theatre, a playwright, the editor of a newspaper, Copenhagen's *Flying Post*, and a critic as well as the earliest and most faithful exponent of the philosophy of G. W. F. Hegel in Denmark. His career was marked by an increasing isolation from the public he sought to save and serve through all these means. His increasing elitism and dogmatism in the operation of the theatre led to his increasing contemptuous attitude toward the public. At his height in 1830s and 1840s, he is now remembered more for his refusal to permit the plays of Ibsen to be performed in the National Theatre than for his own achievements.

Fru Heiberg was the most famous actress of the age, beloved by all for her ability, grace, charm and physical beauty. The three lived together from 1831 when Heiberg married Miss Pätges until 1856 when Fru Gyllembourg died. They lived, wrote, criticized together in what was then known as "the Heiberg factory." After the death of her husband, Fru Heiberg had an independent acting career and achieved some literary reputation herself.

Fru Gyllembourg began her literary career in 1827 with the first of twenty-four of the fictive letters which were later collected under the title of *The Polonius Family*. "A Story of Everyday Life" also attracted Kierkegaard's attention as the opening pages of *Two Ages* show. She also wrote some of the plays that the world received as Heiberg's as well as numerous anonymous pieces in the *Flying Post*. *Two Ages* closed her writing career. In it she set forth a treatment of the main tensions that had gripped her life: the contrasted forms of life of the age of revolution (her youth) and the age of the bourgeois (her mature years after the death of Gyllembourg). The contrast between the age of revolution with its aristocratic ideals and its "freer morality" and the leveling, calculating and bourgeois tendencies of the thirties and forties were shown in this novel of great depth, penetration and achievement. *Two Ages* was very well received and is thought of today as Denmark's first realist novel.

Kierkegaard's appreciation of Fru Gyllembourg's literary achievement is profound, but it must be noted that he discovered more than literary merit in her work: he found corroborative evidence of the variety and conflict of various forms of life in all her novels and especially in *Two Ages*. She did not work from a philosophic premise or theory, but rather she transmuted the raw material of her own life into a literary product of some philosophical significance for Kierkegaard at least. It was her own independent discovery that the conflict of personalities is socially mediated, that there is indeed a temper of the times, a social environing of the ego that so impressed Kierkegaard and which is in complete agreement with his own views. This may come as a surprise to some, but we will let the following essays speak in detail to this issue.

I

Passion
Reflection
and Particularity

by John W. Elrod

In the nineteenth century, Denmark became a modern nation state. It experienced the rise of the middle class, the dissolution of guilds and communal agriculture, the emergence of laissez-faire economics, a bloodless revolution in 1848 that established it as a constitutional monarchy, the flourishing of experimental science, the appearance of freedom of the press, and the displacement of the clergy and the nobility by professors, scientists, and businessmen as the chief advisers and architects of economic and political policy. After the collapse of the Danish economy in 1813 and a military defeat by the British in that same year, the country quickly rebounded from economic and military humiliation to become a moderately thriving Scandinavian country with few, if any, significant problems for its middle-class citizenry.

Danes in the middle of the nineteenth century quietly settled into an uneventful and undemanding middle-class comfort that challenged them to accomplish little more than to pay their debts. In quest of economic security and well-being as the highest achievement of human life, the nineteenth-century Dane learned to be guided by the lights of prudence and common sense. All sensible actions were those directed toward managing oneself in the new marketplace in which the modern Dane resided. It was not possible for the emerging Danish middle class to imagine an alternative superior to its newfound way of life, so the calculating sensibleness of the age argued against any thought of insurrection, revolution, or world renunciation. In spite of the self-assured smugness of this marketplace mentality, the inward life of the nineteenth-century Dane was troubled by the sufferings of bourgeois comfort, namely, boredom and envy. The "present age" was in fact quite petty and trivial, or so it seemed to Kierkegaard. This unflattering perception of his age first appeared in 1846 in his *Two Ages*.

This bourgeois marketplace mentality troubled Kierkegaard not because of its capacity for great evil; he was convinced that the age lacked the passion for anything great, either good or evil. What disturbed him was the spiritual banality of modern Denmark. Self and society were withered versions of what they were potentially capable of becoming. He thought that the spirit of the marketplace was not to be identified or confused with the realization of the human spirit. In *Two Ages*, Kierkegaard addresses this dilemma in terms of the dichotomous categories of reflection and passion. Simply put, the problem with modern Denmark was that it had become a reflective age that was utterly devoid of passion. The purpose of this paper is to explore the meaning of this claim as it is developed in the third and concluding part of *Two Ages*.

Reflection and Particularity

This concern in *Two Ages* that reflection is a problem for contemporary Denmark is not new to Kierkegaard's writings. In *Concluding Unscientific Postscript* Kierkegaard's pseudonym, Johannes Climacus, attacks the prevailing philosophical wisdom of speculative philosophy that asserts the identity of thought and being. Climacus complains that "speculative thought repeatedly attempts to reach reality within its own domain, assuring us that whatever is thought is real, that thought is not only capable of thinking reality but of bestowing it, while the truth is the direct opposite" (CUP, 283). The speculative philosophers are simply mistaken insofar as human existence is concerned, because "existence involves first and foremost particularity, and this is why thought must abstract from existence, because the particular cannot be thought, but only the universal" (CUP, 290). In fact, "the only thing-in-itself which cannot be thought is existence, and this does not come within the province of thought to think" (CUP, 292). These passages convey Climacus's well-known opposition to the reflective identification of thought and being in speculative idealism. Climacus argued that the ontology, epistemology, and ethics of this version of idealism arbitrarily distort our understanding of the nature and destiny of the self. According to Climacus, idealism denies the ontological status of the particular, of that which individuates each self and makes it distinctive. This denial of the ontological value of contingency is reflected in the epistemology and the ethics of speculative idealism with its claim that self-knowledge and moral obligations are universalizable. Self-knowledge is a knowledge of a transcendental and universal self, and moral obligation is conceived in terms of those duties that are shared in common by citizens of the state. This universalizing tendency of speculative idealism in its analysis of the self provoked Climacus into a defense of the individual against the hegemony of idealistic reflection. The passages quoted above contain the philosophical core of that defense.

Climacus also argued that those who insist on the identity of thought and being are not only philosophically in error but also existentially "fantastic" (CUP, 293). Reflective philosophers live in a fantasy world, ignoring or forgetting their particularity. Climacus describes Hegel in this sense as a fantastic individual who even becomes comical, because he constructs a palatial system of thought and yet is compelled by existence to live in a hovel next door. Preoccupied as the reflective philosopher is with philosophical system building, he fails to attend to the lusts, passions, despair, selfishness, faith, obligation, responsibility, anxiety, envy, fear, freedom, past, present, and future that individuate him as a particular human being. Since Climacus understands particularity ontologically, he realizes the importance of developing a mode of thinking that does not in principle rule out the ontological character of the non-universalizable. Hence a long section of *Concluding Unscientific Postscript* is devoted to a discussion of the existential, as opposed to the reflective, thinker, who gains a knowledge of himself as a particular being through interest, passion, imagination, and choice (CUP, 312-22). Self-knowledge requires an awareness of oneself as a particular being, and this awareness can be mediated only through those modes of knowing that are themselves commensurate with the particular. If the particular is the real, then Climacus argues for the identity of passion and being rather than the identity of thought and being. To ignore this fact is to make an error philosophically and to fall into a fantastic mode of existing.

In *Two Ages*, Kierkegaard continues Climacus's attack on reflection. He begins by describing nineteenth-century Denmark as an "age of reflection" in which "the single individual has not fomented enough passion to tear himself out of the web of reflection" (TA, 69). This reflective web is, however, one that is spun not exclusively, or even primarily, by philosophers but by the processes of modernization mentioned in the opening paragraph of this paper. Climacus's defense of the individual against the hegemony of idealistic reflection is a prelude to Kierkegaard's defense of the individual against the hegemony of the processes of modernization. Kierkegaard interpreted the liberalization of the Danish economy, political institutions, and culture in terms of their influence on the individual's self-consciousness. He realized that these changes in Danish life were not neutral events having no impact on the human spirit. They were, in fact, powerful events that shaped and molded not only economic and political institutions but—and for Kierkegaard this was more important—the self-understanding of individual human beings. Claiming that politics had become "a disastrous caricature of religiousness" (JP 4: 4206), Kierkegaard maintained that politics and economics had become the ultimate concern not only of a few key nobles and advisers of the king but of every Dane at all concerned with his well-being. Sensing his escape from the restrictions of a guild economy, communal agriculture, and monarchical authority, the ordinary Dane took to his newfound political and economic freedom with verve, enthusiasm, and imagination.

The difficulty in this enormous transition was from Kierkegaard's point of view not so much the change to a more liberating secular order but the Dane's ethical-religious interpretation of himself as a human being exclusively in terms of these momentous events and the new political and economic order that they brought into being. Kierkegaard regarded as "obvious nonsense" the position "that the state in a Christian sense is supposed to be what Hegel taught—namely, that it has moral significance, that true virtue can appear only in the state (something I also childishly babbled after him in my dissertation), that the goal of the state is to improve men" (JP, 4: 4238). He also realized that this view of the state as grounding the ethical life was more than a philosophical position in that it had become a way of life in the new liberal order. Throughout his later writings, Kierkegaard repeatedly objects to Christendom's volatilization of ethical and religious categories. Terms like freedom, equality, justice, truth, and happiness became the coinage of Danish liberalism, thereby bestowing upon it the notion of virtue to which these terms had been related in ethical and religious discourse. The blending of these ethical concepts into the economic and political discourse of the state was in Kierkegaard's view an indication of how deeply the individual's self-consciousness had been pervaded by the economic and political processes of modernization.[1]

In his later writings, Kierkegaard uses a variety of terms to describe the individual who has successfully come to terms with the new secular order. In *Judge for Yourselves*, he criticizes the "sober" and "prudent" individual who is exclusively guided in his life by "common sense, discretion, shrewdness, and all that goes with this" (JFY, 115). The same spirit of successful accommodation with the new order is unsympathetically described as "worldliness" in *For Self-Understanding* and is referred to in *Works of Love* and *Training in Christianity* as becoming the "natural man." The thoroughly economic character of the sober and prudent "natural man" is cap-

---

[1]For a full discussion of this point, see my *Kierkegaard and Christendom* (Princeton: Princeton University Press, 1981) ch. 2.

tured in *Two Ages* in which Kierkegaard claims that "ultimately the object of desire is money" and unfortunately it is only "an abstraction" (TA 75). And running throughout this later literature is Kierkegaard's objection to the way in which Christianity has become identified with the new order in the individual's life. "Keeping an eye upon civic rectitude (good—better—best), one makes oneself as comfortable as possible with everything one can scrape together in the way of worldly goods—the Christian element being stirred in with all this as an ingredient, a seasoner, which sometimes serves merely to refine the relish" (TC, 114). This sentiment is reflected more intensely in a journal entry in which Kierkegaard writes that Christianity "has become a divine blessing upon all the trivialities and putterings of finitude and the temporal enjoyment of life" (JP, 4: 4998). It is this ethical-religious interpretation of modernization that enables us to understand that its impact is not limited simply to institutional reform but reaches into the core of human spirit. To give these economic and political reforms the ethical and religious value that they received in Kierkegaard's Denmark is a clear indication that they profoundly transformed the individual's understanding of himself in the new secular order.

As disturbing to Kierkegaard as the appearance of the essentially political-economic individual was the leveling force of this new order. The ethically and religiously sanctioned political and economic self-understanding of the nineteenth-century Dane was in Kierkegaard's view an abstraction that suppressed the individual's respect for himself in terms of those contingent qualities that distinguished him from others. As we have noted above, Kierkegaard believed that in the modern state the individual would be essentially motivated by the desire for money, which he identified as an abstraction. Kierkegaard laments that "a young man today would scarcely envy another his capacities or his skill or the love of a beautiful girl or his fame, no, but he would envy him his money. Give me money, the young man will say, and I will be all right" (TA, 75). Those concrete qualities that literally identify an individual are no longer envied in the new order but only the abstraction of money. This neglect of the concrete as an object of envy and desire reflects for Kierkegaard this leveling power of the new order.

Marx also seems to have shared this view, at least in his early writings. There he makes observations about the leveling power of money in the capitalist order that remarkably resemble Kierkegaard's position. Marx writes

> that which is for me through the medium of *money*—that for which I can pay (i.e. which money can buy)—that *am* I, the possessor of the money. The extent of the power of money is the extent of my power. Money's properties are my properties and essential powers—the properties and powers of its possessor. Thus, what I *am* and *am* capable of is by no means determined by my individuality. I am ugly, but I can buy for myself the most beautiful of women. Therefore I am not *ugly*, for the effect of *ugliness*—its deterrent power—is nullified by money.[2]

Marx offers many examples of the negating power of money and concludes that its essential power is "the overturning and confounding of all human and natural qualifications."[3] In fact, "*money* transforms the *real essential powers of man and nature* into what are merely abstract conceits and therefore *imperfections*" with the result that what we are as well as the nature of our actions are determined by the abstraction of money.[4] This critical observation of the budding capitalistic economies studied by Marx reflects exactly the same suspicions that Kierkegaard harbored about the power of money in liberalized Denmark. While Marx does not explicitly employ the concept of leveling, he would surely have agreed that in capitalist societies money makes us all alike in that it enables individuals to ignore as a basis for self-understanding and action those natural qualities which distinguish us one from the other.

Kierkegaard's fear of the leveling force of money in capitalist economies is complemented by a similar fear of the concept of equality in the new liberal order. He asserted that "the dialectic of the present age is oriented to equality, and its most logical implementation, albeit abortive, is leveling" (TA, 84). He saw in this ab-

---

[2]Karl Marx, *Economic and Philosophic Manuscripts of 1844*, trans. Martin Milligan (New York: International Publishers, 1964) 167.

[3]Ibid., 168.

[4]Ibid., 169.

straction of equality the "representation of *humanity pure and unalloyed*" in which one "becomes a man and nothing else, in the complete and equalitarian sense."[5] Once the individual becomes a person in the complete and equalitarian sense, "he does not belong to God, to himself, to the beloved, to his art, or to his scholarship; no, just as a serf belongs to an estate, so the individual realizes that in every respect he belongs to an abstraction in which reflection subordinates him" (TA, 85). The individual now belongs to a "public [which] is not a people, not a generation, not one's age, not a congregation, not an association, not some particular persons, for all these are what they are by concretions" (TA, 92-93). Indeed, it is the "destruction of the individual."[6] To the extent that the individual exists at all, he only exists in an external sense as "a numeral within the crowd, a fraction within the earthly conglomeration" (PH, 184). Bereft of those qualities that distinguish one individual or group from another, the only identifying attribute remaining is the quantitative one of number.[7]

The reflective identification of thought and being in speculative idealism, then, took a more forceful and consequential form in the reflective identification of the economic and political abstractions of modernization and being. The individual who was only in principle lost in the abstractions of idealism was in practice lost in the abstractions of modernization. Kierkegaard would have strongly concurred with Unamuno's denunciation of the modern state in which he characterizes "the political animal of Aristotle, the social contractor of Rousseau, the *homo economicus* of the Manchester School" as one who is "neither of here nor there, neither of this age nor of another, who has neither sex nor country, who is in brief, merely

---

[5]Søren Kierkegaard, *The Present Age*, trans. Alexander Dru (New York: Harper and Row, Publishers) 55, 57. Kierkegaard's italics. Here is one of the very rare places in which the Hongs' translation does not improve Dru's. For the Hongs' translation, see TA, 87, 88.

[6]Ibid., 54. See TA, 86.

[7]"The trend today is in the direction of mathematical equality so that in all classes about so and so many uniformly make one individual" (TA, 85).

an idea. That is to say a no-man."[8] Using Unamuno's phrase the "no-man" or Heidegger's *Das Man* for that matter, Kierkegaard would have argued that he is a creation of the modern state that ontologically grounds the person in the abstraction, *humanitus* ("pure humanity") (TA, 88), and prudentially guides his actions according to the equally abstract goal of money. Thus like speculative idealism, the institutional processes of modernization deny the ontological positivity of those qualities and attributes that contingently distinguish individuals from each other. The "web of reflection," then, enfolds the individual in a set of philosophical, political, and economic rationalistic abstractions that cause him to appear in a form that is tirelessly replicated in every Danish citizen. Viewed through the institutional lenses of nineteenth-century Denmark, each individual sees in himself only what he sees in the other. As the fabrication of the modern state, this universalized human form is capable of including the particular in only a quantitative sense and, in Kierkegaard's view, this quantification of the particular is the direct consequence of the institutional embodiment of the reflective and rationalistic conception of the individual in the modern nation state.

Passion and Particularity

Now in turning to a discussion of passion, it would be useful to note that *Two Ages* is not a handbook for revolution. It does not propose a scenario that plots the steps to be followed in breaking free of the "web of reflection." In his discussion of passion, Kierkegaard does not in a naive and simpleminded way claim that if individuals will simply become passionate they can break free of their rationalistic imprisonment. Indeed, he is more apt to rely on a certain mode of reflection, which he calls indirect communication, as the proper strategy to be used in combating the age of reflection. Kierkegaard believed that what the age required to set it upon its

---

[8]Miguel de Unamuno, *The Tragic Sense of Life in Men and Nations*, trans. and ed. Anthony Kerrigan, Bollinger Series 85, no. 4 (Princeton: Princeton University Press, 1972) 3-4.

proper course was a Socrates and not a passionate revolutionary. His discussion of passion in *Two ages* is intended rather to provide an alternative to reflection concerning the question of the proper grounding of selfhood. His claim in this book is that it is not through reflection but rather through passion that the individual genuinely becomes himself.

Johannes Climacus had previously made this point in *Concluding Unscientific Postscript*. Opposing the passionate individual to the rationalized individuality of speculative idealism, Climacus textures every step of the individual's subjective development with an essentially passionate dimension. He made this identification of passion and individual subjectivity (CUP, 117, 178, 206) by showing that each stage in the individual's development is grounded in a form of passion. In the aesthetic stage of existence, passion provides the "impulse toward existing" (CUP, 358) and is the form of the individual's initial awareness of himself in his concreteness (CUP, 313). Passion is also the entrance into the ethical stage of existence in that it provides the alternatives or possibilities for choice (CUP, 176). And it is in the religious passion of faith that the individual is elevated to the "highest expression of subjectivity" (CUP, 178). It is by means of this identification of passion and the subjective life in all its forms that Climacus lodged one of his strongest protests against the rationalization of the self by both speculative idealism and the modern state. In *Two Ages*, Kierkegaard follows his line of thought initially proposed by Climacus in *Concluding Unscientific Postscript*.

By giving passion such a fundamental role in his discussion of the individual, Kierkegaard recognized that he was taking a position that easily allowed for caricature and misinterpretation. He stated, therefore, in 1844 that no one should "misinterpret all my talk about pathos (Pathos) and passion *Lidenskab* to mean that I intend to sanction every uncircumscribed immediacy, every unshaven passion" (JP, 3: 3127). It is obvious from this disclaimer that Kierkegaard did not want to be understood as endorsing every fanatical, capricious, or voluntary act that is committed in the name of passion. How, then, should we understand Kierkegaard's use of this term in *Two Ages*? Kierkegaard places it in very good conceptual company by positively associating it with the concepts of ethics, character, choice, sacrality, society, immediacy, form, property, revolution, and revelation (TA, 61-68). Without exploring the nature of all these connections, we can by examining its relations to the concepts of immediacy, ethics, and society gain a purchase on its implications for particularity.

Let us begin our discussion of the passion of immediacy[9] by identifying it as an essential presupposition of the action of self-understanding. The action of self-understanding requires both an object and a form. If self-knowledge is genuinely to be acquired, the form of understanding must be commensurate with this object. If the object of understanding is the individual in his particularity, then there must correspond to it a form of understanding that actually allows for the expression of this particularity. We have already noted that when self-understanding takes the theoretical and practical forms that it took in nineteenth-century Denmark, the result is an abstract and universalizable conception of the individual who becomes by virtue of that understanding an essentially quantifiable being. Having observed this fact, Johannes Climacus concludes that "in every case where the object of knowledge is the very inwardness of the subjectivity of the individual, it is necessary for the knower to be in a corresponding condition" (CUP, 51). Climacus continues that "in order to philosophize [at speculere] he must proceed in the opposite direction, giving himself up and losing himself in objectivity, thus vanishing from himself" (CUP, 55). In order to avoid this disappearing act, Climacus recommends that we adhere to an old philosophical adage which claims that "only the like is understood by the like" (CUP, 51). Kierkegaard has not diverged from this principle in *Two Ages*, and that is why he claims that the individual's passion is the initial material to be examined in his coming to understand himself in his particularity.

This is the first sense in which passion is an essential presupposition to the act of self-understanding. It is the form of the initial act, but it is also its content. And this is the second sense in which it is a presupposition of self-understanding. To speak of the indi-

---

[9]The term *immediacy* in Kierkegaard's writings most generally refers to unreflected states of experience. See the following passages for further discussion of this term: CA, 41ff.; DODE, 148ff.; EO, 2: 190-91, 193; JP, 1: 972; 2: 1942; TA, 64, 66.

vidual as existing in a state of immediacy is to refer to the individual as existing in a state of unrealized potentiality. The immediately existing individual is one who is something definite but in an unactualized state. The immediate individual is also one who exists in a state of innocence in the sense that he is not conscious of himself as the definite being that he is. The immediately existing individual is also identified as a self-interested being. Ignorant of, but interested in, one's particularity, it first erupts in the form of passion. Passion is, writes Kierkegaard, "an energy that unquestionably is a definite something and does not deceptively change under the influence of conjectural criticism concerning what the age wants" (TA, 66). As a "definite something," this energy is the expression of the individual's particularity in the form of an interest in or an enthusiasm for an object that is the externalization of this subjective particularity. In Kierkegaard's words, one's particularity is initially, passionately constituted as an "alter ego." He insists that "only for a completely external and indifferent dialectic is the form not the alter ego of content and thereby the content itself, but rather an irrelevant third something" (TA, 61). Passion as the energy of self-interested immediacy is not a blind, uncircumscribed energy that indiscriminately and arbitrarily expresses itself in the world. It is, rather, a mediated energy whose form is determined by the particularity that constitutes the individual's determinateness. Thus we may say that passion is the energy through which the particular initially finds expression. And, as Kierkegaard notes, it is a definite and specific energy that cannot change with the shifting whims and caprices of the age, because it is a definiteness that partially constitutes the individual's unique nature as an existing human being. As though warning the age against the error of violating the integrity of the individual's particularity, he claims that "fundamentally, essential passion is its own guarantee that there is something sacred, and this gives rise to the determinate priority" (TA, 64). The shifting whims, moods, and curiosities of the present age must not infringe upon the limits of propriety that are revealed in the moment of essential passion. In such a moment, the individual's being is first revealed (TA, 66), and it is in this sense also that passion and particularity are a mutual fit.

The passion of immediacy is, then, the initial expression (form) of the individual's subjective particularity (content). Passion is the initial constitution of the individual in his particularity. This subjective constitution of particularity is not, however, an arbitrary or capricious act but is the expression of the individual's unmediated potentiality. What is now required is an action that will give this particularity a specific determinateness in the form of rules, language, and so forth. This particularity must be transformed into a determinate way of life, and this is the task of ethical passion.

If in passion the individual first becomes aware of himself as a particular being, this awareness cannot be anything more than an immediate knowledge. An interest in or an enthusiasm for an objective externalization of oneself, the "alter ego" is as yet only an immediate mode of self-knowledge. The logic of the passion has yet to be made explicit in language and practice, and until that moment occurs the individual cannot be said to have self-knowledge. Passion is, then, the link between ignorance and self-knowledge, and the disclosing of the logic of passion is the first task of subjective reflection. The individual thinker whose thought takes the form of subjective reflection upon his own particular passion is an ethical thinker. This ethical alliance between passion and subjective reflection is important for a number of reasons.

First, in the moment of passion as the initial constitution of the individual, the individual is elevated above his externally defined locus in both nature and society. Without an essential passion "everything becomes meaningless externality" (TA, 67). In this case, the individual is exclusively heteronomously identified by his place in the natural and social orders. As such, the individual becomes "a flux, a blend of a little resolution and a little situation, a little prudence and a little courage, a little probability and a little faith, a little action and a little incident" (TA, 67). That is to say, there is no sharp definition in the individual's appearance in that he is merely a constantly shifting compromise of the tensions and forces that operate on him from without. Kierkegaard describes such a person as lacking the "tension and resilience of the inner being" (TA, 61) and of being "devoid of character" (TA, 62). This lack of inwardness and character means that the individual has not subjectively reflected upon those moments of passion in which his particularity initially expresses itself against the indeterminacy of the natural and social order in which he dwells.

To reflect subjectively upon passion is to disclose its logic, that is, to make it determinate, for the purpose of being able consciously to identify with it. This moment is nicely described in *Either/Or* by Judge William in the following way.

> He has himself, then, as an individual who has these talents, these passions, these inclinations, these habits, who is under these influences, who in this direction is affected thus, in another thus. Here then, he has himself as a task, in such a sort that his task is principally to order, cultivate, temper, enkindle, repress, in short, to bring about a proportionality in the soul, a harmony, which is the fruit of the personal virtues (EO, 2: 266-67).

Kierkegaard would certainly agree with what Judge William has written here, although he would add that the dimensions of the soul must first be constituted in a moment of passion so that they can become the object of a harmonizing reflection that brings them into a coherent unity. The reflecting subject is then in a position to make determinate this particularity and to identify with this determinacy. To conduct oneself in this manner is to become an individual "who honestly and honorably is constantly prepared to express in his life what he has understood" about himself (JP, 3: 3669).

As we know, Kierkegaard frequently describes this moment as a moment in which the individual must choose either to exist ethically by identifying with his determinate particularity or to exist aesthetically by refusing this identification. He is quite explicit about the centrality of passion in the formation of this choice. "The presence of the crucial either/or depends upon the individual's own impassioned desire toward acting decisively" (TA, 67). Without passion, there can be no legitimate object of reflection and without such reflection there can be no choice. Moreover, if passionate reflection is displaced by a passionless reflection, the either/or can never arise. In Kierkegaard's words, "as soon as the individual no longer has an essential enthusiasm in his passion but is spoiled by letting his understanding [*forstand*] frustrate him every time he is going to act, he never in his life discovers the disjunction [between the aesthetic and the ethical]" (TA, 67). The way in which the individual enters self-reflection is of crucial importance, according to Kierkegaard. Only in passionate reflection can the individual discover himself in his determinate particularity. This is so in the sense that the only way in which his particularity can become an object for reflection is in passion. If the individual falls into a passionless self-reflection, there is no determinate particularity implicitly present to reflection to be disclosed and chosen.

There is yet another sense in which passion is of decisive importance for the way in which the individual begins to reflect upon himself. It makes more certain the connection between the choosing subject and the subject chosen. A subject who is passionately related to the content of his choice is more apt to be choosing what legitimately is self-constituting than a subject who is not passionate about his choice. In the moment of choice, the question concerning the propriety of one's choice always arises and there is no way in which this skepticism can be fully overcome. The choosing individual can always ask, "How can I know with certainty that this idealized self is really *my* self?" There is, of course, no manner of verification that will guarantee absolute certainty. Yet it does seem correct to assume that a strong passion for the idealized self provides a degree of certainty that one's chosen self is one's real self.

Finally, the passionate character of ethical reflection is important because it preserves the vitality and freshness of the choice. In Kierkegaard's words, passion maintains "the originality of the ethical" and prevents it from becoming a "desiccated ruin, a narrow-hearted custom and practice" (TA, 65). Once the logic of one's passion is made explicit as a set of rules, gives rise to certain customs, and establishes routine practices, it can very quickly degenerate into an enervating routine. The coexistence of passion and customs, rules, and practices serves to remind the individual that the ethical life is one in which he as an individual is continually present. The content of the ethical life, so long as it remains passionate, does not lose its subjective grounding in the individual's desire to become a self. Ethical passion serves to prevent the development of a sense of alienation between the individual and the institutions, rules, and customs in which he lives his life. Conversely, the individual who loses his passionate relation to these institutions, rules, and customs must inquire as to whether they any longer reflect his own particularity and hence himself. If he cannot find himself passionately related to the ethical life, then it is possible that there is no longer an essential relation between his particularity and the form of his life. If the ethical way of life becomes a "desiccated ruin" and a "narrow-hearted custom and practice," it is likely that there is no longer an essential relation between the existing subject and his objectification in the ethical form of life.

If in ethical passion, the logic of the individual's particularity is made determinate, it is now necessary to confront the issue of how determinate particularities can and should relate to each other. This is the task of religious passion.[10]

Religious passion is the third mode of passion discussed in *Two Ages*. While it is only briefly discussed in this book (TA, 62-64), it nevertheless establishes the religious basis of Kierkegaard's conception of community. If immediate passion is the initial and prereflective constitution of the individual's particularity and ethical passion reflectively establishes the determinacy of that particularity, the religious passion socially harmonizes individual determinate particularities into a coherent and unified community. There is insufficient time for detailed discussion of Kierkegaard's arguments for religiously grounding community, but it will be useful to draw this essay to its conclusion by briefly amplifying this crucial point.[11] In making this point, Kierkegaard writes, "When individuals (each one individually) are essentially and passionately related to an idea and together are essentially related to the same idea, the relation is optimal and normative. Individually the relation separates them (each one has himself for himself), and ideally it unites them. Where there is essential inwardness, there is a decent modesty between man and man. . . . Thus the individuals never come too close to each other in the herd sense, simply because they are united on the basis of an ideal distance" (TA, 62-63). The ideal dis-

---

[10]While we can theoretically separate schematically the ethical and the religious dimensions of the moment of determinacy, they cannot be so distinct in the existential moment. The ethical and the religious are logically though not existentially distinct, and for this reason Kierkegaard usually speaks of the ethical-religious way of life.

[11]See *Kierkegaard and Christendom*, ch. 5, for a full discussion of this point.

tance between two or more passionate individuals is made possible by the intervention of a "third," that is, the divine.[12] The relation of each individual to the divine must be a passionate one, or else the individual's determinate particularity, which is constituted by immediate ethical passion, will be lost; hence the individual will be lost. Another way of making this point is to say that for an individual to be related to the divine, the relation must by definition be passionate in nature. It is in this sense that the individual's relation to the divine separates him from all others. The socially unifying dimension of this passionate relation to the divine is in the individual's dialectical discovery of that principle according to which the multiplicity of determinate particularities can in principle be communally harmonized. This principle that the individual should love the other as he loves himself is in principle the unifying ground of individual determinate particularities. It is important to note further that in the passionate unfolding of the individual's self-understanding, this principle is dialectically, not authoritatively, introduced into the individual's life. But this point takes us beyond the limits of this paper. In closing, we can note Kierkegaard's faith in the power of religious passion to ground community by noting the social consequences of the failure to appreciate this fact. "Individuals do not in inwardness turn away from each other, do not turn outward in unanimity for an idea, but mutually turn to each other in a frustrating and suspicious, aggressive, leveling reciprocity. The avenue of the idea is blocked off; individuals mutually thwart and contravene each other; then selfish and mutual reflexive opposition is like a swamp—and now they are sitting in it" (TA, 63).

Kierkegaard clearly believed that the present age of reflection was like a swamp. As we have seen, he characterized it as one in which individuals were essentially quantified and leveled by virtue of their participation in the modernization of Danish economic, political, and social institutions in nineteenth-century Denmark. And, as the last quoted passage indicates in its references to frustration, aggression, and selfishness, Kierkegaard clearly believed

---

[12]This concept of a "third" as a necessary condition for the proper grounding of all social relations is at the heart of Kierkegaard's attempt to work out a religious social ethic in *Works of Love*.

that the present age had given rise to moral and psychological problems by virtue of the leveling process. In his second literature (post-CUP), Kierkegaard analyzes at length the selfish, despairing, bored, and envious character of the nineteenth-century Dane in terms of the modernization of its institutions. He is quick to point out the ironical fact that the age of the individual, which is embedded in the liberalization of western European institutions, turns out also to be the age of reflection. As we have seen, in the age of reflection the individual is quantified and distinguished from all others in only a superficially numerical sense.

That the individual became the highest priority on Kierkegaard's philosophical agenda indicates his willingness to take his situation seriously and on its own terms. He thus can be said to have existed contemporaneously with his own age by having made the nature of the individual his deepest ethical and religious concern. And he believed that the ethical and psychological problems generated by the age of reflection could only be resolved by getting the individual to take himself seriously in terms of his own unique particularity. Toward this end, Kierkegaard believed that one of his first tasks was to show the centrality of passion in passing from quantity to quality in the life of the spirit.

II

Towards Apocalypse:
Kierkegaard's Two Ages
in Golden Age Denmark

by Michael Plekon

One solitary man cannot help or save an age; he can only express that it is foundering

(JP, 4: 4157)

Locating and Interpreting Two Ages

Kierkegaard's *Two Ages, a Literary Review*, the focus of this volume of commentary, is a complex, often misunderstood piece of Kierkegaard's social and theological criticism, one with specific historical roots and targets in his Denmark of the 1840s, in the period known as the Danish "Golden Age" of cultural accomplishment.[1] The work was published on 30 March 1846, only a month after the publication of the *Concluding Unscientific Postscript* and during Kierkegaard's feud with the satirical Copenhagen newspaper, *Corsaren*.[2] It was not the first time Kierkegaard addressed sociopolitical matters in print, nor would it be the last, for while most of his largely unsystematic social theory and criticism are located elsewhere in his books, journals, and letters, *Two Ages* remains one of the most explicit and concentrated of his writings in these areas. Further, *Two Ages* stands at a crucial position in his life and literary career. Not a few commentators—among them Kresten Nordentoft, Bruce Kirmmse, and John Elrod—have observed that *Two Ages* marks the crucial shift in Kierkegaard's productivity.[3] *Two Ages*, as

[1]Assistance instrumental in the preparation of this essay and in the Kierkegaard research upon which it is based was provided by a fellowship from the National Endowment for the Humanities that allowed me to work at the Institute for Systematic Theology of the University of Copenhagen during 1979-1980, and by a grant of release time for research from the Dean and School of Liberal Arts and Sciences, Baruch College, CUNY. I also want to express gratitude to those who encouraged and guided my work on Kierkegaard, among others, Peter Berger, Niels-Jørgen Cappelørn, Howard and Edna Hong, Bruce Kirmmse, Paul Müller, and Julia Watkin.

[2]On Kierkegaard's literary work in general, and in particular with respect to *Corsaren*, see: CA; *Corsaren*, 6 vols., repr., ed. Uffe Andreasen (Copenhagen: Det Danske Sprog- og Litteraturselskab and C. A. Reitzel, 1977-1979); Uffe Andreasen, Susanne Nyegaard, Marianne Bjørn Olsen, Bjørn Westerbeek Dahl, *Corsaren 1840-1846: Efterskrift og Registre* (Copenhagen: Det Danske Sprog- og Litteraturselskab and C. A. Reitzel, 1982); Elias Bredsdorff, *Corsaren, Goldschmidt og Kierkegaard* (Copenhagen: Corsarens Forlag, 1977); Aron Meier Goldschmidt, *Livs Erindringer og Resultater* (Copenhagen: Gyldendal, 1877); Ulf Kjær-Hansen, *Søren Kierkegaards pressepolemik* (Copenhagen: Berlingske Forlag, 1955); Paul V. Rubow, *Dansk litterær Kritik i det 19de Aarhundrede indtil 1870* (Copenhagen: Munksgaard, 1921; *Goldschmidt og Søren Kierkegaard* (Copenhagen: Munksgaard, 1952); *Søren Kierkegaard og hans Samtidige* (Copenhagen: Munksgaard, 1950); Sven Møller Kristensen, *Digteren og Samfundet*, 2 vols. (Copenhagen: Athenaeum, 1942); Henning Fenger, *The Heibergs* (Boston: Twayne, 1971); *Kierkegaard, The Myths and Their Origins* (New Haven: Yale University Press, 1981); F. J. Billeskov-Jansen, *Studier i Søren Kierkegaards litterær Kunst* (Copenhagen: Gyldendal, 1951); Merete Jørgensen, *Søren Kierkegaard som kritikker* (Copenhagen: Gyldendal, 1975); Søren Gorm-Hansen, *H. C. Andersen og Søren Kierkegaard i dannelseskulturen* (Copenhagen: Medus, 1976).

[3]See Kresten Nordentoft, *"Hvad siger Brand-Majoren?" Kierkegaards opgør med sin samtid* (Copenhagen: Gad, 1973), the most authoritative Danish study of Kierkegaard's social theory and criticism, to which I am deeply indebted. In particular, see the provocative analysis of TA on 35-66. Nordentoft's two other Kierkegaard

Kierkegaard also observes himself, signals the end of the early or "first" pseudonymous authorship, concluding with the *Postscript*. It also marks the beginning of a transitional phase in Kierkegaard's thinking, one in which he contemplated ending his literary work to seek ordination and work in a country parish.[4]

However, the shifts in Kierkegaard's thinking were to be far more complex and momentous, involving, as has been argued elsewhere, profound changes in his social and theological thinking.[5] The period after 1846 saw the publication of *Works of Love*, Kierkegaard's principal examination of ethics and also his fullest statement of an affirmative theology, rooted in the assumption that love abides as an *a priori*, as the permanent possibility of grace and mercy, as the "sprout in the grain," in the heart of God and of humankind (WL, 202-11).[6] This same period was also a time of ges-

---

studies should also be cited: *Kierkegaard's Psychology* (Atlantic Highlands NJ: Humanities Press, 1978) especially 240-55 and his collection of essays, *Søren Kierkegaard. Bidrag til kritikken af den borgerlige selvoptagethed* (Copenhagen: Dansk Universitets Presse, 1977) especially 69-122. Also see John W. Elrod, *Kierkegaard and Christendom* (Princeton: Princeton University Press, 1981); and the magisterial study by Bruce Kirmmse, "Kierkegaard's Politics: The Social Thought of Søren Kierkegaard in its Historical Context" (Ph.D. dissertation, Berkeley, 1977) especially 501-28 on TA. Other important studies of the late Kierkegaard include P. G. Lindhardt, *Søren Kierkegaards angreb på folkekirken* (Århus: Aros, 1955); "Søren Kierkegaards opgør med kirken," in *Øieblikket* (Copenhagen: Hans Reitzel, 1962); Gregor Malantschuk and N. H. Søe, *Søren Kierkegaards Kamp mod Kirken* (Copenhagen: Munksgaard, 1956); Hermann Deuser, *Dialektische Theologie: Studien zu Adornos Metaphysik und zum Spätwerk Kierkegaards* (Munich: Kaiser-Grüenwald, 1980); and Johannes Sløk, *Da Kierkegaard tav. Fra forfatterskab til kirkestorm* (Copenhagen: Hans Reitzel, 1980). Finally, see my essays, "Anthropological Contemplation: Kierkegaard and Modern Social Theory," *Thought* 55 (September 1980): 346-69; "Kierkegaard and the Interpretation of Modernity," *Kierkegaard-Studiet* 11 (1981): 3-12.

[4]See Gregor Malantschuk, "Søren Kierkegaard, Poet or Pastor?" (AN, 3-24).

[5]See Nordentoft, *Brand-Majoren*, 160-260; *Kierkegaard*, 102-22; Kirmmse, "Kierkegaard's Politics," 501-947. Also see my essays, "The Late Kierkegaard: A Reexamination," Papers of the Nineteenth Century Theology Working Group, *American Academy of Religion* 7 (1981): 13-40; "Moral Accounting: Kierkegaard's Social Theory and Criticism," *Kierkegaardiana* 12 (1983): 69-82; "Kierkegaard, the Church and Theology of Golden Age Denmark," *The Journal of Ecclesiastical History* 34 (1983): 245-66; and "Introducing Christianity into Christendom: Reinterpreting the Late Kierkegaard," *Anglican Theological Review* 64 (1982): 327-52.

[6]See Nordentoft, *Kierkegaard's Psychology*, 365-86; Kirmmse, "Kierkegaard's Politics," 586-633; and my efforts to describe the late Kierkegaard's "incarnational op-

tation for both Kierkegaard's social and theological criticism, which underwent a slow process of experimentation and profound transformation that unfolded in his large journals for the years after 1846. Along with the theological affirmations of *Works of Love*, Kierkegaard came to a new understanding of God's grace, mercy, and forgiveness. Personal religious experiences from Holy Week and Easter of 1848 were related to this theological breakthrough (JP, 5: 6131-35, 3: 2465, 2: 1942, 1213-14, 1123). Moreover, in the same time span he arrived at the Christological rediscovery of the figure of Jesus, the suffering servant, in contrast to Enlightenment and romanticist Christologies (JP, 3: 2503, 2481, 2: 1391, 1852, 1862, 1848, 1877, 1: 334). *Training in Christianity*, from 1850, became the fullest expression of Kierkegaard's Christological shift, other statements coming in *For Self-Examination*, *Judge for Yourselves*, and finally in the literature of the public attack on the Danish church and society in 1854-1855 (TC, 33-37, 44, 40-60, 86-126, 127-44). Integral to this Christological recognition was Kierkegaard's own renewed conviction that "imitation" (*Efterfølgelse*) of this suffering Christ, that is, "existential expression," as he repeatedly put it, of faith in everyday life, was the New Testament's demanding requirement for Christian discipleship (TC, 61-72, 140-43, 194-96, 219-46).[7] For Kierkegaard, in the years after 1846, such theological transformations became inseparable from rigorous social criticism—of the Copenhagen upper and middle classes, their values, piety and life-styles, of the intertwined church and state, of the clergy and their preaching, indeed of the entire Danish society he called "Christendom."[8]

---

timism" in the essays cited in 5n. above, and in "Protest and Affirmation: The Late Kierkegaard on Christ, the Church and Society," *Quarterly Review* 2 (1982): 43-62, and "Blessing and the Cross: The Late Kierkegaard's Christological Dialectic," *Academy: Lutherans in Professions*, forthcoming.

[7] See JP, 2: 1833-1940, 7:48, and the following studies: Per Lønning, *Samtidighedens Situation* (Oslo: Land og Kirke, 1954); Valter Lindström, *Efterföljelsens Teologi* (Stockholm: Diakonistyrelsens Bokförlag, 1956); Bradley A. Dewey, *The New Obedience: Kierkegaard on Imitating Christ* (Washington DC: Corpus, 1968).

[8] See, for example, JP, 1: 236, 386, 3: 3215, 3498, 4: 4518, 4685, 6: 6469, 6498, and untranslated entries 10, 2 A55 and 10, 3 A135 in *Søren Kierkegaards Papirer*, ed. Niels Thulstrup, index by Niels-Jørgen Cappelørn, 2nd ed., 25 vols. (Copenhagen: Gyldendal, 1968-1978).

Authentic New Testament Christianity did not exist any longer. There was nothing to reform and so, strange as it may have sounded, Kierkegaard saw his task as that of "introducing Christianity into Christendom" (JP, 1: 388, PV, 22-23). This fusion of sociotheological criticism and affirmation culminated in the well-known public attack of 1854-1855 (KAUC).

All of this brings us far beyond *Two Ages* in time and content. Yet it is well worth noting, at the very beginning, in the effort to locate *Two Ages* as a crucial text at a critical point in Kierkegaard's life and writing. I am arguing that Kierkegaard's social, political, and theological positions in *Two Ages* reflect his thinking *at one crucial point* in his life and literary career. *Two Ages* should not be taken as his final position in these areas. Neither should it be understood as a normative nor completely representative statement of his social, political, and theological perspectives. In what follows, I shall argue that in *Two Ages* we see a great deal of Kierkegaard's earlier and rather conservative sociotheological thinking quite accurately reflected, while at the same time we also receive indirect hints of the turns in his thought which were to come in the later years. More specifically, I want to inspect some of Kierkegaard's earlier social criticism and its sociohistorical context. In so doing, some of the connections between his early criticism and that of his contemporaries in Copenhagen of the 1840s will be analyzed, particularly his connections with Johan Ludvig Heiberg. Then I want to examine the criticism in *Two Ages* itself, especially the theological underpinnings of the social critique there, to see how *Two Ages* shares views with other Danish conservative positions and also how it sharply diverges into a distinctive position. Particularly in the "apocalyptic" view in the closing pages, we will see social and theological perspectives Kierkegaard came to reject and discard in the years after 1846, as well as some hints of the positions which he adopted in the period leading up to the public attack.

Social Criticism in Golden Age Denmark:
Precedents and Contemporaries of Two Ages

For some time, when *Two Ages, A Literary Review* has been read, it has been studied in a somewhat fragmentary and dislocated manner. Non-Danish readers who have not gone to other translations have had to be content with Alexander Dru's rendering into English of only the last portion of the text. Howard and Edna Hong have now resolved this difficulty, not only by a complete, dynamic translation of the entire text, but also by providing translations of portions of the novel, *Two Ages*, upon which Kierkegaard's review is focused, and of material from the journals intimately related to Kierkegaard's text (TA, 119-57). In addition, they have supplied us with a brief but helpful historical essay locating the text. How many readers were previously sensitive to the fact that Kierkegaard was providing an extended review of the novel, *Two Ages*, by the pseudonymous "Author of A Story from Everyday Life?" In reality, this was Thomasine Gyllembourg (1773-1856), former wife of the exiled critic, Peter Andreas Heiberg (1758-1841), and mother of the notable critic, dramatist, Royal Theater director and Hegel proselytizer, Johan Ludvig Heiberg (1791-1860). Fru Gyllembourg has her own important place in nineteenth-century Danish literary history for the moral criticism and realism of her short stories and novels and for the sheer drama of her own long life. Johan Ludvig was connected with Kierkegaard in many and complicated ways throughout the latter's career, as we shall soon see. My point here is that not unlike the reading of other Kierkegaard texts, the interpretation of *Two Ages* has very often been carried out in a historical vacuum. Too often it is forgotten that the "present age" (*Nutiden*) of which Kierkegaard writes is not all of modernity, not in essence the twentieth century with its wars and political transformations but the very small world of Golden Age Denmark's Copenhagen. In claiming this I am certainly not saying that applications of Kierkegaard's criticism in *Two Ages* have no bearing whatsoever on later periods. Rather, I am arguing that it is important to maintain some historical fidelity and specificity at least at the start of analyzing this text.

To be sure, the place of this text in Kierkegaard's authorship has frequently been discussed, Kierkegaard himself having made a number of references to this in his journals and in other places (TA, 119-52; PV, 13, 148). *Two Ages* was published in Kierkegaard's own name and thus, as he observes, it stands outside both the early pseudonymous writings and the religious ones, the edifying and other specifically religious discourses. Although it was explicitly a review of a novel, it was not simply an esthetic work but also had to do with Kierkegaard's time and society in contrast to the "revolutionary age" of the late 1700s described by Fru Gyllembourg. Yet this was by no means the first time Kierkegaard had expressed in print criticism of his period and his contemporaries, both in his own name and pseudonymously, as was very much the style in the Copenhagen literary world.[9] As early as 1834 Kierkegaard began to appear in print in such publications as *Kjøbenhavns flyvende Post, Fædrelandet, Kjøbenhavnsposten, Statsvennen,* and *Humoristiske-Intelligentsblade.*[10] In addition to these early newspaper articles, there are Kierkegaard's first longer published work from 1838, *From the Papers of One Still Living* (SV, 13: 41-92)—a rather ruthless review of Hans Christian Andersen—and his academic dissertation of 1841, *The Concept of Irony* (CI). Later there were more newspaper articles and letters, mostly in *Fædrelandet,* with a few in *Berlingske Tidende,* and one in *Ny Portefeuille* dealing with the authorship from 1842 to 1851, the last being the "Open Letter" to A. G. Rudelbach (AN). There was, of course, the large authorship itself and finally the *Fædrelandet* articles and numbers of *Øieblikket,* Kierkegaard's own periodical, that constituted the literature of the public attack. It would be far beyond the limits of this essay to attempt to analyze all of this early literature in detail. Still, at least some description can help us to understand both Kierkegaard's earlier efforts in social criticism and their relationship to *Two Ages,* as well as something of the period leading up to the 1840s in Denmark.

Danish historians paint a picture of a complex, conflict-ridden Denmark in the early years of the nineteenth century.[11] After notable land, school, and social reforms in the late 1700s guided by the Reventlows and the future king, then regent, Frederik VI, Denmark experienced one catastro-

---

[9]See the studies of Kierkegaard's literary work and connections cited above in 2n.

[10]All of these, as yet untranslated, are to be found in the first Danish edition of *Søren Kierkegaards Samlede Værker* (hereafter SV) ed. A. B. Drachmann, J. L. Heiberg, H. O. Lange, 14 vols. (Copenhagen: Gyldendal, 1901-1906). See SV 13: 1-40. This volume is forthcoming in *Kierkegaard's Writings* as vol. 1, to be translated by Julia Watkin. Also see Teddy Petersen, *Kierkegaards polemisk debut: Artikler 1834-36 i historisk sammenhæng* (Odense: Universitetsforlag, 1977).

[11]The account here is based on the following sources, among others: Marcus Rubin, *1807-14 Studier til Københavns og Danmarks Historie* (Copenhagen: Gyldendal, 1892); *Frederik Vis Tid* (Copenhagen: Gyldendal, 1895); Villads Christensen, *København, 1840-1857* (Copenhagen: Gyldendal, 1912); Otto Borchenius, *Fra Fyrrene,* 2 vols. (Copenhagen: Gyldendal, 1878-1880); Jens Vibæk, *Reform og Fallit,* 1784-1830, vol. 10; Roar Skovmand, *Folkestyrets Fødsel,* 1830-1870, vol. 11; *Danmarks Historie* (Copenhagen: Politikens Forlag, 1978); Sigurd Jensen, *Fra Patriarkalisme til Pengeøkonomi* (Copenhagen: Gyldendal, 1950); Hans Christian Johansen, *En samfundsorganisation i opbrud 1700-1870,* vol. 4: *Dansk socialhistorie* (Copenhagen: Gyldendal, 1979); Ole Feldbæk, *Denmark and the Armed Neutrality* (Akademisk Forlag, 1980); Martin Zerlang, *Bøndernes klassekamp i Danmark* (Copenhagen: Medusa, 1976).

phe after another. The wrong alliances and a futile effort at neutrality in
the Napoleonic conflicts cost Denmark the British attack on Copenhag-
en's harbor in 1801, then the city's devastating bombardment and loss of
the fleet in 1807. Then came state bankruptcy in 1813, the loss of Norway
at the Congress of Vienna in 1814, and succeeding years of poor commerce, crop failures, and food shortages in the 1820s. From an economic
perspective, Denmark came crawling out of the Middle Ages at the turn
of the nineteenth century and ended up limping in poverty into that same
century's first few decades. By the 1830s the formerly progressive Frederik
VI had become a rigidly conservative absolute monarch. Despite his establishment of advisory assemblies at long last in 1835, after over a decade
of pressure from the signatories at Vienna, every suggestion of liberalism
or criticism in Frederik VI's Denmark was suspect. Harsh criminal justice
prevailed and a wall of various ordinances limited the press and any political organizing or protest, just as the old seventeenth-century earthen
ramparts encircled Copenhagen and stifled its growth. Yet this period of
economic decline and political repression was also the Danish "Golden
Age," illumined by such stellar figures as the sculptor Thorvaldsen, paint-
ers Købke, Eckersberg and Marstrand, the brothers A. S. Ørsted, a renowned jurist, and H. C. Ørsted, internationally known for his work on
electromagnetism. Perhaps the true glory of the Golden Age was the ver-
itable pantheon of literary figures who stretched from the century's beginning to its midpoint: Oehlenschläger, Baggesen, Blicher, Grundtvig,
Ingemann, Hauch, Fru Gyllembourg, J. L. Heiberg and his circle, called
"Familien," Frederik Paludan-Müller, Bagger, Hans Christian Andersen,
and of course, Kierkegaard himself.[12] Few among these could by any
stretch of the imagination have been called political or cultural liberals, at
least in the 1820s and 1830s.

By the late 1830s Heiberg had become one of the dominant literary figures
in Copenhagen. In the Heiberg circle, presided over by Fru Gyllembourg
and Heiberg's wife, the most renowned actress in Scandinavia at that
time, Johanne Luise (1812-1890), were gathered a number of personalities,
with professor, later bishop, Hans Lassen Martensen (1808-1884), as the
leading clerical figure. In addition, a flock of younger writers stood at the
margins waiting for acceptance. As Henning Fenger and Teddy Petersen
convincingly argue, a great many of Kierkegaard's early literary efforts,

---

[12]See F. J. Billeskov-Jansen and Gustav Albeck, *Fra Ludvig Holberg til Carsten
Hauch*, vol. 2; and Oluf Friis and Uffe Andreasen, *Fra Poul Møller til Søren Kierkegaard*, vol. 3; *Dansk Litteratur Historie*, 6 vols. (Copenhagen: Politikens Forlag,
1976).

certainly the very earliest articles on up to and including *Either/Or* in 1843, bear the marks of orientation toward Heiberg's perspectives and thus were potential means of admission to "Familien."[13] Thus it is no surprise that in the early newspaper articles we find a number of social, political, and literary issues handled by Kierkegaard in a conservative manner.

Lest there be any quarrel about the term "conservative" here, I mean by it Kierkegaard's early allegiance to what the consensus of Danish historians refer to as "konservative" and what Bruce Kirmmse has called the "conservative mainstream."[14] Quite a broad spectrum of the leading figures of the Danish Golden Age, indeed the majority of statesmen, clergy, and academics were to be found within the ranks of the conservatives. In the Danish church, most of the clergy leaned toward this position. Jakob Peter Mynster (1775-1854), as bishop of Zealand and primate, was the foremost ecclesiastical spokesman for the conservative mainstream and he was joined by other members of the Danish episcopal college and the university's theological faculty, with the exception of H. N. Clausen. Well into the 1840s even Grundtvig would have counted himself in the company of the conservatives, along with Jacob Christian Lindberg, who established working relationships between Grundtvig's followers and the revival movements that had sprung up throughout the country in the 1830s. Others in the conservative camp included Kierkegaard's old philosophy professor, F. C. Sibbern, his beloved mentor and friend, Poul Martin Møller, the economist C. N. David, Count Wilhelm Sponneck, Prime Minister P. C. Stemann, the writer B. S. Ingemann, and as we shall see, J. L. Heiberg. In their number, the National Liberals could also count notables such as the businessman L. N. Hvidt, officer A. F. Tscherning, jurist T. Algreen-Ussing, academics J. F. Schouw, H. N. Clausen, P. G. Bang, J. N. Madvig, later church minister and bishop D. G. Monrad, and in the lead, the dynamic young political strategist Orla Lehmann. Later in the 1840s more crossed over from conservative to liberal positions, particularly those associated with Grundtvig and the revival movements.

Central among the conservatives' social and political positions was support for a paternalistic, or as they put it, a "fatherly" absolute monarchy. Their view of monarchy remained tainted with divine right beliefs and was greatly solidified by the excesses of the French Revolution, not least

---

[13]Henning Fenger and Teddy Peterson both convincingly argue that Kierkegaard's earliest writing is oriented toward Heiberg's views and seems to be seeking his acceptance.

[14]See Kirmmse, "Kierkegaard's Politics," 155-391.

by the horrifying act of regicide. The monarch's central authority, encircled by elite groups—cabinet ministers, aristocrats, landholders and royally appointed civil servants—crowned an ordered hierarchy in Denmark's social structure. The conservatives understood their society through the Lutheran view of "call and station," as one clearly and with good reason stratified by God in terms of income, education, and occupation. The conservatives thus saw politics as the domain of the monarch and of a cultured elite, composed of royally appointed officials (including academics, clergy, and other intellectuals), the leaders of business and finance, aristocrats, and the holders of large estates. In the majority of Danish communities, which were rural towns, the pattern of local social organization had remained relatively unchanged for centuries. In many cases, both the parish church and its property were owned by the local landholder, who either directly or indirectly was responsible for the appointment of the parish pastor and schoolmaster. The pastor, moreover, fulfilled a variety of roles. He was, of course, the spiritual "father" of his "parish children," responsible for the preaching of the Word, the proper administration of the sacraments, and for religious education. In addition, he was, as a royal official, responsible for the maintenance of vital statistics: the recording of births, deaths, marriages, and migration. He was also the local historian, economist, and agricultural agent, very often the disseminator of new techniques in farming, veterinary science, and medicine. In most villages he was the only public official with a university education and thus also the holder of the sole library in the community. The parish pastor then served as the end station of a hierarchy that led back to God and the king. He presided over the rituals of passage in the life of most people, not the least of which was the passage into adulthood through their church confirmation. For both God and the king, the earthly terminus of the hierarchy lay back in Copenhagen, the capital city and official seat of government, the home of culture and learning, of Denmark's only university (and school of theology for pastoral training), and the episcopal seat of the Danish primate, the bishop of Zealand.

Thus despite the reformist legislation of the late eighteenth century and early nineteenth century, which broke the peasant's bondage to the landholders' estates and established a rudimentary system of public education, Denmark in Kierkegaard's time was really just emerging from the patterns of a medieval society. With the exception of her commercial fleet and trading companies, both severely damaged by the British in 1801 and 1807, Denmark was still essentially an agrarian society even into the 1830s and 1840s. Industrialization was thirty years away. Copenhagen, with only about one-tenth of the entire population—120,000 residents—held the monopoly on political, cultural, and economic life. This was the Denmark that the "conservative mainstream" knew, loved, and sought to preserve. A maze of law held the professions, crafts, and trade in check through taxation, a guild system, print censorship, and ordinances prohibiting extraecclesial religious activities and political organizing. In culture as well as in politics, the conservatives saw learning and the arts as the preserve of an elite. A catchword of theirs to describe this was *Dannelse*, the cultivation or refinement enjoyed by the leading few, the intellectual aristocracy.[15] Further, the conservatives assumed their state and culture to be Christian—evangelical Lutheran, to be precise. Religious toleration, through law, came only with the new constitution in 1849. Though the church's position had never been formally established in an ecclesiastical constitution, the church was understood as an essential social institution alongside the state.

In light of these conditions it is possible to see why the conservatives resisted proposals for social and political change, even those mandated by the Congress of Vienna. Such changes called for the formation of advisory assemblies in Slesvig-Holsten, still part of the Danish realm, and in Zealand, Jutland, and for Funen and the other islands. Similarly, one can also understand the conservatives' opposition to press criticism of the state and cultural elites, particularly that launched by Goldschmidt in *Corsaren*. And it is equally understandable that the conservatives would find the interloping of outsiders into the political sphere, particularly that of the reformist liberals, at best loathsome meddling and at worst, treason against God and king. In the 1830s and 1840s, then, the conservatives consistently opposed the liberals' demands for a constitution and an elected legislature, for male suffrage and for further social reform, including the dismantling of the guild system. The conservatives not only feared the events of the French Revolution, but were further shaken by the July revolution in France in 1830, and by growing language and political conflicts with Prussia over Slesvig and Holsten. The problems of the urban poor and the peasants, they believed, could be best solved by paternal benevolence from above, rather than by any efforts to redistribute income or to "level" society from below. Danish historian Jens Engberg, among others, has chronicled the measures the conservative government took in these first decades of the 1800s to control and even brutally repress any challenges to

---

[15]Nordentoft, *Brand-Majoren*, 67-139; *Kierkegaard*, 69-85; Sløk, *Da Kierkegaard tav*, 41-52.

the prevailing order.[16] These ranged from press censorship, which drove J. L. Heiberg's father into exile in 1800 and which constantly plagued Goldschmidt's *Corsaren*, to the life imprisonment of a very unlikely political critic, Dr. Dampe, in 1820, and to the execution of rebellious inmates of the prison in Christianshavn in Copenhagen in the same decade. Paradoxically, during these years of material economic depression, conservative political paranoia, and repression, Denmark's "Golden Age" blossomed forth in the arts and in literature. It is not impossible to recognize the flourishing of poets Oehlenschläger, Ingemann, P. M. Møller, Blicher, and Grundtvig; of the Rahbeks' literary salon; and, of course, in the 1830s and 1840s, of J. L. Heiberg's criticism and theater productions as responses, perhaps even antidotes to or diversions from the growing sociopolitical tension. Heiberg's vaudevilles, Grundtvig's romanticizing of Denmark's past, and the games and amusements of the old Deer Park were not enough. In 1843 Georg Carstensen opened a new amusement park in Copenhagen, Tivoli. Yet despite these diversions and the conservatives' opposition to reform, profound changes were gradually but inexorably taking place throughout Denmark. The peasants were increasingly becoming owners of their farms and, in large part due to the revival movements and school reforms, were also becoming more literate, aware, and critical of the political, cultural, and religious monopoly of absolutism's state and church. Revivalist lay preachers eventually joined forces with Grundtvig and his followers. Calls for reform became more frequent: for better schools and hospitals; for loosening of parishioners' bonds to their parishes; for freedom of a congregation to call its own pastor; for greater freedom in the professions, trades, and labor movement; and of course, increasing demands for a constitution and an elected legislature to make all the rest possible.

Against this background of social and political ferment in the 1820s, 1830s, and 1840s, what wonder that the young Kierkegaard should be called a conservative, in light of the positions he supported. In the early newspaper articles noted above, he came down solidly against Orla Lehmann, the National Liberals' leader. He opposed most of the proposals for reform, supporting instead continued press censorship. He satirized calls for the social and political emancipation of women. He attacked the liberal press as morally irresponsible and dangerous, such a line of criticism culminating much later, of course, in his conflict with *Corsaren*. Kierkegaard, as did others in the conservative mainstream, found the liberals lacking in

---

[16]Jens Engberg, *Dansk Guldalder eller Oprøret i Tugt-, Rasp- og Forbedringshuset* (Copenhagen: Rhodos, 1973).

passionate commitment to ethical principles. He saw liberals as illegiti-
mate poachers in the political arena, the preserve of the cultural elite.
Worst of all, the liberals were pragmatic opportunists in politics. They
stooped to utilize the daily press to create and manipulate a public which
would support their proposals for social and political change. In these
early writings, we find Kierkegaard interested in literary, social, and political issues *without* any of the religious motives and positions of his later
pseudonymous authorship (PV, 10-43, 142-51). Here Kierkegaard does little more than affirm the conservatives' arguments against the liberals'
proposals. He reiterates the conservatives' legitimations of their own positions without the ethical and religious embellishments he would later
contribute. As both Fenger and Petersen suggest, the esthetic and sociopolitical conservatism expressed in these early articles, along with the evidence of other literary efforts by the young Kierkegaard in the 1830s,
resemble the positions put forward by other young writers such as P. E.
Lind and H. P. Holst, also friends of Kirkegaard, who were making their
starts in Copenhagen's literary world. All set their sights on acceptance
by and entrance into the Heiberg circle.[17]
Of course, a great flood of writing was to flow from Kierkegaard's pen between these early articles and *Two Ages*. In the intervening years came his
attack on Hans Christian Andersen in *From the Papers*, his academic dissertation on irony with constant reference not only to Socrates but also to
Heiberg-approved Hegelianism, and then the two-pronged series of pseudonymous works and edifying/religious discourses. A detailed accounting
of Kierkegaard's social theory and criticism in these writings is not possible here.[18] It is perhaps enough to recall the cavalcade of commentary

---

[17]Petersen, *Kierkegaards polemisk debut*, 20-28. Unfortunately, an important essay
on Kierkegaard's relationship to the Copenhagen literary world in the 1830s and
1840s was not included in the recent translation of Fenger's *Kierkegaard, The Myths*.
This essay can be found in the Danish edition, *Kierkegaard-Myter og Kierkegaard-
Kilder* (Odense: Universitetsforlag, 1976) 171-254. Also see Fenger's article, "Søren
Kierkegaard, P. E. Lind og 'Johan Gordon,'" *Kierkegaardiana* 7 (1968).

[18]See Nordentoft, *Kierkegaard's Psychology*; Josiah Thompson, *The Lonely Laby-
rinth: Kierkegaard's Pseudonymous Authorship* (Carbondale: Southern Illinois Univer-
sity Press, 1967); *Kierkegaard* (New York: Knopf, 1973); Louis Mackey, *Kierkegaard,
A Kind of Poet* (Philadelphia: University of Pennsylvania Press, 1971); "The Poetry
of Inwardness" (1-102), "The Loss of the World in Kierkegaard's Ethics" (266-88),
"The View from Pisgah" (394-428), in *Kierkegaard: A Collection of Critical Essays*, ed.
Josiah Thompson (Garden City NY: Doubleday-Anchor, 1972). "A Ram in the
Afternoon: Kierkegaard's Discourse of the Other" (193-234) in *Kierkegaard's Truth:
The Disclosure of the Self*, ed. Joseph H. Smith, vol. 5: *Psychiatry and the Humanities*

from that company of characters, the pseudonyms. Think, for example, of the "Life-views" (*Livs-Anskuelser*) enacted by the various young esthetic types, of the protracted considerations of Judge William on marriage, on social, political, and personal selfhood (EO, 2: 171-81, 343-56). There is the cutting delineation of "spiritlessness" (*Aandløshed*) (CA, 17-72, 83-86) and of Copenhagen's cultural and religious life and illuminati (SLW, 97-178; ET, 45-52, 65, 78-91; SUD, 170-80; CUP, 415ff., 486-87).[19] In addition, the pseudonymous literature provides valuable depictions of the human self, the interpenetration of its biological, social, and psychological dimensions, along with painstaking analyses of angst, despair, guilt, and the therapy of the Spirit (FT; CA).[20] In this respect, too, the understudied edifying and religious discourses should be mentioned as Kierkegaard's efforts, in his own name and in a well-respected genre of his time, to more explicitly present his social and theological perspectives as he developed them.

Heiberg and Kierkegaard

Basic to the tasks of this essay is my claim that Kierkegaard's singularity of vision and ingenuity do not negate his kinship with his contemporaries.[21] He shared the perceptions of Mynster, Grundtvig, Heiberg, and Martensen, among others, that the modernity of the early nineteenth century was fraught with problems. Of course, this kinship was not always mutually acknowledged, in fact, rarely so; and it was qualified by clear differences in both di-

---

(New Haven: Yale University Press, 1981); Johannes Sløk, *Kierkegaard—humanismens tænker* (Copenhagen: Hans Reitzel, 1978); Stephen D. Crites, "Kierkegaard's Pseudonymous Authorship as Art and as Act" (183-229) in Thompson, *Kierkegaard: Critical Essays*. Also see my *Thought* and *Kierkegaardiana* articles cited in notes 3 and 5 above.

[19]See Nordentoft, *Kierkegaard's Psychology*, 240-55; Kirmmse, "Psychology and Society: The Social Falsification of the Self in *The Sickness Unto Death*" (167-92) in Smith, *Kierkegaard's Truth*; Mark C. Taylor, *Journeys to Selfhood: Hegel & Kierkegaard* (Berkley: University of California Press, 1980) 23-70.

[20]Nordentoft, *Kierkegaard's Psychology*, 51-239.

[21]See my forthcoming article in the *Journal of Ecclesiastical History*, cited in 5n. above. Also see Hal Koch, *Den Danske Kirkes Historie, Tiden 1800-48*, vol. 6 (Copenhagen: Gyldendal, 1954); P. G. Lindhardt, *Den Danske Kirkes Historie, Tiden 1849-1901*, vol. 7 (Copenhagen: Gyldendal, 1958); and Niels Knud Andersen, Jens Glebe-Møller, Knud Banning, and Leif Grane, *Københavns Universitet 1479-1979*, vol. 5: *Det Teologiske Fakultet* (Copenhagen: Gad, 1981).

agnosis of the age and ideas about correctives. Not suprisingly, the kinship was closer with some than with others; and, perhaps typical of Kierkegaard, his connection with his dead predecessors (Socrates, Hegel) was usually clearer in his self-reflection than that between himself and the living. The latter connections were far more complex and ambivalent. One can mark, for example, convergences of vision between the theological personalism of Mynster's sermons and that of Kierkegaard's edifying discourses. With others, such as Grundtvig, Lindberg, and Martensen, the clashes of personality and expression between them and Kierkegaard are all too obvious and often obscure the more subtle, perhaps even deliberately understated or denied convergences of language and viewpoint. I would mention, in passing, the uncanny resonance between Lindberg's attack on the pastors of the Danish church in the 1820s and Kierkegaard's polemics of some thirty years later, a connection observed by Jørgen Bukdahl. Grundtvig (1783-1872) railed against the church of Golden Age Denmark, starting as a theological candidate with his 1810 trial sermon, "Why Has the Word of the Lord Disappeared From His House?" and continuing with his attack on university theologian H. N. Clausen, "The Church's Reply," in 1825. In the next several decades, Grundtvig found himself censored and his pastoral duties curtailed. But later he became perhaps the most influential figure of his time in the Danish church and society. In his historical chronicles, and in numerous lyrical and prose works over the span of more than half a century, Grundtvig spoke out against not only the church, in which he remained as a pastor, but also against industrialization, and earlier on, against the reformism of the liberals.[22] In his works he sought to deepen the relationship of Danish culture to Christianity by connecting Den-

---

[22]See N. F. S. Grundtvig, *Værker i Udvalg*, ed. Georg Christensen and Hal Koch, 10 vols. (Copenhagen: Gyldendal, 1940-1949) especially 1: 250-60, 335-480, 2: 317-49, 4: 1-126, 199-233, 234-352, 5: 1-232, 242-51, 6: 1-273. Major works are selected and translated in *N. F. S. Grundtvig*, ed. and trans. Johannes Knudsen, Enok Mortensen, Ernest D. Nielsen (Philadelphia: Fortress Press, 1976). For overviews, see P. G. Lindhardt, *Grundtvig* (London: SPCK, 1952); Hal Koch, *Grundtvig* (Yellow Springs, Ohio: Antioch College Press, 1952); Ernest D. Nielsen, *N. F. S. Grundtvig: An American Study* (Rock Island IL: Augustana, 1955); Kaj Thaning, *Menneske Først. Grundtvigs opgør med sig selv*, 3 vols. (Copenhagen: Gyldendal, 1963); the leading recent study and the English abridgement, *N. F. S. Grundtvig* (Copenhagen: Det Danske Selskab, 1972).

mark's historical past and future with the faith. Later he supported the political changes of 1848-1849 and eventually took a seat as a member of the parliament, where he was a strong backer of church reform, adult education, and Danish nationalism, particularly during the conflicts with Prussia. While Kierkegaard did not share Grundtvig's romanticism, historicism, and nationalism, or his theological vision of the "living word," he nevertheless concurred with Grundtvig's view that the nineteenth century was a critical point in the history of the Christian community. One can see the entangled connections between Kierkegaard and Grundtvig during and after the former's public attack on the Danish church and society most clearly in Grundtvig's sermons for 1854-1855 and in his *Christian Childhood Teachings*.

One of Grundtvig's early supporters, the scholar and later pastor J. C. Lindberg, linked the Grundtvigians' criticism of the church with that coming from the predominantly lay revivals or awakening movements (*Vækkelser*) in the 1820s and 1830s.[23] As noted, Kierkegaard could well have taken some of Lindberg's polemical tracts and speeches as models for his own vicious criticism of the clergy in 1854-1855.[24] The revivalists were also critical of the social structure and policies of the Golden Age, as P. G. Lindhardt has argued.[25] In these awakenings, criticism ranged from concern for the preservation of Lutheran orthodoxy to what might be called radical populism, that is, attacks upon the church's monopoly over religious and educational activities.[26] The revivalist movements to some extent served as schools of political socialization, with some lay leaders eventually becoming political spokesmen for the peas-

---

[23]Kaj Baagøe, *Magister Jacob Christian Lindberg* (Copenhagen: Gad, 1958).

[24]Jørgen Bukdahl, *Søren Kierkegaard og den menige mand* (Copenhagen: Munksgaard, 1961); Carl Weltzer, *Peter og Søren Kierkegaard* (Copenhagen: Gad, 1936); *Grundtvig og Søren Kierkegaard* (Copenhagen: Gad, 1954).

[25]P. G. Lindhardt, *Vækkelser og kirkelige retninger*, 3rd ed. (Århus: Aros, 1978).

[26]See *Vækkelsernes Frembrud i Danmark i Første Halvdel af det 19. Aarhundrede*, ed. A. Pontoppidan Thyssen, 6 vols. (Copenhagen: Gad, 1960-1974).

ants and eventually members of parliament. A particularly good example of such would be the schoolteacher, Rasmus Sørensen.[27]

The period in which Kierkegaard wrote, especially the 1840s, can be accurately characterized as a time of crisis and response.[28] Despite the image of Kierkegaard created by hagiographers such as Lowrie (and to some degree by Kierkegaard himself) of a singular voice of ethicoreligious protest crying in the desert of a spiritless, passionless age, there is abundant historical evidence to the contrary. Among Grundtvig, Lindberg, Mynster, and other intellectuals of this period there was a common perception of social, political, cultural and, to be sure, religious crisis. Even two of the specific targets of Kierkegaard's public attack, Mynster and Martensen, wrote, preached, and lectured about the problems the modernity of the early nineteenth century was bringing to Denmark and both tried unsuccessfully to spare the Danish church from change.[29] Others would include *Corsaren's* editor, A. M. Goldschmidt (1819-1887), the leading liberals Orla Lehmann and H. N. Clausen, Monrad and the social critic Frederik Dreier.[30] Clearly these did not all share the same diagnosis of the age or plans for reform, but to regard Kierkegaard as the only critic in this period is

---

[27]Knud Banning, *Degnekristne* (Copenhagen: Gad, 1958); *En Landsbylærer* (Copenhagen: Gad, 1958); *Forsamlinger og Mormoner* (Copenhagen: Gad, 1960).

[28]Again, see my *Journal of Ecclesiastical History* article, cited in 5n., above.

[29]J. P. Mynster, *Meddelelser om mit Levnet* (Copenhagen: Gyldendal, 1852); *Blandede Skrifter* (Copenhagen: Gyldendal, 1854); *Kirkelige Leiligheds Taler* (Copenhagen: Gyldendal, 1854); *Yderlige Bidrag til Forhandlinger om de kirkelige Forhold i Danmark* (Copenhagen: Gyldendal, 1851); *J. P. Mynsters Visitatsdagbøger*, ed. Bjørn Kornerup (Copenhagen: Gad, 1937); H. L. Martensen, *Af mit Levnet*, 3 vols. (Copenhagen: Gyldendal, 1882-1883); *Biskop Hans Martensens Breve*, ed. Bjørn Kornerup (Copenhagen: Gad, 1955): *Den christelige Dogmatik* (Copenhagen: Gyldendal, 1849); *Den christelige Etik* (Copenhagen: Gyldendal, 1871-1878).

[30]H. N. Clausen, *Catholicismens og Protestantismens Kirkeforfatning, Lære og Ritus* (Copenhagen, 1825); *Optegnelser om mit Levneds og min Tids Historie* (Copenhagen: Gyldendal, 1877); Frederik Dreier, *Folkenes Fremtid*, ed. Finn Hauberg Mortensen and Johannes Nymark (Copenhagen: Gyldendal, 1973); Svend Erik Stybe, *Frederik Dreier* (Copenhagen: Munksgaard, 1959); Poul Bagge, "Akademikerne i dansk politik i det 19. Århundrede," *Historiske Tidsskrift* 12:4:3 (1970): 423-70; Kirmmse, "Kierkegaard's Politics," 472-83.

at best erroneous and at worst wishful thinking. Quite simply, the truth of the Danish literary historian and critic Paul Rubow's comment is proved the closer one looks at the sources: "One cannot place Kierkegaard and the Copenhagen intellectual life of the years 1830-1850 in close enough connection with each other."[31] To recognize that Kierkegaard dropped his early allegiances to the conservative mainstream after 1848 and steered an independent course, as Bruce Kirmmse has so convincingly argued, is quite another matter.[32] Moreover, as we shall see, it is similarly misguided to take the social and religious criticism of *Two Ages* as representative of Kierkegaard's position throughout his career or even at the end of his life. It is best understood as an authentic expression at a particular time, a position that was to change radically after 1848.

In the case of *Two Ages*, perhaps no connection is more telling than that between Kierkegaard and J. L. Heiberg.[33] In particular, Sven Møller Kristensen underscores a number of Heiberg's views which are startling in their similarity to those of Kierkegaard in *Two Ages*, especially that of "the public."[34] In a number of reviews and essays, particularly one called "The People and the Public," although the target was originally the Copenhagen reading and theater public, Heiberg goes beyond these immediate groups to touch upon the deeper social, political, and cultural processes at work producing a new "public" in the Denmark of the 1840s.[35] Heiberg writes, earlier on:

> The subjective entitlement, which is the principle of all the age's actual struggles, is the same that leads it astray. In politics this

---

[31]Rubow, *Kierkegaard og hans Samtidige*, 10.

[32]Kirmmse, "Kierkegaard's Politics," 484-87.

[33]Credit for illumining the relationships between these and other Golden Age writers and their society is due in the first place to Rubow and then to Møller Kristensen, F. J. Billeskov-Jansen, Fenger, Petersen, and Andreasen. See their studies cited in notes 2 and 10, above. Also see *Dansk litteratur Historie*, 3: 191-247, and Kierkegaard's essay on Johanne Luise Heiberg (C).

[34]Kristensen, *Digteren*, 1: 35-38, 64-76, 87-90, 154-60, 209-28.

[35]Johan Ludvig Heiberg, *Prosaiske Skrifter*, 11 vols. (Copenhagen: C. A. Reitzel, 1862) 6: 263-82, 284-87.

wrong way is clearly recognizable in all the many of equally entitled subjects, each of whose opinions must be considered. It is authority that they want to abolish, without realizing that this cannot happen by placing themselves beyond it but rather by freely acknowledging and assimilating it. It is actually a striving to transform a people into a public, for a people is an organism in which the single atom is not valid by itself but by its relationship to the whole, but a public is a mushy mass, in which all the distinctions of the organism have vanished.[36]

Several themes and viewpoints of concern common to both Kierkegaard and Heiberg surface in this passage and throughout this and other of Kierkegaard's and Heiberg's writings. Fundamental to Heiberg's (as well as Kierkegaard's) quasi-Hegelian sociopolitical theory at this point in the 1840s was the view that authority is centrally located in the state. All the rest of social structure and culture, including religion, should be harmoniously subsumed into a higher unity with the state. No primitive authoritarian theory of the state is this; rather, it is one which views the ideal state as the epitome and collection of the "cultured" (*Dannede*). Furthermore, this pattern of society forms a well-ordered and ordering hierarchy. Authoritative figures and elite groups "represented" the interests of the remainder of society. They also were to serve the rest of society by educating, inspiring, and leading them in the path of the Spirit. It is interesting that the word used by both Heiberg and Kierkegaard for "educating" here (although with different meanings as we shall see) is "upbringing" (*Opdragelse*). Heiberg's conservatism allows room for progressive social change from above, that is, through the leadership and pedagogy of a cultural (and as it turns out, political) elite. Møller Kristensen, following David Daiches, characterizes Heiberg's position as a modified conservatism, more like the "cultural liberalism" of later nineteenth century intellectuals, including the National Liberals in Denmark later on.[37]

---

[36]Heiberg, *Prosaiske Skrifter*, 4: 401; also cited in Kristensen, *Digteren*, 1:66. The translations here are mine. Also see Rubow, *Dansk litterær Kritik*, 78-197; and Nordentoft, *Brand-Majoren*, 38-46. Kirmmse's analysis of Heiberg's theology, social theory, and politics is outstanding: "Kierkegaard's Politics," 271-329.

[37]Kristensen, *Digteren*, 1: 69.

Equally fundamental to Heiberg's position was his diagnosis of the present age, that is, the events and trends of Denmark in the 1830s and 1840s. Throughout his writings, Heiberg describes his age as one of profound crisis, cultural but also ethical and religious.[38] The ideal unity of culture, state, and religion was not being achieved. Instead the social organism was breaking down. It was being challenged by deviant new sociopolitical theories and groups. These forces wanted to destroy the state as it existed under the monarchy and level society into a public of individuals, thereby creating a society open to debate and decision by balloting. These tendencies toward equality and democracy were rejected by Heiberg as against the best interests of the people. Nothing good could come from the destruction of tradition and authority; the upheavals in France served as convincing examples of the repulsiveness of mob rule. These tendencies toward disintegration, in Heiberg's view, could be seen throughout society—in the arts, in the university and the church, and in the political realm as well. In his estimation, the result of such tendencies would be most tragic. Mob rule rather than the representational and educational leadership of the intellectual elite would produce an atomistic or fragmented mass instead of a society. Individuals would be cut loose only to be lost in spiritlessness, in a mediocre, bourgeois world.

On the basis of such a description and diagnosis, one which sees little of worth coming from liberal reformers, Heiberg proposes his own model of the directions in which society can and should progress. The path to authentic cultural and political emancipation he puts forward assumes the progress of the human spirit. It also presupposes an enlightened monarch under whose protection society will follow the lead and tutelage of the cultured elite.[39] Otherwise, "the public's own passage from an organic representative to an atomistic mob, representing nothing, is, as with every disorganization, a retrogressive step.[40]

For Heiberg, the basic model of society is precisely the organism, composed of interrelated and interdependent, albeit differ-

---

[38]Heiberg, *Prosaiske Skrifter*, 1: 384.

[39]Heiberg, *Prosaiske Skrifter*, 6: 200, 266.

[40]Heiberg, *Prosaiske Skrifter*, 6: 267.

ent parts. Any tampering with such an organism disturbs the delicate balance among components and threatens the whole with death. Only by changes from within, an almost primitive version of evolutionary theory, can the organism further develop and be perfected. Although allowing room for change, this model is nevertheless a conservative one, certainly one employed by a number of social theorists later on, not the least of whom were Emile Durkheim and Talcott Parsons.

Several other of Heiberg's writings should also be examined. Often noted in discussions of his efforts to introduce Hegelianism into Denmark is his essay, "On the Significance of Philosophy for the Present Age," from an earlier period in 1833.[41] Here the crisis of the age is identified in much the same manner as in the essays we have already inspected. The present age sorely lacks religiosity and thus morality. To this demoralized, fragmented age Hegel is summoned as a corrective, as the provider of a comprehensive view of world history and its unfolding in consciousness and in every sector of society: the state, university, theater, and church. Similar criticism of leveling and of atomistic tendencies is pursued in even greater detail in the essay, "On Authority."[42] Such criticism, as well as Heiberg's affirmative views, is also evident in his lyrical works, in particular the *Reformation Cantata*, from 1839, and the *New Poems*, from 1841. In the *Cantata* and in the portions of *New Poems* called "Divine Services" and "Protestantism in Nature," Heiberg expresses his theological position. Although it cannot be discussed at length here, this highly poeticized theology is striking in its lack of specifically Christian, let alone Lutheran, features. In preference to the worship and preaching of the institutional church, Heiberg celebrates the ideal church of nature, the home of a benevolent but rather distant and impersonal God. Heiberg affirms Protestantism's liberation of the spirit rather than any Christian dogma. His theology reverberates with echoes of Goethe, Hegel, and Oehlenschläger. His vision of the presence and movement of God in nature and in consciousness travels close to but does not cross over

---

[41]Heiberg, *Prosaiske Skrifter*, 1: 381-460.

[42]Heiberg, *Prosaiske Skrifter*, 10: 328-49.

into pantheism or deism. Fortunately for Heiberg, these works received enthusiastic reviews and thus a kind of ecclesiastical approbation from his good friend, then theology professor Hans Martensen. Yet in contrast to Kierkegaard, who used a great many natural elements in the edifying and religious discourses, and to Grundtvig, whose poetry and hymnody were suffused with nature imagery, Heiberg's theology was really quite distant from biblical and orthodox patterns. His God was essentially the spirit progressing through history. Only the few, truly enlightened souls could perceive this God, while most still had to cling to the primitive God of the church, as preached by the pastors. In sum, Heiberg's theology parallels his sociopolitical thought in elitism and in its cautious optimism about humankind, social change, and progress.

Of special note in this same collection, *New Poems*, is the satirical five-act play, "A Soul After Death," in which Copenhagen society, its bourgeois values, life-styles, and institutions are submitted to witty scrutiny and lampooning.[43] After flunking the appropriate examinations for both the Christian heaven and the Greek Elysium, Mr. Soul, a superficially educated, mediocre "bourgeois-philistine" is taken to hell by Mephistopheles. It is a hell of insipid theater and literature, a flat, dull world populated by like-minded boors. It is none other than Copenhagen. In what he subtitled as an "apocalyptic comedy," Heiberg thus pokes fun at the liberals seeking reform, the press, the university, his fellow authors, in short, at the entirety of Copenhagen society outside his own circle. Like Kierkegaard and many other Golden Age writers, Heiberg found in the bourgeois the target for his ridicule and the foil to attack the public and celebrate the cultured few.[44]

---

[43]Heiberg, *Poetiske Skrifter*, 11 vols. (Copenhagen: C. A. Reitzel, 1862) 10: 183-264.

[44]Kristensen, *Digteren*, 1: 216-17; Nordentoft, *Kierkegaard's Psychology*, 240-55; L. L. Albertsen, "Hr. Sørensen. Den personificerede dansk Biedermeier," *Kritik* 7 (1968): 68-82; and Kirmmse, "Psychology and Society," 177-83. On the Hegel-Kierkegaard connection, see Taylor, *Journeys*, and Niels Thulstrup, *Kierkegaard's Relation to Hegel* (Princeton: Princeton University Press, 1980); Stephen Crites, *In the Twilight of Christendom: Kierkegaard vs. Hegel on Faith and History*, AAR no. 2 (Chambersburg PA, 1971); and the Crites-Roberts L. Perkins exchange in Papers of the Nineteenth Century Theology Working Group, *AAR* 7 (1981): 41-71.

Although Heiberg's conservatism is clearly evident in his basic social theory and politics as well as in his diagnosis of the present age, it is richer and more elastic than that of other conservatives who rejected all change. Grundtvig's and Lindberg's earlier conservatism in the 1830s would be examples of rigidity compared to Heiberg. As a Hegelian, Heiberg was hardly rigid or reactionary in his sociopolitical or cultural perspectives. The march of the spirit was through history toward higher unity and perfection. There was an inherent optimism in Heiberg's outlook, despite his understanding of the crisis of that age. What sets Heiberg apart is the significance he grants to the spirit's ambassadors and apostles, namely the cultured elite. True progress was only possible through their guidance. Thus it is not surprising that Heiberg would have found the liberals' proposals, moderate and elitist as these were, to be repugnant. To open politics to a voting public was to unleash chaos and further atomization. Such reform would establish a tyranny of the mob. Perhaps Heiberg's own sinking popularity with the reading and theater public in the later 1840s further encouraged his vision of an intellectual oligarchy and hardened his contempt for liberal reform and democratic procedures.

Kierkegaard and Two Ages

Now these elements of Heiberg's social and political thought and his concerns about the crisis of the present age are striking when compared and contrasted with Kierkegaard's thinking early on in the latter's life as well as in *Two Ages*. There is more at stake than mere linguistic and conceptual similarities. On a number of issues I would argue that there is true convergence of viewpoint. Yet at the same time, I would also maintain that there is significant divergence in their perspectives. Both the similarities and differences suggest more than coincidental intellectual kinship and imply a complex, ambivalent relationship between them. As noted earlier, Kierkegaard seems to have circled hopefully around the Heiberg "family" in the 1830s. As Fenger observes, a great deal of Kierkegaard's early writing displays features resonant with Heiberg's own perspectives. Several pieces of evidence suggest that Kierkegaard's first book, *From the Papers of One Still Living*, was intended for one of Heiberg's journals, *Perseus* (LD, 54-55).[45] But Kierkegaard was never admitted into the Heiberg circle. He never received unqualified, serious or extended critical approval from Heiberg for *Either/Or* or any of his other writings.[46] In fact, Kierkegaard went on to lampoon Heiberg in a number of places in his writings; for example, Dr. Hjortespring's (Heiberg's) almost religious experience of Hegel's system in a Hamburg hotel room (CUP, 163-64) and the small volume *Prefaces* and its satire of Heiberg's *Urania* (SV, 5:5-71). Kierkegaard's relationship to Heiberg could be described, as the years progressed, as a mixture of distant, somewhat stilted respect yet subtle, often vicious contempt. Despite the satire of him in the pseudonymous writings, Kierkegaard regularly sent copies of his books to Heiberg (LD, 429-34). On 29 March 1846, the day before its publication, Kierkegaard sent two copies of *Two Ages, A Literary Review* to Heiberg, who had served as the editor of the novel. One copy was for the novel's pseudonymous "Author of *A Story from Everyday Life*," Fru Gyllembourg, and one for Heiberg himself (LD, 191-92, 437; TA, 142) along with a copy of the *Postscript*. Heiberg's comment on Kierkegaard's review, in his letter of response is revealing (LD, 192-93; TA, 143-44). In part Heiberg says: "I consider your description of the present age as contrasted with the preceding century a small masterpiece of penetrating and acute comprehension and pointed and pertinent satire. I am especially grateful for the description of the public and its dog, but even more so for the excellent development of the concepts of 'to be silent' and 'to speak.'"

But beyond this there was little commentary on Kierkegaard's emphasis on the ethicoreligious problems of the present age, his stress on the individual, or his prophetic-apocalyptic vision at the end of the review. Heiberg promised to forward a copy to the novel's author, and she sent Kierkegaard a pseudonymously written reply which was gracious and warm (LD, 196-98; TA, 146-49).[47] In-

---

[45]Fenger, *Myths*, 15-18, 132-49; *Myter*, 171-254.

[46]See SV 13: 407-15, and Fenger, *Myths*, 1-31.

[47]For Kierkegaard's response to Heiberg's letter, see LD, 193-94, TA, 145-46.

cidentally, Heiberg begged off any extended commentary on the copy of *Postscript* Kierkegaard had sent him.

In *Two Ages*, a great deal of what Kierkegaard has to say by way of social criticism resonates not only with Fru Gyllembourg's perspectives on the present age but also with those of her Johan Ludvig. All three are kindred spirits in contrasting the spiritless, passionless 1840s with the revolutionary last decades of the eighteenth century. The authentic cultivation (*Dannelse*) of the age of revolution is singularly lacking in the present age (TA, 61, 64), which erupts in "superficial, short-lived enthusiasm" only to dissolve into indolence (TA, 68). Over and over within the text Kierkegaard rejects the collective political activity of the National Liberals. He condemns their politicization of culture and the press, noting that their "sociality" was dehumanizing (JP, 4: 4126, 4144, 4149). What Kierkegaard implies here in *Two Ages* is stated more openly in the pages of his journals. Kierkegaard saw no need for political or social change in Denmark at this point. There could be no greater tyranny, nothing more debased than a popular government established by balloting (JP, 4: 4134, 4135, 4140). Mob rebellion against the rule of the monarch is the parallel to the present age's treason against divine governance.

Thus Kierkegaard can argue that although the present age wants to overthrow everything, everything apparently remains the same but is disintegrating from within. In the present age, specifically among the liberals, there is publicity but no action, spectators but no participants, public opinion created by the press, but no passionately held principle (TA, 70-77). Reformers call for equality, but instead level. For Kierkegaard, leveling is the creation of false equality. It is the undermining of society's bonds and order, the smashing of relationships between teacher and student, between parent and child, between priest and parishioner, between king and subject, and ultimately between the individual and God (TA, 84-87). Political activity is misguided in seeking to eliminate differences among people in the attempt to establish equality, for authentic human equality is rooted neither in social likeness, nor difference, but in the common identity of God's creatures. It is not just society's hierarchical structure and microlevel webs of interpersonal relationships that are being destroyed in the present age.

Leveling makes ethical and religious individuality impossible; thus the age looks in vain for true heroes, reformers, or leaders (TA, 88-89).

Numerous convergences between Kierkegaard and Heiberg in conservative perspectives on society and politics are expressed in *Two Ages*: mistrust of reformism; fear of the effects of political transformation; the diagnosis that the present age is being taken over by bourgeois philistines and the mob rather than being educated and led by true heroes and reformers. Perhaps nowhere is the Kierkegaard-Heiberg consensus more evident than in the depiction of "the public, a monstrous abstraction, an all-embracing something that is nothing, a mirage . . . " (TA, 90). As for Heiberg, so for Kierkegaard: this public corresponds to no particular class or interest group in society but cuts through, or better, undercuts them all (TA, 90, 92-93). The public, created by the press, can be found everywhere and nowhere, for it has no identity or permanence (TA, 93-96).

Kierkegaard's critique closed with a prophetic, even apocalyptic, vision (TA, 105-109). Noting that the present age experiences no dearth of "prophecies, apocalypses, signs and insights," most likely with Grundtvig's visionary pronouncements on the future of Denmark and Christendom, and perhaps Heiberg's own apocalyptic farce in mind, Kierkegaard observes that his own prophecy is modest, as all modern prophecies, lacking the endorsement of governance, must be. It will either happen or it will not happen (TA, 106). The present age cannot expect its salvation from social movements, from petitions sent to the government, from political rallies and marches, from public opinion or voting, and certainly not from its alleged leaders. Help will only come through the activity of "unrecognizable" individuals, God's own "plainclothes policemen" and "secret agents" (TA, 107). These extraordinary incognitos, unlike the ancient prophets and judges, will give no direct help, instructions or leadership. They cannot aid even their loved ones. Rather, following the orders of an angry yet merciful God, these invisible reformers will suffer at the hands of the present age. Suffering is their mark and this easily can be misunderstood as a sign of failure. But those who have made the leap into God's hands may be able to see that the unrecognizable ones will ultimately defeat the present age and its leveling by helping indirectly and by their suffering service and example (TA, 109). It is not without significance that Socrates, Kierkegaard's great hero and a great unrecognizable one, is mentioned by name in the brief concluding remarks that Kierkegaard devotes to the novel.

It is hard to characterize Kierkegaard's social criticism here as anything but a continuation of his early opposition to the National Liberals. That is, Kierkegaard's critique remains in the spirit and even in the language of the Golden Age's "conservative mainstream." How is this the case? Later commentators, including Lowrie, Stark, Johnson, and Malantschuk, among others, emphasize Kierkegaard's attack here in *Two Ages* on the "mass society" features of the present age: the ruthless dismantling of traditional institutions and values; its godlessness; mob psychology; the totalitarian possibilities of democracy and socialism; the alienation and anonymity of the present age; the tyranny of bureaucracies, particularly those of modern social welfare states; and the institutionalization of what Helmut Schelsky has called "continual reflection."[48] More recently, Sløk has presented Kierkegaard as the indefatigable defender of the individual against all ideologies and institutions that threaten human freedom.[49] In fact, there is much resonance between Kierkegaard's social criticism in *Two Ages* and that of later social theorists such as Max Weber, Emile Durkheim,

---

[48]Helmut Schelsky, "Can Continued Reflection Be Institutionalized? Thoughts on a Modern Sociology of Religion," *Cross Currents* 15:2 (Spring 1965): 171-89. Also see Gregor Malantschuk, "Kierkegaard and the Totalitarians," *American-Scandinavian Review* 34 (September 1946): 246-48; *The Controversial Kierkegaard* (Waterloo, Ontario: Wilfred Laurier University Press, 1980); Werner Stark, "Kierkegaard on Capitalism," *Sociological Review* 42:5 (1950): 87-114; *Social Theory and Christian Thought* (London: Routledge & Kegan Paul, 1959); Howard A. Johnson, "Kierkegaard and Politics," in Howard A. Johnson and Niels Thulstrup, eds., *A Kierkegaard Critique* (Chicago: Regnery, 1962): 79-84; Walter Lowrie, *Kierkegaard* (New York: Oxford University Press, 1939).

[49]Sløk, *Humanismens tænker*, 8-13, 95-140, 175-86, 229-39; *Da Kierkegaard tav*, 129-37.

and Georg Simmel in the "classical" period as well as contemporary critics Arnold Gehlen, Robert Nisbet, and Peter Berger.[50]

On close inspection, though, it is not simply what Kierkegaard attacks that makes his perspective conservative, but also what he both explicitly and implicitly supports. In addition to what was mentioned earlier, that is, that he opposed balloting, political parties and other collective efforts at "external" social reform (JP, 4: 4121, 4126), it is worth considering what Kierkegaard advocated. He supported an orderly hierarchical structure reflecting God's rule over creation, one in which the monarch rules with authority in matters of state and the church governs in the religious realm. Kierkegaard's basic view of social structure at this point in time is shaped both by the Lutheran doctrine of the two kingdoms and Hegelian elements, as was so with Heiberg. Authoritative individuals represent the people, first and foremost the monarch (JP, 4: 4097-99, 4116). In contrast to the liberal tyranny of mob politics, of a "people's government," authentic equality is possible only when, in an ordered society, there is a dialectical relationship between the individual and the social group (JP 4: 4144, 4110). However, in such a situation the individual is not, as in Hegel's view, fused, evaporated, or swallowed up into the mass. In fact, this very dialectic between the society and the individual is, for Kierkegaard, the high point of modern world-historical development, a progress from antiquity and the Middle Ages. By the process of "individualization" the social structure of the past will be fragmented in the present age, but now in a positive, truly helpful sense (JP, 4: 4109, 4128, 4129). The path toward the authentic reformation of modernity is also one toward authentic ethical and religious individuality (PV, 107-38).

---

[50]See Arnold Gehlen, *Urmensch und Spätkultur* (Bonn: Athenaeum, 1956); *The Self in Technological Society* (New York: Columbia University Press, 1981); Robert Nisbet, *The Twilight of Authority* (New York: Oxford University Press, 1975); Peter L. Berger, *The Homeless Mind* (New York: Random House, 1973); *Pyramids of Sacrifice* (New York: Basic Books, 1974); *Facing Up to Modernity* (New York: Basic Books, 1977). Some of the convergence noted here is examined in my *Thought* article cited in 3n., above, and in my "From Angst to Ambivalence: Kierkegaard's Social and Theological Modernity Reconsidered," *Dialog* 20 (Winter 1981): 45-51.

We can now qualify Kierkegaard's position. It is true that up until 1846 he is a loyal supporter of Denmark's absolute monarchy and state-church and a rigorous critic of the reformist orientations of the National Liberals (JP, 4: 4115-17). But he is not a pure, "party-line" conservative mainstreamer or a dogmatic Hegelian, precisely because his social theory focuses so nearly on the individual. For some time afterwards, even through 1848-1849, Kierkegaard would refer back to the text of *Two Ages*, particularly to the prophetic-apocalyptic ending, as an accurate foreshadowing of the political events of 1848 and thereafter (JP, 4: 4134, 4167; PV, 129-30, 148). Thus it is valid to claim, as Nordentoft, Kirmmse, and Elrod do, that Kierkegaard opposed Danish liberalism.[51] But it is quite another matter to conflate this admittedly antidemocratic, monarchist opposition with opposition to every other modern social and political movement, indeed with modernity *tout court*, even with social and political events of the last half of the twentieth century, as some commentators imply. To be sure, Kierkegaard's earlier social criticism, including much of that in *Two Ages*, easily lends itself to use by conservatives of social, political, or theological bents. Many Kierkegaard scholars have employed him in just such ways, including, among others, Malantschuk, Lowrie, Johnson, Stark, the Thulstrups, and Sløk. Great thinkers can be and are used to support diverse positions. But careful attention to historical details allows us to recognize that Kierkegaard was hardly a dogmatic or even an orthodox conservative, certainly not the reactionary some make him out to be. Further, such historical sensitivity also permits us to see that the liberalism Kierkegaard opposed was hardly so radical and expansive as he and later scholars sometimes imply. It is certainly not comparable with late twentieth-century fascism, state socialism, or for that matter, with contemporary Scandinavian social welfare democracy. It is misleading to treat the targets of Kierkegaard's criticism in the abstract. The Danish liberalism of the 1840s that he attacked, led by his fellow University of Copenhagen intellectuals, was quite moderate; indeed, as Kirmmse has shown, it was hardly less elitist than the "conservative mainstream," and

---

[51]Elrod, *Kierkegaard and Christendom*, 47-85, 193-248.

still very much committed to the synthesis of Christianity and culture, and to a capitalist political economy.[52] Perhaps this is why
Kierkegaard later came to oppose not only the National Liberals but
also the positions of the conservative mainstream, to which he had
earlier been loyal.

At least as far as *Two Ages* is concerned, though, a good deal of
Kierkegaard's criticism can still be accurately described as conservative. There is more than accidental agreement, more than merely
verbal similarity between his views here and those of Heiberg and
Mynster, among others. There are, of course, significant differences. Kierkegaard's criticism, while as taken up with the moral
and cultural disintegration of the present age as Heiberg's, diverges precisely at those points at which his social criticism merges
with his theological perspectives. In *Two Ages* this convergence is
most easily read in the prophetic-apocalyptic vision at the end of
the text. There, in the chaos of a leveled society, with its "broad
vista of abstract infinity," in a landscape as barren and desolate as
the Jutland heath, as Nordentoft observes, the decisive instant is
reached.[53] "That is the time when the work begins—then the individuals will have to help themselves; each one individually" (TA,
108). Then, when "everything is ready," the "abyss of the infinite"
opens up and "the sharp scythe of leveling permits all, every single
one, to leap over the blade . . . into the embrace of God" (TA, 108).
Here in rather dramatic form we still have the familiar Kierkegaardian view of the individual before God in the decisive "instant" or
"moment," the *kairos* or *Øieblikket*. Looking back over the pages of
Two Ages, the "single individual" and the "instant" are woven
throughout as the dominant themes in the diagnosis of the age and
its corrective. Individuality is threatened by the age's hyper-reflec-
tivity, by its envy, by the leveling public, by chatter. Most important, ethical and religious individuality, the relationship with God,
is made extremely difficult when the crucial human quality, passion, is stifled. Yet this tumultuous point in time, this leveling and
passionless present age is, according to Kierkegaard, God's deci-

---

[52]Kirmmse, "Kierkegaard's Politics," 472-87; Nordentoft, *Brand-Majoren*, 139-
59; *Kierkegaard*, 69-101.

[53]Nordentoft, *Brand-Majoren*, 56-66.

sive moment. God uses this *kairos* of chaos as his instrument, along with the individual, to effect authentic ethical and religious transformation, just as God used his only Son to make atonement, to win back fallen creation. There is a profound theological insight here implied, subtly stated beneath the upper layer of the text of *Two Ages*. It is Kierkegaard's recognition of an actual incarnational encounter, a meeting of God and humankind, a merging of *Geschichte* and *Heilsgeschichte*.

The convergence of human and sacred history in the apocalyptic vision is signaled by the emergence of the "unrecognizable" ones, God's "secret agents," sent to indirectly help the age, to serve in suffering (TA, 109). There is none of Heiberg's elitism here, nothing corresponding to his view of a moral oligarchy of the cultured few. If anything, there is a total reversal of such an elitist perspective and in its place a biblical view of the' authentic prophets and reformers as suffering, powerless witnesses or martyrs. Furthermore, these unrecognizable ones are suffering servants of salvation for every person, for each single individual, in particular for the poor, the sick, and all others at the fringes of respectable society. To be sure, glimpses of these figures are available earlier, in the portraits of Socrates (CI), of Abraham,and the knight of faith (FT, 49-61; CUP, 364ff., 415ff., 446ff.) and his "hidden inwardness." There are also the images of Kierkegaard himself in the struggle with *Corsaren* (JP, 5: 5891; CA) and later in the public attack on the Danish church and society (FSE, 35-36, 47-49; KAUC, 283). The unrecognizable individuals of *Two Ages*, with their decisive roles and missions in bringing about the age's healing and salvation, become the "martyrs" of Kierkegaard's later writings. Most important, the figure of the unrecognizable God, the suffering servant Christ, becomes the Christological focus of those later years. The God-in-time, the paradox is God incognito, *Deus absconditus*, covered not only with humanity but with degradation and pain (TC, 33-37, 40-60, 86-144; FSE, 78-90). This is also the Jesus who identifies himself and his Gospel with the poor, the sick, with prostitutes, criminals, and all the others at the margins of a "Christian society" (FSE, 64-67; JFY, 116).[54] This is the reviled, tortured man of sorrows who

---

[54]Also see the texts cited in 11n., above.

makes the terrible invitation to the would-be disciple to follow, to imitate him in suffering (JFY, 161-217). Yet in the dialectics of the late Kierkegaard's Christology, in what I have called his "incarnational optimism," this Christ is also God come to save, God's gift and sacrament.[55] The theological underpinnings of the end of *Two Ages*, although dimly and incompletely stated, form the groundwork for the shifts in Kierkegaard's thinking in the last years.

Towards Apocalypse: Kierkegaard's Later Years

> In these times politics is everything. Between this and the religious view the difference is heaven-wide [*toto caelo*] as also the point of departure and the ultimate aim differ from it *toto caelo*, since politics begins on earth and remains on earth, whereas religion, deriving its beginning from above, seeks to explain and transfigure and thereby exalt the earthly to heaven . . . "unpractical" as he is, the religious man is nevertheless the transfigured rendering of the politician's fairest dream. No politics has or ever can, no worldliness ever has or can think through or realize to its furthest consequences the thought of human equality [*Menneske-Lighed*]. To realize complete equality in the medium of worldliness [*Verds-Lighed*] i.e. to realize it in the medium the very nature of which implies differences, and to realize it in a worldly way, i.e. by positing differences—such a thing is forever impossible, as is apparent from the categories. . . . It is only religion that can, with the help of eternity, carry human equality to the utmost limit—the godly, the essential, the non-worldly, the true, the only possible human equality. And therefore (be it said to its honor and glory) religion is the true humanity [*Menneskelighed*]. (PV, 107-108)

Although not published until 1859, after Kierkegaard's death, these lines above were written much earlier, perhaps as early as 1846 or 1847, to serve as the preface for "The Individual—Two Notes Concerning My Work as an Author." On the one hand, Kierkegaard's sentiments in this passage accurately reflect his social, political, and theological positions in 1846, points of view that were, as we have seen, essentially conservative. In the passage, disdain for politics is not very heavily veiled. Politics and religion are worlds

---

[55]See my essays cited in 5n., above.

apart. No amount of political maneuvering will ever effect authentic human equality, which is to be found only in the realm of religion, before God. Indeed, with respect to Fru Gyllembourg's novel, and in light of the events of 1848-1849 in Denmark, the vision at the close of *Two Ages, A Literary Review* can appear as a flight of prophetic imagination, an apocalyptic fantasy.[56] Yet on the other hand, both the sentiments in this passage above and the apocalyptic vision of *Two Ages* were to be actualized in far different ways. I mean here the shifts recorded in the journals and published works after 1846 and the events of the last year of Kierkegaard's life, his public attack on the Danish church and society in 1854-1855. It is therefore premature judgment to take Kierkegaard's social and theological views in *Two Ages* by themselves, as typical or final positions. *Two Ages* is not "the" statement of his sociotheological criticism but a version, an expression at roughly the midpoint of his literary career. As I have argued elsewhere, what was to follow, in the years 1846-1855, was not merely a continuation of the earlier authorship. I do not concur with Kierkegaard's own retrospective views of 1848 and 1851 (PV, 5-138, 141-51) published respectively in 1859 and 1851, or with the views of later commentators that there is essential unity of purpose and content throughout the entirety of the writings, from *Either/Or* to the literature of the public attack.[57] Rather, along with other interpreters, Nordentoft and Kirmmse in particular, I would argue that in the years after 1846, Kierkegaard's social criticism and theology take the turns suggested earlier in this essay, turns only dimly and indirectly signaled by *Two Ages* or by the passage I have just cited. The prophetic-apocalyptic vision was quite inaccurate as a preview of the events of 1848-1849, unless one remained a social, political, and theological conservative as Kierke-

---

[56]Nordentoft, *Brand-Majoren*, 243-56.

[57]Gregor Malantschuk, *Kierkegaard's Way to the Truth* (Minneapolis: Augsburg, 1963); *Kierkegaard's Thought* (Princeton: Princeton University Press, 1969); *Fra Individ til Den Enkelte* (Copenhagen: C. A. Reitzel, 1978); Marie Mikulová, "Kierkegaards 'onde verden,'" *Kierkegaardiana* 1 (1955): 42-55; "Søren Kierkegaards martyrbegreb," *Dansk teologisk Tidsskrift* 27 (1964): 100-14; "Kierkegaard's Dialectic of Imitation," in Johnson and Thulstrup, *A Kierkegaard Critique*, 266-85. Also see Nordentoft, *Brand-Majoren*, 9-24, for a review of Kierkegaard scholarship.

gaard did until somewhat later in the early 1850s. Otherwise the change in Denmark from absolute to constitutional monarchy and the establishment of a legislative body hardly qualify as apocalyptic events (PV, 129-30, 148). The closest to such would have been the severe food shortages in 1847, the disastrous three-year war between Denmark and Germany from 1848-1851, the reactionary attitudes of the A. S. Ørsted cabinet in 1853-1854, or perhaps the incredible housing and sanitation conditions in Copenhagen that led to the terrible cholera epidemic there in the summer of 1853. None of these received more than passing mention, if that, in Kierkegaard's late journals. Yet in another sense, the apocalyptic vision did prove true and the sentences about religion as the true humanity were fulfilled—in the pages of Kierkegaard's later journals and books and in the literature of the public attack.[58] Although Kierkegaard joined ranks with neither the conservative nor the National Liberal-Grundtvigian-Friends of the Peasants coalition in the years after 1846, he nevertheless became convinced that "religion, deriving its beginning from above, seeks to explain and transfigure and thereby exalt the earthly to heaven" (PV, 107). In the end, *Two Ages, A Literary Review* is more than just a provisional statement of Kierkegaard's views on the Danish church and society in the 1840s. It also points us forward, albeit indirectly and vaguely, to the time when Kierkegaard would become an "unrecognizable" critic for whom social and theological protest were inseparable, a subversive "secret agent" of the kingdom of God, both in eternity and in the waning "Christendom" of mid-century Denmark. In short, Kierkegaard's "one-man revolution," as Sløk has called it, would culminate in the apocalypse of the public attack but also establish Kierkegaard as the first revolutionary theologian of the modern period.

---

[58]The late Kierkegaard is treated in greater detail in my essays cited in 5n., above, and in a monograph in progress. Also see Stanley R. Moore, "Religion as the True Humanism: Reflections on Kierkegaard's Social Philosophy," *Journal of the American Academy of Religion* 37:1 (1969): 15-25, as well as my essay, "Prophetic Criticism, Incarnational Optimism: On Recovering the Late Kierkegaard," *Religion,,* forthcoming (1983).

III

Kierkegaard's Two Ages: An Immediate Stage on the Way to the Religious Life

by Lee Barrett

Søren Kierkegaard is both praised by friends and criticized by enemies for reducing the evolution of an individual's passional existence to a highly standardized pattern. Many commentators do recognize that the aesthetic, ethical, and religious stages need not follow a strict chronological sequence, and they note that Kierkegaard often suggests a direct translation from some variety of the aesthetic stage to the religious, completely omitting any reference to the ethical. Nevertheless, many interpreters continue to speak of a necessary progression through the various moods and stages in Kierkegaard's works. It is commonly alleged that the road to true selfhood must pass through an orderly sequence of melancholy, irony, anxiety, and so forth. Each of these moods are alleged to be necessary prerequisites for the religious stage of life. For example, it is often proposed that one must pass from simple aesthetic immediacy through reflective aestheticism before one can attain the self-consciousness necessary for making ethical and religious decisions. At this point Kierkegaard's critics object that the roads to spiritual maturity are diverse and idiosyncratic. No single pattern of development can capture their nuanced variety.

I will argue that Kierkegaard was far from denying the multitude of nonuniform ways in which individuals can win mature selves. He does not insist upon any standard developmental pattern in the life history of an individual. Kierkegaard's *Two Ages* provides evidence to support this contention. *Two Ages* is Kierkegaard's appreciative tribute to an avenue leading to the religious life that is relatively neglected in his other writings. The singularity of this path helps suggest the wide spectrum of approaches to true selfhood which Kierkegaard was able to entertain.

Viewed in the light of his total authorship, *Two Ages* is a puzzling book. Not only is the pattern of passional development atypical of his other works, but it is also difficult to harmonize with the description of the stages of life contained in Kierkegaard's pseudonymous literature. I shall propose that the differences between *Two Ages* and the pseudonymous works are not irreconcilable discrepancies. All of Kierkegaard's remarks about the stages of life must be considered in their particular contexts, attending to the special purpose of each remark. This need becomes acute when dealing with the pseudonymous productions. The pseudonyms express only what they can discern from their own unique perspectives. Each imaginary author exemplifies a certain life view, writes with a definite polemical or artistic purpose, and addresses a unique situation. Of course, the points that these authors make are not contrary to Kierkegaard's own proper attitudes. But their analyses of their own and other's lives are colored by their limited perspectives. Consequently, Kierkegaard's definitive treatment of any given issue cannot be discovered by indiscriminately collating the scattered remarks of the pseudonyms. The effusions of Johannes about life and love cannot be added without further ado to the pronouncements of Judge William concerning the same subjects. Kierkegaard's understanding of such controversial topics as "immediacy," "the ethical," "actuality," and "inwardness" cannot be adequately appreciated without taking into account the contexts of the relevant statements in his authorship. By attending to the environment of a remark, apparent discrepancies can be resolved. The interpretive problems become insurmountable only when one takes all remarks at face value and tries to integrate them into a cohesive system.

Put starkly, the ostensible problem here is that *Two Ages* suggests an "immediate" access to the religious life. Kierkegaard claims that the "life-view" of the author of *A Story of Everyday Life* and *Two Ages* "lies on the boundary of the aesthetic and in the direction of the religious" (TA, 14). Speaking in his own voice, Kierkegaard insists that this life-view is not ethical, but is aesthetic, and, as such, "immediate" (TA, 39-40). At the same time he claims that genuine "inwardness" is to be found here and that the religious life is not far away. He commends *A Story of Everyday Life* as a "place of rest, or if you please, a place of prayer, for a certain religious tinge is unmistakable" (TA, 21). This opinion contrasts with the prevalent theme in the pseudonymous works that any "inwardness" requires a decisive breach with immediacy, actuality, and the aesthetic life. (However, the pseudonyms admit that a "concentricity" of the aesthetic and the ethical and religious dimensions can be established after such a breach.) *Two Ages* seems to present a life-view that has close affinities with the religious life, but which is not characterized by any "mediated" passage through melancholy, irony, guilt, or even ethical seriousness.

A careful reading of *Two Ages* and the relevant pseudonymous literature may reveal that such concepts as "immediacy," "actuality," and "aesthetic" have different nuances in different contexts. What Judge William means by "immediacy" may differ from what Kierkegaard, speaking in his own voice, may want to suggest. Even in Kierkegaard's nonpseudonymous uses, the connotations of such a rich concept as "aesthetic" may vary significantly. If these uses can be sorted out, the apparent discrepancies in his work may dissolve and the temptation to over-systematize his remarks may disappear. Variety may be discerned rather than conflict. I shall explore the uses of Kierkegaard's crucial concepts in *Two Ages*, not allowing their nuances in his other works to intrude. Here the meaning of his concepts will be shown through his analysis of the story. At this stage of my argument Kierkegaard's other writings will only be considered insofar as they reiterate some theme independently discernible in *Two Ages*. After this step I shall examine the divergent employment of these same concepts in his other writings, considering the mood and purpose of each work. This will enable us to appreciate the distinctiveness of the life view of *Two Ages*, recognizing how it differs from the more familiar moods and stages, and how it can be an inroad to the religious life. Keeping these differences in mind, we shall see how Kierkegaard's thought permits a plurality of patterns of passional maturation.

Kierkegaard delights in *A Story of Everyday Life* and *Two Ages* because they present a consistent "life-view." In this context a life-view is a comprehensive attitude and behavioral policy toward life as a whole. It is a distinctive way of acting, feeling, desiring, and thinking, a unique style of integrating and giving significance to the diverse components of a life. With the possession of a life view, a special demeanor informs everything an individual does and undergoes. Life views are long-term characterizations of a personality, forging the discrete episodes and particular aspects of a life into a unity.

Kierkegaard discerns such unity and coherence in these novels. He writes of them, "The disquietude is essentially the same, the quietude is essentially the same, the movement in all the stories is essentially from the same to the same; the discord introduced has essentially the same resilience, the peacefulness and relaxation are also the same—that is, the life-view is the same" (TA, 14). The author of the novels expresses her own life-view through the histories of her main characters. Whatever her distinctive life-view is, it must be visible in the constancy manifested by the two heroines of *Two Ages*.

The same life-view can exhibit itself in strikingly different ways, through seemingly different sets of behavior. The pattern of manifestation of a life-view depends upon the character of the social environment and the natural endowments of the individual. Kierkegaard observes, ". . . what is born is greatly influenced by conditions, the environment with its psychological predisposition" (TA, 49). For example, the differing attitudes and sensibilities of the two historical ages affect the behavior of the two heroines. Although most of Kierkegaard's *Two Ages* is concerned with elucidating the differences between the present age and the age of revolution, he repeatedly insists that the two heroines, living in different ages, nevertheless exhibit the same pathos. Claudine's surroundings encouraged a romantic impetuosity, inclined to action. The heroic atmosphere of the French legation supported a positive orientation to the world, expecting a happy resolution of desire. On the other hand, Marianne's environment, with its triviality and reflective indecisiveness, accustomed her to disappointment and resignation. Her situation fostered a personality inclined to recollection, to the mere thought of the beloved, rather than to the active enjoyment of him. Nevertheless, in these two quite different examples Kierkegaard insists that the "inwardness" of the life-view is qualitatively identical. He remarks, " . . . that inwardness may be the same, for example, whether it is someone who goes out on the balcony and gazes at the starry night or is a prisoner for life who steals a glance at a single star through a crack" (TA, 49). The internal cohesion of a life-view can encompass such seemingly diverse sets of behavior.

Not every life possesses a life-view, and not every author has a life-view to express in her literary productions. Kierkegaard repeatedly contrasts the constancy and self-identity of the author of *A Story of Everyday Life* and *Two Ages* with the lack of unity in the productions of other contemporary authors (TA, 7-16). Just as an author's corpus can lack cohesion, so also an individual's life can be nothing more than a congeries of particular, atomistic episodes. A person can simply react in a random, disconnected way to external situations. A life can dissolve into a chaos of immediate opportunities, pains, pleasures, desires, and fears. A subject's energies and attentions can be thoughtlessly squandered upon whatever fortune casts in its path. Such a life is lived within the category of necessity, fully determined by forces over which it has no control. Both the individual's own welter of conflicting natural desires, and the multiple values and expectations of society can dominate the subject. In such a state the self is unconscious of itself as something distinguishable from its natural and social environment, and is incapable of true responsible, purposeful activity. Such a life has no self-imposed task to give significance to its movement from past to future. It is a succession of discrete episodes rather than a cohesive history.

Kierkegaard repeats this theme in *Purity of Heart Is To Will One Thing*: "Neither can he be said to will one thing when that one thing which he wills is not in itself one: is in itself a multitude of things, a dispersion, the toy of changeableness, and the prey of corruption" (PH, 56). In *Two Ages*, those lives that are determined by the fluctuating requirements of the "age" epitomize this absence of coherence. Part of Kierkegaard's project as literary critic is to draw attention to this lack of a unifying life-view in those who only react to the demands of the age. The emphasis falls upon the difference between constancy and random activity.

However, not every life that exhibits consistent behavior necessarily possesses a life-view. A life-view requires a second condition in addition to consistent behavior. An individual might instinctively happen to behave in a consistent manner. Some very consistent patterns of behavior are attributable to mere natural endowments. Such a life might qualify as a "stage," namely, the immediate aesthetic, but it would not constitute a life-view. This is the case with Don Juan in *Either/Or*. Don Juan's life certainly has a sort of unity, for his actions are highly regular and predictable. But Don Juan is completely naturally determined. His life has the unity of a natural force, of an immediate sensuous power. He did not consider various possibilities and decide to embody erotic energy. The unity is not an achievement on his part; it is given to him by the sheer force of his dominating instinct. He is utterly devoid of self-concern and the capacity to determine his own life. The unity that he seems to have is not subject to his control; it is an accident. His life is not a true history of the responsible actualization of an ideal, but is a numerical sum of similar but nevertheless disjointed moments (EO, 1: 93-96).

The necessary condition for true self-unity that Don Juan lacks is a passionate concern for the quality of his own life. This requisite self-concern, according to Kierkegaard, arises in a special way in Mrs. Gyllembourg's *Two Ages*. Here the process of passional maturation is catalyzed by a passionate relation to a single object. One highly selective desire dominates the individual, giving order to the flux of passing fancies. No longer is the self dispersed in a stream of nonspecific immediate energy. To desire a single object is an advance beyond the condition of Don Juan. Although Don Juan does have one paramount type of desire that does give some order to his existence, his one desire can be satisfied with a plurality of similar objects. Appropriately, his desire is characterized as extensive rather than intensive (EO, 1:93). Any woman will satisfy him; his happiness depends only upon generic considerations. But the more object-specific a desire becomes, the more focused the desiring self becomes. The self is drawn even farther out of the flux and multiplicity of its environment. The desired object is no longer an amorphous manifold, but has assumed a specific shape and content. The specificity of the object helps collect the straying energies of the self, unifying and defining it. Those who lack a single passion directed toward a single object are doomed to reflect the ceaseless flux of their environment. In *Fear and Trembling* Johannes de Silentio echoes this theme that Kierkegaard has affirmed in his own voice, "If a man lacks this concentration, this intensity, if his soul from the beginning is dispersed in the multifarious, he never comes to the point of making the movement, he will deal shrewdly in life like the capitalists who invest their money in all sorts of securities, so as to gain on the one what they lose on the other—in short, he is not a Knight" (FT, 53). Similarly, in *Purity of Heart Is To Will One Thing* Kierkegaard emphasizes the category of "the wish," the concentration of all one's desire for happiness upon a singular object (PH, 148-52). To stake one's worldly happiness upon the single object of a single desire gives the immediate self its highest concentration and intensity.

In these novels the necessary unifying, object-specific passion is romantic love. Through the focus provided by the beloved person, the lover consolidates her interests and energies. This concentration of all one's hopes and fears upon a specific object has a peculiar reflexive character. The passionate concern for an object motivates a passionate interest in the quality of the subject's own life. Self-concern and concern for the object are mutually dependent. Kierkegaard remarks, "Being in love is the culmination of a person's purely human existence . . . being in love is simultaneously just as much inwardness as it is a relation directed outward to actuality" (TA, 49). Through love, "inwardness" is "born" (TA, 49). Similarly, Climacus in *Philosophical Fragments* reiterates this view, claiming that the paradox of self-love is awakened in an individual in the form of love for another (PF, 48). This self-concern, or inwardness, can evolve from concern for the externalities of love to concern for love's internalities. One commences with the hope that one will be loved in return, and with the fear of separation from the beloved, and matures to the earnest desire that one's own self will be worthy of love, that one will remain constant and faithful to the beloved. This inwardness becomes a quality of all the lover's activities and passivities in relation to the beloved.

In *Two Ages* this passionate concern is exhibited primarily by Claudine and Marianne. It is significant that in both instances the passion is a matter of "immediacy." The exact ways in which their passion deserves this description must be determined. At the very least, "immediacy" suggests that the object of love is "given" to the subject. Both of them fall in love; neither of them decides to love. Their passions are not the fruit of their own free self-determination. In this respect they are just as much determined by natural necessity as was Don Juan.

Moreover, their love is not mediated by reflection. Their passions are not any type of self-conscious pursuit of an aesthetic ideal, as is the reflective aestheticism expressed in "The Rotation Method" and "Diary of the Seducer" of *Either/Or* and "In Vino Veritas" of *Stages on Life's Way*. They are not deliberately devoting themselves to the task of appropriating some aesthetic concept, be it the "beautiful," the "pleasurable moment," or the "interesting." Furthermore, the two women are not inspired with any reflective appreciation of the need for some beloved object to give coherence to their lives. They do not first desire to be integrated selves and then, as a consequence, go search for a suitable object to give their lives the longed-for unity.

Similarly, the passion of *Two Ages* is not mediated by ethical concepts or ethical decision. Claudine and Marianne do not project the possibility of ethical existence for themselves. The stability and coherence that can be won through the appropriation of such ethical concepts as "marriage," "honor," and "duty" are not what they desire. Kierkegaard pointedly insists that the life-view in *Two Ages* is not ethical but aesthetic. The women are oriented to their own particular immediate happiness, not to the struggle to live according to "universal" categories. The moral predicates "good" and "evil" are not decisive for their lives.

To summarize, the inwardness of Claudine and Marianne is "immediate" in that it is not a function of any decision to actualize an ideal form of life presented to them by reflection, be it aesthetic, ethical or religious. The self that is the object of concern here is not any ideally possible self, but is the self of immediate actuality. These individuals are not interested in any possible ways of life that are not immediately present to them. Rather, their concern is to preserve the selves that they already are, to preserve that quality of love that they find in themselves. Any abstract self-qua-self is not the object of their passionate attention. The actual self, enmeshed in all its concrete relationships, dominates their field of vision. This is a striking divergence from the general pattern of *Either/Or*, *Stages on Life's Way*, and *Repetition*, in which inwardness seems to require some variety of mediation as a necessary condition. In *Two Ages*, on the other hand, inwardness is generated by the same natural inclination that was operating in Kierkegaard's depiction of the immediate aesthetic stage. In the pages of Mrs. Gyllembourg, Kierkegaard recognized that the intensification and concentration of immediacy itself, through the reflexive power of a specific natural passion, could stimulate genuine inwardness.

Even so, such a unified inwardness does not necessarily constitute a life-view. As we have already seen, the passion upon which a life-view can be based must be not only intensive but also extensive. The passionate inwardness must be so expansive that the relation to the beloved object comes to determine the subject's relation to everything else. The passion must be capable of engendering a comprehensive attitude and behavioral policy toward all of life's joys and sorrows. It could be possible for an individual to be passionately devoted to a beloved object, and yet never extend that buoyant love to encompass all of existence. In fact, one could love a single object and hate or fear everything else. Surely this would not qualify as a "loving" life-view. In order to become a life-view, the intensive passion must extend itself into a general stance toward "actuality." It cannot rest content with those particular aspects of life directly involving the beloved object. The acquisition of a life-view requires a dual movement on the part of the self. First it must contract itself to an intense point, and then, from that point, it must expand again to reclaim all the territory it had evacuated.

In *Two Ages* the crucial factor in the extension of the intensified inwardness is the conflict of the passion with actuality. Some obstacle to the happy resolution of the passion motivates the lover to adopt a distinctive stance toward actuality as a whole. The self is confronted with the question of what it should do, how it should feel, in a world that does not reward its single, most constant desire with satisfaction. For the life-view of *Two Ages* to develop, "the intrinsic immediate coherence of happiness and immediacy" must be "broken" (TA, 20). In this sense Kierkegaard does admit that the immediacy of this life-view has suffered a "breach." This need not happen as an actual calamitous event, for an imaginative grasp of the fragility of one's earthly happiness would suffice to provoke the split. Any awareness of the possibility of losing the beloved object or even one's own love for the object would introduce the necessary tension, would create a breach between actuality and the immediacy of desire. The possibility of unhappiness forces a confrontation of the self with the underlying indifference of the world to human desires. As long as desires are either unfocused or immediately satisfied, the recalcitrance of the world might not be fully appreciated. The concentration of the self's desires upon one object, an object that is caught up in all the uncertainties of actual existence, makes the confrontation of the self with actuality unavoidable.

The individual needs to achieve a general policy for dealing with the possibility of unhappiness in the world. In fact, the true quality of an individual's life-view is discernible in his manner of coming to grips with the "pain of actuality" (TA, 15). Concerning this pain of actuality, Kierkegaard writes, "Every life-view knows the way out and is cognizable by the way out that it knows. The poet knows imagination's way out; this author knows actuality's way out; the religious person knows religion's way out. The life-view is the way out" (TA, 15). The unhappy and bruised immediate passion needs healing, and the formation of a life-view is its salve.

This is the key to Kierkegaard's enthusiasm for the life-view of *A Story of Everyday Life* and *Two Ages*. Its method of dealing with the pain of actuality has powerful attractions for Kierkegaard. It differs dramatically from the pain-coping strategies of the life-views that

Kierkegaard elaborates elsewhere. For one thing, Claudine and Marianne do not succumb to a thoroughgoing despair. Actuality as a whole does not assume a meaningless or hostile guise for them. Their life-view draws back from a complete rupture with actuality. In this sense Kierkegaard can claim that their life view remains within immediacy. Reflection does not generalize from the experienced frustration of desire to conclude that happiness and actuality are utterly incongruous; no choice is made of a completely new life presented by a reflective imagining of alternative possibilities. Accordingly, the two heroines do not grasp for the life-views of the aesthetic poet or the religious individual, each of which requires becoming a "stranger and an alien to actuality" (TA, 20). The poet's life-view is an escape from the disappointments of actuality into the realm of imaginative possibility, into an ideal world constructed by the poet himself. The reflective aesthete abandons actuality in favor of possibility, contemplating ideals rather than actualizing them.

The differences between the life-view of *Two Ages* and the religious life are more subtle, for both involve an element of profound resignation. In order to appreciate these finely textured differences, we must recall the portrayal of the Knight of Infinite Resignation in *Fear and Trembling*. There the young swain, like Marianne and Claudine, realizes that actuality will not bless his love. Also like Marianne and Claudine, the swain persists in focusing all his passion upon the cherished thought of the beloved princess. At the same time, he does abandon all hope of attaining her in this world. The recollection of the princess remains "the whole content of life and the whole significance of reality" (FT, 53). He is not overpowered by unwelcomed and unsolicited attacks of poignant memory, but deliberately cultivates his recollection of her. At this point the "religious" quality is evident in the swain's pathos. The intensity and constancy of his love no longer require actual contact with, much less possession of, the princess. The swain gains an insight into his own subjectivity, recognizing that the internal powers of his love can sustain themselves whether fortune grants him the princess or not. He has won an enduring happiness that the world cannot disturb, and thus reveals that he has made the "infinite movement." Immediacy has been completely shattered; actuality no longer determines him at all. Kierkegaard writes, "He has comprehended the deep secret that also in loving another person one must be sufficient unto oneself" (FT, 55). The perduring quality of his own disposition, immune from all external dependencies, is the presence of the "eternal" in him.

The resignation in the works of Mrs. Gyllembourg is not such an "infinite" movement away from actuality. Of course, the resignation of Claudine and Marianne is quite real and is not to be taken lightly. Here too the one thing giving life significance and promising happiness must be renounced. Here too this renunciation does not involve any diminution of passionate attachment to the beloved. Marianne and Claudine do not forget their loved ones; they are not fickle souls given to fleeting, superficial attachments. Nevertheless, they do not make the movement of infinity. They do not rest content in the constancy of their own loving dispositions. Claudine continues to long for the apparently hopeless union with Lusard, while Marianne, although quietly resigned to her separation from Bergland, still dreams of marriage to him. Possession of the beloved object, although its unavailability is recognized, is still the focal point of the pathos. The women would infinitely prefer a happy reconciliation with actuality. The relation to external actuality remains their essential orientation. They have not made their inwardness, the enduring quality of their love, sufficient unto itself.

Furthermore, the frustration of their passion does not lead to a complete breach with actuality as a whole. Although reality is seen to be incommensurate with the fulfillment of their highest desire, they do not reject the actual world as such. They do not universalize their disappointment in their relation to the beloved into a disappointment with life in general. This certainly does not mean that they forget their loves or try to convince themselves that things are not really so bad. Such a resolution would be the evaporation of the newly won inwardness. Rather, while remaining faithful to their original passions, their strategy is to welcome and embrace whatever solace actuality can afford. Accepting the fact that their ultimate happiness has eluded them, they retain the capacity to appreciate the restorative aspects of the situations in which they find themselves. Claudine cultivates the consolations of motherhood, and Marianne, as she has always done, has recourse to the secret enjoyment of her recollection. Although their specific tactics differ according to their world-historical context, their basic strategies are the same. (In this respect, however, Marianne's inwardness more closely approximates that of the Knight of Infinite Resignation than does Claudine's, but even Marianne does not find contentment in the possession of a loving disposition. Her comfort remains the fond recollection of the beloved object, imagining how good it would be to share a life with him, and thus she betrays her orientation to an actual happiness.) The life-view presented here is a rapprochement with the way things are.

This battle-scarred appreciation of actuality is very different from the "first immediacy." Now the immediate, naive unity of desire and happiness, of aspiration and actuality, has been broken. Because this life-view still "bears the marks of having been bruised" (TA, 20), it can perceive old, familiar things in a new way. It neither takes the pleasures of actuality for granted, nor harbors any illusions about them. Rather, it deliberately cultivates whatever nourishment can be gleaned from the "more merciful aspects of suffering," "the patience which expects good fortune to smile once again," and "the resignation which gives up—not everything, but the highest" (TA, 19). The individual does not just happen to enjoy isolated episodes of gratitude, resignation, sympathy, and patience. Such moods and emotions are no longer determined by externalities beyond the subject's control, as they were in the first immediacy. Now the individual understands the deep value of these things and seeks them out on every occasion. The qualities of gratitude, resignation, patience, and sympathy characterize the individual's life in all respects. The actual world has become an object of reflection, and a choice has been made to intend that world in a definite way. The immediate passionate attraction to a single object has been tempered into a set of dispositions that can embrace the entire world in a distinctive way.

Even so, these dispositions do not constitute a qualitatively "new" life. The mastery of patience, resignation, gratitude, and sympathy does not require the refashioning of the self. As we have seen, no special concepts suggesting new and unsuspected possibilities need to be learned. For this reason, Kierkegaard can regard this life-view as remaining within the aesthetic sphere. The ability to attain and sustain such a life-view is a deepening of natural en-

dowments. The capacities that this life-view calls for normally arise
in the course of a human life in response to various ordinary situations. Human lives are such that gratitude, sympathy, and resignation are often elicited in the appropriate circumstances. One
does not decide to have them; they are called forth. The life of these
novels is the systematic extension of such episodic emotions and
natural capacities into an attitude toward life in general. Although
a reflection upon the self and its world and a choice of that world
are present, both the self and the world that are the objects of reflection and choice are the self and world of actuality. The immediate cohesion of desire and actuality has been disrupted, but
actuality has not yet been disturbed by the introduction of novel,
reflective possibilities. Consequently, Kierkegaard can describe
this way of intending the world as an "immediate" life-view. Its immediacy does not prevent it from fostering true inwardness and a
resolute and comprehensive grasp of one's life as a whole.

In Kierkegaard's *Two Ages* the pattern of a self's maturation begins in undifferentiated, externally determined immediacy, moves
to an immediate passion focused upon one specific object, proceeds to a breach with actuality, and concludes with a resigned acceptance of actuality. Through the passion for the beloved object
the self concentrates its energies, collects itself out of multiplicity,
and acquires concrete definition and unity. At this point its concern
for the object is reflected back upon itself, and it achieves inwardness. The breach with the beloved object provokes the self to consider its relation to actuality in general. With this last movement the
two necessary conditions for the formation of a life-view are present. The self has the requisite internal cohesion and self-consciousness that are a function of its partial breach with actuality. The self
has an internal principle of unity as well as a synoptic grasp of external actuality.

The ostensible problem with these conclusions is that they seem
to conflict with the analysis of passional development suggested by
portions of the pseudonymous literature. Most significant are the
remarks of Judge William concerning the "first love" and the young
girl who is "heart and soul in love" (EO, 2: 20, 21, 43, 48, 171, 187).
In these passages Judge William expresses his concern that the
seeming constancy of immediate love is illusory. The perseverance

of the lover in his emotion depends entirely upon the continued strength of the feeling of love, over which the individual can exercise no control. Nothing guarantees that the passion will endure. Judge William explains, "The lovers are sincerely convinced that their relationship in itself is a complete whole which never can be altered. But since their assurance is founded only upon a natural determinant, the eternal is thus based upon the temporal and thereby cancels itself" (EO, 2:21). As long as love is only determined immediately, it cannot be trusted.

Later the Judge grows more strident and announces that constancy can only be achieved through ethical decisions, for only ethical decisions can remove the self from the uncertain flux of natural determinants and elevate it to the secure sphere of responsible self-determination. In fact, only a choice made in the light of ethical categories is a genuine expression of inwardness and freedom. Judge William remarks, "Thus, when a young girl follows the choice of her heart, this choice, however beautiful it may be, is in the strictest sense no choice, since it is entirely immediate" (EO, 2:171). His conclusion is that true self-unity must be mediated by ethical decisiveness. Immediate love must summon duty to its aid to command that permanence that it yearns for but cannot actualize by itself. Only the universally applicable categories of ethics can ground the true inwardness and coherence of a self.

How can Judge William's rejection of aesthetic choice be reconciled with Kierkegaard's praise of the inwardness and coherence of an aesthetic life-view in *Two Ages*? Kierkegaard grants the main contention of Judge William, that immediate passion is a natural determinant. Kierkegaard even admits that Claudine's "constancy is mainly a natural endowment, a matter of immediacy and romantic erotic love, for the ethical is not decisively contributory" (TA, 39-40). Yet throughout *Two Ages* Kierkegaard praises the integrity of a singular immediate passion and contrasts it to the inconstancy of all who lack a unifying passion. One would never guess from Kierkegaard's panegyric to immediate passion that it is fundamentally incapable of giving true unity to a self.

Perhaps Kierkegaard and his own pseudonym are using such terms as "aesthetic" and "natural endowment" in slightly different ways. Judge William is addressing a highly reflective aesthete who is at the mercy of his own unruly imagination. Completely determined by his naturally given whims and moods, the young aesthete is incapable of making a decision and acting upon it. The possible life-styles that the aesthete imagines are suggested to him by his uncontrollable fancy. In this context it makes sense to emphasize the difference between ethical decisiveness and aesthetic loss of self-possession. Here the aesthetic appears as the realm of natural determination, in which human beings are buffeted by external and internal forces they cannot master.

Kierkegaard the literary critic, however, can discern another aspect of immediacy and aesthetic existence. In *Two Ages* the danger is not riotous reflective aestheticism, but the dissolution of potential individuals into the amorphous "public." Immediate passion serves to arrest this process, for at least the exemplars of passion are concerned about their concrete actuality. As we have seen, an object-specific passion differentiates subjects from their environments, giving them definition. In this process of individuation a new aspect of immediacy comes to light, an aspect that Judge William's sharp distinction of ethical freedom and aesthetic necessity had obscured.

Unlike the Judge, Kierkegaard can speak of "natural endowments," "immediate passion," and responsible "choice" in the same breath. In *Two Ages* he does not treat the natural endowments and passions of an individual as powers that automatically determine the otherwise free agent. The natural components of the subject do not appear as uncontrollable externalities in which responsible self-determination can play no part. Certainly it is true that natural endowments and immediate passions are not created by individuals ex nihilo. But this does not mean that impersonal necessity rules in the aesthetic sphere. We have seen how a naturally given passion for a single object is reflected from the object back upon the subject in its given, determinate actuality. The immediate passions, enthusiasms, proclivities, and quirks of the "actual self" are the sorts of things that can be cultivated, cared for, neglected, and even extinguished. As such, they can become the basis for a coherent life without the help of the "universal" ethical categories of a social group. Through inwardness, an individual's own concrete actuality can be present to him as a task. One can choose to appropriate one's own immediate attributes, or one can allow them to atrophy.

However, Judge William is justified in insisting upon a distinction between ethical and aesthetic choices. In an ethical choice the self appropriates a projected possibility; it becomes something qualitatively new. This is not the case with the aesthetic choices of *Two Ages*. As we have seen, the life-view here is "immediate" in that the possibilities presented by reflection have not yet made an appearance. Only the rift between desire and actuality had disturbed the peace of immediacy. Until "more decisive categories" are made available, the only self that the self can choose is the actual self. By choosing itself, the self deepens and extends that which it already is. This choice of one's actuality is as much a challenge as is the choice of an ethical possibility. Both choices can serve as preparation for the religious life. In both the ethical view and the life-view of *Two Ages*, the self can win the unity and constancy necessary for the consideration of religious categories. As Kierkegaard the appreciative literary critic remarks, "And whether or not we can come to rest in the identical life-view, there nevertheless is peace here and the incorruptibility of a quiet spirit" (TA, 16).

In the *Two Ages* we see that an "aesthetic," "immediate" life-view can bring a self to the "boundary" of the religious life. The two heroines have acquired many of the passional prerequisites necessary for the move into the religious life. Their immediate passion has given the self definition, a reflexive self-concern and inwardness, and the breach with the highest happiness has prompted the self to deliberately cultivate an expansive life-view. In a sense the self does choose and is self-conscious, but the self of which it is conscious and chooses is the self of actuality. It does not reflectively entertain or project any possibilities that are not immediately presented to it in the life of actuality. Consequently, it cannot experience the highly reflective moods of irony, melancholy or ethical guilt. Its coherence has been achieved without the projection and choice of a qualitatively new life. The self has deliberately cultivated the kind of resignation that is inherent in the life of actuality.

The fact that the self remains oriented toward actuality separates this life-view from the religious stage. The individual still looks for comfort in actuality and would prefer a happy relation to actuality. In *Edifying Discourses*, Kierkegaard describes similar lives that have reduced their empirical wants to a minimum, and thus have a minimal attachment to actuality. This chastened attachment to actuality means that this life-view is still subject to some minimal external necessity. The continued dependence upon factors external to the self can provide the motive for the movement into the religious life proper. The self cannot be fully integrated and content until it recognizes that happiness depends upon nothing except the Eternal. In order to advance into the religious sphere, Marianne and Claudine would have to discover that they do not need worldly solace of any sort, that the "eternal" is sufficient. Their resignation would have to extend from being qualified to being infinite. Such an extension would require a decisive breach with actuality in every respect. A new life in which the Eternal alone is sufficient for happiness would have to be imagined and deliberately chosen. Here the self would not simply choose to cultivate its natural endowments and attitudes toward the world, but would decide for a fundamentally new orientation.

Although this new life requires more than the deepening of aesthetic capacities, it does bear some continuity with the life-view of *Two Ages*. The life-view of *Two Ages* has been a helpful "education" in resignation. The qualified resignation of *Two Ages* is useful practice for the more dramatic infinite resignation of the religious life. Kierkegaard remarks in *Purity of Heart Is To Will One Thing*, "love, from time to time, has in this way helped a man along the right path. Faithful, he willed only one thing, his love. . . . Yet the act of being in love is still not in the deepest sense the Good. But it may possibly become for him a helpful educator, who will finally lead him by the possession of his beloved one or by her loss, in truth to will one thing and to will the Good" (PH, 66). This theme of resigned suffering in actuality as "educator" appears frequently in Kierkegaard's edifying literature. As Kierkegaard notes in "Man's Need of God Constitutes His Highest Perfection," life can educate a person in resignation by stripping away an individual's sources of happiness one by one until the individual recognizes that God alone is sufficient (ED, 4). In "The Narrowness Is the Way" Kierkegaard suggests that life teaches a child that its task is to bear misfortune (GS, 97-117). The child does not discover this by entertaining reflective possibilities; life itself makes this abundantly clear. The adult can build upon what the child has learned and come to see that resignation is the path to the Eternal. The adult can freely welcome what the child has humbly accepted. Like the child, Marianne and Claudine accept their suffering, which does educate them in the art of resignation. This pedagogy can bring an individual to the point where he can appreciate and appropriate resignation as the way to God.

IV

The Levels of
Interpersonal Relationships
in Kierkegaard's Two Ages

by Pat Cutting

Introduction

K ierkegaard used the writing of a literary review of Thomasine
Gyllembourg's novel, *Two Ages*, not only as the occasion for a
scathing criticism of the present age, but also for a presentation of
the levels of interpersonal relationships. Although the main concern of Kierkegaard's authorship is the stages of the development
of the individual, this writing shows that he does not rule out the
possibility of genuine relationships between individuals. In the final analysis, for Kierkegaard, the authentic individual need not remain isolated in his or her own subjectivity but can choose to
actualize genuine relationships with others.

Like all of Kierkegaard's published writings, this work is incredibly complex and multileveled. Whereas Gyllembourg's descriptions of everyday life reflect the spirit of the age of revolution and of the present age, Kierkegaard's review offers a double reflection that not only reflects the major themes of Gyllembourg's novel, but also reflects some of the major themes of his own pseudonymous writings. And as the novel stresses interpersonal relationships of everyday life in the two ages, so Kierkegaard's reflections bring out the possibilities of interpersonal relationships within the stages of life depicted in his pseudonymous writings.

The description of the stages of life in Kierkegaard's pseudonymous writings is developed along two lines—the concrete and the abstract. The concrete line develops in a way analagous to that of Gyllembourg's reflections of the ages in everyday lives, that is, for Kierkegaard, various individuals within concrete situations reflect the characteristics of the stages of life. This line moves through *Either-or, Repetition, Fear and Trembling,* and *Stages on Life's Way.* The abstract line of Kierkegaard's pseudonymous writings goes a step further than Gyllembourg's novel by describing and analyzing the fundamental existential structures that are depicted in the concrete line. The abstract writings include *Johannes Climacus or De Omnibus Dubitandum Est, Philosophical Fragments,* and *Concept of Anxiety.* The *Concluding Unscientific Postscript* aims at a fusion of the abstract and concrete orientations.[1]

In *Two Ages* Kierkegaard interweaves the abstract and the concrete lines by giving abstract descriptions of the fundamental characteristics of the ages, as well as reflections of these characteristics in his interpretations of the concrete everyday lives of Gyllembourg's novel.

Following the structure of Kierkegaard's *Two Ages,* the second section of this essay will describe in abstract terms the fundamental characteristics of each of the ages of interpersonal relationships and some of the ways in which these fundamental structures are reflected in the interpersonal relationships of the characters of Gyllembourg's novel, as interpreted by Kierkegaard. Also, some of the

---

[1]Gregor Malantschuk, *Kierkegaard's Thought,* trans. Howard V. Hong and Edna H. Hong (Princeton: Princeton University Press, 1971) 214.

reflections of the stages of intrapersonal development for the individual as depicted in Kierkegaard's pseudonymous writings will be shown. And to further elucidate Kierkegaard's observations, especially as they pertain to the individual's relationships with others, some of the similarities between Kierkegaard's levels of interpersonal relationships and Heidegger's authentic and inauthentic modes of Being-with-Others will be pointed out.

The third section will use Kierkegaard's law of repetition and theory of reduplication to illuminate some of the complex structures of moments of choice for the individual, some of which involve interpersonal relationships. And it will conclude by showing that Kierkegaard's concern for the possibilities of genuine interpersonal relationships is not restricted to *Two Ages* but is foreshadowed in earlier writings and further illuminated in later ones.

Reflections of Gyllembourg's Two Ages,
Kierkegaard's Stages of Individual Development
and Levels of Interpersonal Relationships

The main purpose of this section is to elucidate Kierkegaard's description of the levels of interpersonal relationships as given in *Two Ages*, especially the level of individuality in community. Second, it will show some of the characteristics of the individuals that are involved at each level. And incidentally, it will point out some of the ironic twists that Kierkegaard gives to the reflection of the stages of life of his pseudonymous works in the ages of interpersonal relationships.

The ages of interpersonal relationships include an earlier age of provisional immediacy, in which outstanding individuals determine the values and norms for the others; the present age, which levels the outstanding individuals but establishes an abstract public that dictates the norms and values of the society; and the highest stage of the second immediacy[2] in which the authentic individual can establish genuine interpersonal relationships.

---

[2]Immediacy is often used by Kierkegaard in this basic schema: aesthetic stage = first immediacy; ethical stage = reflection/other mediating agent; religious stage = second immediacy. (See fn. 6, below, for an explanation of Kierkegaard's

Kierkegaard relates the earlier age of interpersonal relationships to Gyllembourg's age of revolution, which he describes, in part, in terms of the society of "antiquity" in which there were two classes of people: (1) the few outstanding individuals who were "the men of excellence," and (2) the many lesser members of society. "The host of individuals existed, so to speak, in order to determine how much the excellent individual was worth . . . the crowd had no significance whatsoever; the man of excellence stood for them all" (TA, 84-85).

Unlike the abstract mass of the public of the present age, the groups in antiquity and the age of revolution consisted of distinct individuals with passionate loyalties, which gave them a degree of inwardness and depth. However, the majority of the people subordinated their values and choices to others—to outstanding orators, to superior officers, to leaders of the revolution, and others.

According to this description, the existential experiences of Being-with-Others were not genuine relationships in which each individual is free to project and choose which possibilities to actualize in his or her existence. Rather, in Heideggerian terms, Being-with-Others at this level is in an inauthentic mode in which the outstanding individual "leaps in" and takes over the cares of the others, disburdening them of the responsibility of making choices, and thus, depriving them of authentic selfhood.[3]

For Kierkegaard, the outstanding individuals, as well as the lesser members of society, have not reached the highest stage of development. This is true because the person at the highest stage of individual development respects the freedom of each and every person so that everyone can become an authentic individual. "The

---

multiple use of the term "reflection.") This basic schema is used in a variety of ways such as: "The individual as the individual is higher than the universal, but it is the universal precisely which is mediation. . . . Faith is not the first immediacy but is a subsequent immediacy. The first immediacy is the aesthetical" (FT, 92); and "The immediacy of love recognizes only one other immediacy as of equally noble birth, that is the immediacy of religion; love is too maidenly to recognize any party as privy to it except God. But religion is a *new* immediacy, it has reflection betwixt it and the first immediacy" (SLW, 159).

[3]Martin Heidegger, *Being and Time*, trans. John Macquarrie and Edward Robinson (New York and Evanston: Harper and Row, Publishers, 1962) 158.

bleakness of antiquity was that the man of distinction was what others could not be; the inspiring aspect (of the modern era) will be that the person who has gained himself religiously is only what all can be" (TA, 92).

In concrete terms, the people from Part One of Gyllembourg's *Two Ages* are essentially passionate, and therefore, have an inwardness and immediacy that is lacking in those of the present age. However, this is a provisional inwardness and immediacy, and unlike that of the highest stage, "it can be transformed by one single deviation into untruth" (TA, 65). For example, just as there is something sacred about the worshiping of an idol because devoutness itself is sacred, even though it is devoutness to a false God; so there is something essential about the passion between Madam Waller, the merchant's wife, and Dalund because passion itself is essential, even though there is also an untruth about the affair. Devious, false behavior towards others is made necessary because the affair must be concealed from her husband. Also, she lacks personal integrity because she tries but "cannot completely master an inner voice that reminds her that she is treading a forbidden path" (TA, 46).

The heroine of the age of revolution, Claudine, has the constancy to will one thing—a marriage with Lusard—and remaining true to the idea, she remains true to herself in inwardness (TA, 42-43). Thus, the "denouement in the relation between Claudine and Lusard is romantically created by constancy" (TA, 39). However, this is a relative constancy, similar to that of the ethical stage as depicted in Kierkegaard's pseudonymous writings[4] (see EO, SLW), so it does not have the absolute stability of the religious stage.

Also in Part One of the novel, among the noncommissioned officers, as well as among the company commanders and generals, there are outstanding heroes, men of excellence (TA,107). These outstanding individuals are recognizable as having actualized the idea of the revolution in their own existences, and thus, they are authorities on the revolutionary values that others are expected to actualize in their lives.

---

[4] See below and fn. 7.

The passionate willing of one thing, whether it is a personal re-lationship or a revolutionary idea, provides a basis for the inward-ness that is required for individuality. However, the crucial fact at this preliminary stage is in regards to the constancy of the passion. At this level the object of the willing is something relative, so the passion provides only a provisional immediacy and inwardness. Even though some people live out their lives in this provisional way, for Kierkegaard it is not the highest stage possible. This is true be-cause the passion for something relative can wax and wane as the circumstances change—"a person finds definitive rest only in the highest idea, which is the religious" (TA, 65).

During the second stage of interpersonal relationships, the present age, it is the abstract crowd, namely, the public, rather than the outstanding individual, that leaps in and takes over the respon-sibilities and the choices of the members of the society. In Heideg-gerian terms, this is the level of the "they- self,"[5] and like Heidegger's "they," Kierkegaard's "public" is an abstraction. There are no distinct individuals to enter into an essential relation-ship. Rather, the public is "made up of unsubstantial individuals who are never united or never can be united in the simultaneity of any situation or organization" (TA, 91).

As the individuals themselves evaporate into the anonymity of the abstract public, all hope of genuine interpersonal relationships also evaporates. Instead of the qualitatively distinguishing pas-sions that provide inwardness and thus distinct entities that can re-late to each other, the present age provides only enervating infinite reflections that produce superficial abstractions that cannot enter into genuine relationships but can only reflect on the problem. The citizens of the present age "watch each other instead of relating to each other and count as it is said, each other's verbal avowals of re-lation as a substitute for resolute mutual giving in the relation" (TA, 79).

---

[5]Heidegger, *Being and Time*, 164.

The present age, as an age of reflection,[6] is an age devoid of vitality. It has "no hero, no lover, no thinker, no knight of faith, no great humanitarian, no person in despair" (TA, 75) who has had the primitive experience that gives validity to the reflections and utterances of an age. Rather, both the intrapersonal development and the interpersonal transactions are like paper money that is traded off as though it were the real precious metal.

As usual, Kierkegaard's reflections are not straightforward mirror images, but repetitions with a difference (see TA, 14). The reflections of the stages of life (of the pseudonymous writings) in the first two ages of interpersonal relationships, take an ironic twist.[7] The individuals from the first of the two ages, the age of revolution, are viewed as having many of the characteristics of the ethical stage, which is the second stage of the pseudonymous writings; and the people of the present age, the second of the two ages, are seen as having many of the characteristics of the aesthetic stage, the first stage of the pseudonymous writings. Only the stage of religion remains constantly in its place—at the highest level of both intrapersonal development and interpersonal relationships. The only difference is that in *Two Ages* there is an emphasis on individuality in community rather than on the development of individuality.

In concrete terms, the present age produces superficially "plated people" (TA, 53) such as the Mrs. Waller of Gyllembourg's present age, that is, the commercial councilor's wife, who is not a pure, essential person, but is superficially plated over a core of less

---

[6]See the Hongs' *Historical Introduction" to Two Ages*, ix. Their explanation of Kierkegaard's two uses of the term *reflection* (Danish: *Reflexion*) aids in understanding some of the subtle meanings in *Two Ages*. When the present age is depicted as a mediating reflective age Kierkegaard is using "reflection" to mean "calculating prudence or procrastinating indecision lacking in the passion of engagement" (TA, ix). In *Stages on Life's Way* (see fn. 2 above) he uses the term *reflection* in its meaning of "contemplation" when he describes the ethical stage as a mediating reflective stage. Also see fn. 7 below.

[7]Much of the irony of *Two Ages* is due to Kierkegaard's reversal described, in part, in this paragraph. Also involved is a reversal of the role of mediation. In *Two Ages* the present age is the reflective mediating agent, whereas in the pseudonymous writings the ethical stage played this role, but with a difference—see note 6 above.

pure metal. This lack of integrity leads to false interpersonal relationships as represented by her transitory relationships with men,
the encounters with her stepdaughter, the maid, and others.

The love affair of Marianne and Ferdinand reflects the superficial quality of the present age. Like the age itself, the relationship
was "essentially devoid of passion from the standpoint of inwardness and the romantic" (TA, 53). Marianne and Ferdinand were so
caught up in the worrisome calculations of the age that neither of
them were able to overcome the anxieties the age that neither of
them were able to overcome the anxieties brought about through
reflection on their financial situation. Lacking the enthusiasm of
passion between Claudine and Lusard of the age of revolution, the
relationship between Marianne and Ferdinand could be threatened
by mundane pecuniary anxieties.

According to Kierkegaard, the present age is a necessary mediating stage between the earlier age and the age of genuine interpersonal relationships (TA, 108). In the forward movement through
the ages, one of the most important lessons that is learned is that
of genuine equality. In the earlier age there was no real equality because the heroes, the leaders, the outstanding individuals, chose
the values that the lesser members of the society were expected to
actualize in their own lives.

The leveling process of the present age introduces the concept
of equality, but it is an alienating, abstract, mathematical equality
(TA, 84-85). Like all averages, the average norms of the public,
which all members of society are expected to strive for, level outstanding individuals to the mediocrity of the average. Thus, society
"grinds smooth the individual's angularity and essential acciden-
tality" (SUD, 33), so that the present-day member of the public
"finds it too hazardous to be himself and far easier and safer to be
like the others, to become a copy, a number, a mass man" (SUD,
34). Thus, equality, like all values at this stage, is relative to the values and size of a given society at a given time.

In the age of genuine interpersonal relationships, the highest
stage in the dialectical movement, there is absolute, essential equality, rather than the relative, accidental equality of the intermediate
present age. According to Kierkegaard, true equality can only be
achieved at the highest level where there is authentic individuality

capable of genuine community with others. Here, each individual, rather than relating himself or herself to the relative norms of the public, relates absolutely to the absolute. And "it is true that before God and the absolute *telos* we human beings are all equal" (CUP, 359). Thus, the person who "reaches the top does not become the man of distinction, the outstanding hero—this is forestalled by leveling. . . . He only becomes an essentially human being in the full sense of equality. This is the idea of religiousness" (TA, 88).

This essential and absolute equality is the basis for one of the main requirements for genuine interpersonal relationships: Thou shalt love thy neighbor with a nonpreferential love (WL, pt. 1, sec. 2B). "Love to one's neighbor is therefore eternal equality in loving, but this eternal equality is the opposite of exclusive love or preference. . . . Equality is just this, not to make distinctions, and eternal equality is absolutely not to make the slightest distinction" (WL, 70). Thus, authentic nonpreferential love "means, while remaining within the earthly distinctions allotted to one, essentially to will to exist equally for every human being without exception" (WL, 92).

A person at the highest level of maturity has learned well the lessons of the previous ages. He or she will have been educated to actualize individuality at the highest level in such a way as to respect the freedom and responsibilities of others. Not one of the persons at the highest stage will give direct help by assuming "decisive leadership of the crowd (instead of giving negative support and helping the individual to the same decisiveness he himself has)" (TA, 108). The law of existence at this stage is "not to rule, to guide, to lead, but . . . to serve, to help indirectly" (TA, 109).

Although the aid is not direct, the individual does work diligently to aid others through non-coercive, indirect methods, so that each person can see his or her potential for authentic individuality and for harmonious, genuine relationships with others. One such method is involved in Kierkegaard's theory of reduplication, which includes the possibility of indirectly teaching values through the actualization of these values in one's own life. By choosing to actualize possibilities that incorporate, for example, the values that are involved in a genuine marital relationship, a person makes others aware of the possibility of reduplicating such values in their own lives—yet each person is left free so that he or she might choose such a relationship, as did Fru Gyllembourg, or not, as did Kierkegaard.

Also, both the novel by Gyllembourg and its interpretation by Kierkegaard can be viewed as indirect communications that aid individuals in their development of authentic individuality and genuine relationships with others. Since these writings involve fictionalized individuals related in fictionalized situations, the indirectness is a step further than the actual existential communication of one's own life.

In Heideggarian terms, in genuine interpersonal relationships the authentic individual leaps ahead of the other and "helps the Other to become transparent to himself *in* his care and to become *free for* it."[8] That is, each person aids the other to see through the inauthentic they-self and view the possibilities of authentic existence. In becoming free from the "they" each individual becomes free from each and every other person, including the one who is giving the indirect assistance. For Heidegger, the "mode of being" for authentic individuality in genuine community is anticipatory resoluteness that takes into account authentic care. This is a "kind of solicitude which does not so much leap in for the other as *leap ahead* of him in his existentiell potentiality-for-Being, not in order to take away his 'care' but rather to give it back to him authentically as such for the first time."[9]

For Kierkegaard, this stage can only be reached by way of a leap away from the crowd to a solitary position face to face with God (TA, 108). Here, the individual escapes the abstracting and leveling relativity of the public and relates the self to the self with the absolute as a measure (SUD, 14, 79, 210). However, this does not mean that the individual must necessarily remain isolated. Rather, "the single one" (*den Enkelte*) can reaffirm relationships with others, but at a qualitatively higher level than that which was possible at the lower stages of individual development.

As the author of the literary review, Kierkegaard offers some observations on the general characteristics of authentic individuality

---

[8]Heidegger, "Being and Time, 159.

[9]Ibid., 158-59.

in genuine community, such as those described above (see also TA, 111-112). However, partly due to the fact that the novel he is reviewing extends only to the present age, he does not give examples of specific individuals who reflect the general characteristics of the highest stage. Thus, the concrete line of the review points to, but does not extend into, the age of genuine relationships with others.

However, Kierkegaard does give additional insight into the possibilities of specific genuine interpersonal relationships in *Purity of Heart Is to Will One Thing*, one of the *Edifying Discourses in Various Spirits* that he wrote in 1846 just after finishing *Two Ages*.[10] Here, he expands on the possibilities of remaining an authentic individual while entering into such specific relationships as those between husband and wife and between parent and child. In this writing Kierkegaard unequivocally states that the individual at the highest stage of life need not remain isolated, for it is the person who has gained the stability and the insight given by a consciousness of the eternal who is capable of genuine interpersonal relationships (PH, 197).

The following section of this article will attempt to give additional insight into the possibilities of genuine interpersonal relationships for the individual at the highest stage of life by showing how this theme, which is so prevalent in *Two Ages*, relates to Kierkegaard's theory of reduplication and law of repetition and to other of his writings such as *Fear and Trembling* and *Works of Love*.

*The Reaffirmation of Genuine Interpersonal
Relationships for the Individual at the Highest Stage of Life*

The ages of interpersonal relationships and the stages of the development of the individual are so closely interrelated that they can often be considered as two aspects of one existential experience. This section will attempt to clarify the interrelationships of these two aspects by using Kierkegaard's theory of reduplication and law

---

[10]Alistair McKinnon and Niels Jørgen Cappelorn, "The Period of Composition of Kierkegaard's Published Works," *Kierkegaardiana* (Copenhagen: Munksgaard, 1974): 9:139.

of repetition to describe some of the fundamental characteristics of the complex structures of moments of choice.

The law of repetition requires that as each new stage of life is achieved by the existing individual, the content of previous experience is retained, but it is repeated;[11] that is, it is "re-viewed" in the light of the perspective of the new stage. The individual's life has continuity because in repetition "his history goes forward in continuity with his own past."[12] Also, the viewing of one's experience according to a new perspective leads to the opening up of new possibilities for the person at the higher stage that were not available to him or her at the lower level.

Reduplication gives the individual's life the content that is retained and repeated under the law of repetition. The theory of reduplication, which was mentioned in a different context in the second section of this essay, maintains that the existing individual can decisively institute a transition from thought possibilities to actuality. Kierkegaard describes reduplication in a journal entry of 1847:

> No doubt there have been keener and more gifted authors than I, but I would certainly like to see the author who has reduplicated his thinking more penetratingly than I have in the dialectic raised to the second power. It is one thing to be keenly penetrating in books, another to redouble the thought dialectically in existence. . . . The dialectic in books is merely the dialectic of thinking, but reduplication of such thinking is action in life (JP, 3:3665).

Thus, according to the theory of reduplication, the claim of existence for the existing individual is "not that he should be a contemplative spirit in imagination, but an existing spirit in reality" (CUP, 108). The existing individual's task is not to remain abstract possibility but to choose which specific possibilities to actualize.

The interrelationship of the law of repetition and the theory of reduplication can be explained in terms of Kierkegaard's multiple use of the word "leap." As well as the leap between major stages of

---

[11]Malantschuk, *Kierkegaard's Thought*, 135-36.

[12]Søren Kierkegaard, *Søren Kierkegaards Papirer*, P. A. Heiberg, V. Kuhr, and E. Torsting, eds. (Copenhagen: Gyldendal, 1908-1948) 4:263-64. The translation is mine.

life, which signifies a breaking with an old viewpoint and the reorientation of the self according to a new perspective, there is also a leap from thought possibilities to actuality.[13] Thus each moment of choice includes: (1) the choice of whether to remain at the current stage of life and retain the viewpoint of that level or to leap into the next stage and adopt a new perspective, and (2) the choice of which specific thought possibility to actualize, that is, which possibility to assist in its "leap" from the realm of thought to the realm of actuality. Of course, the choices of which possibilities to actualize are limited to a set of live options[14] available for the person making the choice.

The range of possibilities that are live options for a specific person at a specific moment of choice is determined not only by the person's potential for actualizing the possibilities, but also by his or her awareness of such potential. When the individual has reached the highest stage of maturity there are moments of choice that include both a potential for genuine interpersonal relationships and an awareness of such potential. Thus, at the highest stage the individual's set of live options includes possibilities of authentic individuality in genuine community.

Repetition and reduplication at the highest stage of individual maturity involves the reaffirmation of relationships with others, but at a qualitatively higher level than was possible at the lower stages. The possibility of reaffirmation of relationships with others for "the single one," that is, for the religious person, is not restricted in Kierkegaard's writings to *Two Ages*. Rather, it is foreshadowed in the earlier writings, especially in *Fear and Trembling* (1843), and is repeated again in the later writings, especially in *Works of Love* (1847).

In the pseudonymous writing of *Fear and Trembling* Kierkegaard describes the two steps of resignation and reaffirmation in terms of the double movement of the knight of infinite resignation and the knight of faith. The knight of infinite resignation renounces all temporal and finite relationships in return for an eternal conscious-

---

[13]Malantschuk, *Kierkegaard's Thought*, 133.

[14]William James, *The Will to Believe and Human Immortality* (New York: Dover Publications, 1956) 2.

ness (FT, 59). The knight of faith makes the second part of the double movement by reaffirming temporal and finite relationships. "A purely human courage is required to renounce the whole of the temporal to gain the eternal. . . . But a paradoxical and humble courage is required to grasp the whole of the temporal by virtue of the absurd, and this is the courage of faith" (FT, 59). The isolated, lonely knight of infinite resignation has not yet reached the highest stage of faith that includes possibilities of authentically reaffirming relationships with others. And further, "the knight of faith is the only happy one, the heir apparent to the finite, whereas the knight of resignation is a stranger and a foreigner" (FT, 61).

In 1847, the year after he wrote *Two Ages*, in the non-pseudonymous writing of *Works of Love*, Kierkegaard repeats the description of the reaffirmation of relationships with others, but this time he describes it in specifically Christian terms: To love thy neighbor, who is each and every person, is not to remain isolated in the blissfulness of eternal consciousness, as did the knight of infinite resignation, but to reaffirm relationships with others as did the knight of faith. "In Christ perfection looked down to earth and loved the person it saw. We ought to learn from Christianity. . . . To descend from heaven means limitlessly to love the person you see just as you see him. If, then, you will become perfect in love, strive to fulfill this duty, in loving to love the person one sees, just as you see him" (WL, 170).

The new translation of *Two Ages*, may well lead the English reader of Kierkegaard's writings to more awareness of the possibilities of interpersonal relationships for the existing individual at the various stages on life's way. The reader of *Two Ages* will see that it is the relationships of the earlier ages/stages that Kierkegaard views as immature and false and that the individual at the highest stage of life can choose to actualize possibilities of genuine relationships with others. This aids the reader to see an additional level beyond the level of resignation in other Kierkegaardian writings and makes more understandable his statement of 1843: "If I had had faith I would have stayed with Regine"[15] (JP, 5:5664).

---

[15]This refers, of course, to Regine Olsen to whom Kierkegaard was engaged from 10 September 1840 to 11 October 1841. He learned in July 1843 that she was engaged to Friedrich Schlegel.

V

Passion
and Reflection

by Robert C. Roberts

The ideas of passion (or pathos) and reflection (or thought) loom large in the thought of Søren Kierkegaard. They seem to be for him an important key to authentic ethics and Christian faith as well as to understanding what is wrong with his own age. I propose to examine the relations between these notions. This subject is complicated by the fact that Kierkegaard uses "passion" in two quite distinct (though related) leading ways, and that he assigns reflection both a villainous and an angelic role in his story. I propose to consider the following questions in this essay: (1) What are the leading senses of "passion" in Kierkegaard's thought, and how are they related? (2) How does reflection become an enemy of passion? (3) How is reflection an ally of passion? (4) What are the main passion-engendering features of Kierkegaard's own thought?

Passion and Emotion

Let me begin with some general comments about these concepts, and then apply what we learn to Kierkegaard. In everyday usage, there are at least two different concepts that can be expressed by the word "passion." When we speak of a neighbor as having a passion for antique automobiles, we are pointing to something quite different about him than when we say he flew into a passion upon seeing the neighborhood children making mudpies on the hood of his 1922 Rolls Royce. Having a passion for something, and being in a passion over something are different phenomena. The passion our Rolls Royce owner flew into was an emotion—anger. But a man with a passion for antique cars is not, by this token, having any particular emotion. Instead, he has a relatively abiding *interest* in such cars, an interest that has a marked effect on his behavior when car shows come to town, and which manifests itself in the subjects he chooses for conversation and in his propensity for sticking his nose in antique car magazines. Here we are talking about something approaching a character trait of the man, a pattern of caring, an interest, a concern, an enthusiasm.

The main connection between an enthusiasm and an emotion, or having a passion and being in a passion, is that the former is the disposition to the latter. A passion is a disposition to pathos. An interest is a disposition to emotions. One can easily see how the passion for antique cars, while not itself an emotion, is a disposition to a wide range of emotions: anger about the ill-placed mudpies, joy and anticipation at seeing one's car magazine in the mail box, envy of the neighbor's new Bearcat, disappointment at the rain on the day of the auto club's city tour, and so forth.

In Kierkegaard's writing and those of his pseudonyms, "passion" is used in both of the senses distinguished above. When Kierkegaard accuses his age of being "a sensible, reflecting age, devoid of passion, flaring up in superficial, short-lived enthusiasm and prudentially relaxing in indolence" (TA, 68), he is claiming that people lack sustained interests that are deep enough to shape consciousness and behavior decisively. Thus this *lack of passion* is at the same time a lack of character (see TA, 77-78). "Even a relative end," says Johannes Climacus,

> transforms a man's existence partially. But since the speculative nineteenth century has unfortunately made existence tantamount to a thinking about everything, we rarely see an existence that devotes itself energetically even to a relative end (CUP, 352).

The present age, through its reflectiveness, has become dissipated in interests; most people are not capable of prolonged and focused enthusiasm. Instead, they are dilettantes, interested in everything and therefore deeply interested in nothing, neither in political reform, nor learning, nor religious renunciation. (cf. TA, 70-71). The highest and most deeply integrated human passion is the infinite passionate interest in one's own eternal happiness. Passion as enthusiasm or interest or concern is the sense in which this word is most frequently used in Kierkegaard's writings.

But we also find "passion" used in the sense of emotion. For example, Climacus says this:

> I have often reflected how one might bring a man into a state of passion. I have thought in this connection that if I could get him seated on a horse and the horse made to take fright and gallop wildly, or better still, for the sake of bringing the passion out, if I could take a man who wanted to arrive at a certain place as quickly as possible, and hence already had some passion, and could set him astride a horse that can scarcely walk (CUP, 276).

When Climacus speaks here of bringing a man into a state of passion, he is not talking about giving a man an interest, but about giving him an emotion that he could not have unless an *interest* were already present in him. The emotion of the man seated on the frightened and wildly galloping horse may be assumed to be fear, a fear arising from the perception that his life and safety (about which he passionately cares) are threatened by his mode of transportation. The emotion of the hurried man astride an old nag will be anxious frustration or impatience, and it arises from the perception that his interest in getting somewhere quickly is being contravened. Let me now make two points about the relation between passion as emotion and passion as interest.

First, emotion is one of the chief ways that passion is manifested in human beings; emotions are symptoms and fruitions of passions. Kierkegaard's emphasis on passion (in the sense of interest) is understandable both in relation to his role as a moralist and as a Christian communicator. For the ethics he desires to foster is not of the utilitarian variety, with social results as the focus of interest and criterion of success. His is instead an ethics of the *heart*, and consequently finds its criterion not only in individual action, but perhaps even more basically in emotion. The individual who seeks the good with a passion approaching purity of heart is known not by his social programs (for these can be motivated by the desire for prominence or political advancement or something else extraneous), but by the fact that he grieves at the sight of corruption and indifference and rejoices at the sight of justice and love; and above all by the fact that he himself is a *penitent*. All such emotion is impossible apart from a passion for the good.

What is true of ethics is perhaps even more obviously true of Christianity. For the mark of the Christian is the fruit of the Holy Spirit, and this fruit is largely a range of emotions: joy, hope, peace, gratitude, love of neighbor, in response to the news that God so loved us that He became one of us and redeemed us, by his own blood, for an eternal life of righteousness. But no one responds to the gospel with such emotions unless he has a passionate interest in eternal life and freedom from sin. Only he who hungers and thirsts for righteousness will find satisfaction here; only he who in the requisite way labors and is heavy laden will find rest in the presence of the Lord. The emotions of the Christian life, arising from an assessment of the world in terms of the gospel, presuppose a passionate desire for what is offered in that gospel. If the fruits of the Spirit are the aim (as they must be for any Christian communicator), the strategy must be Kierkegaard's: to arouse a concern, an infinite passionate interest in an eternal happiness.

My second point from Climacus's equestrian analogy is that emotions always involve some *assessment of one's situation*, and that with respect to any of the more spiritual and peculiarly human emotions such as we find in ethics and Christianity, this assessment will always involve some *reflection*. In the cases of Climacus's fearful and frustrated riders, the assessment is very simple and requires little or no reflection. But to assess a situation as deficient in justice, or to assess oneself as falling short of an ethical ideal, or again to assess oneself as a sinner redeemed by the blood of Jesus Christ and destined for eternal fellowship with God—such assessments are essentially reflective, determined by *thought* from the very bottom up. Indeed, the thought in terms of which the assessment is made determines the identity of the emotion which the individual experiences. As Kierkegaard remarks, in critique of Magister Alder, who had a religious experience of some sort, but one which was not determined by the Christian concepts,

> Upon this common basis of more universal emotion the qualitative difference must be erected and make itself felt, for the more universal emotion has reference only to something abstract: to be moved by something higher, something eternal, by an idea. And one does not become a Christian by being moved by something indefinitely higher, and not every outpouring of religious emotion is a Christian outpouring. That is to say: emotion which is Christian is checked by the definition of concepts (OAR, 163).

Thus, spirituality of the sort that Kierkegaard discusses and seeks to engender through his writing is essentially thought-determined, essentially conceptual, essentially reflective. And this reflection is directly related to passion in both of the senses that we have determined: Passion as interest is thought-determined in that one must have some conception of what one is interested in, if one is to have a passion; and passion as emotion is thought-determined in that any emotional assessment that the subject makes of his situation must be in some terms of other.

In light of this fact, it is perhaps surprising that in *Two Ages* most of Kierkegaard's discussion of reflection in relation to passion is *critical*: that is, he sees reflection as the cause of the passionlessness of his age. In the next section I want to expound Kierkegaard's analysis of the deleterious effect of reflection on passion and then in the following section to set this existentially degenerate thinking in contrast with what Climacus calls subjective thinking in the *Postscript*.

Passion and Reflection

Kierkegaard's chief diagnostic theses concerning the present age in *Two Ages* are that it is "without passion" and that it is "reflective." The theses are correlative: the present age is passionless because it is so reflective, and so reflective because it is devoid of passion.

"Reflection" (to be distinguished in the present translation from "reflexion" [see p. ix]) is ambiguous. Roughly, it seems to have three different meanings. First, it is sometimes almost only a synonym for "deliberation"—meaning thinking about what to do (though it sometimes broadens out to encompass a non-deliberative thinking). Thus Kierkegaard says, "Reflection is not the evil . . ." (TA, 96), meaning, I take it, that there is nothing wrong with deliberation per se. Second, the word sometimes means the *misuse* of deliberation as a strategy for avoiding decisive action. For example, he completes the sentence begun above, ". . . but the state of reflection, stagnation in reflection, is the abuse and corruption that occasion retrogression by transforming prerequisites into evasions" (TA, 96). Third, "reflection" denotes an ethos, or group spirit, or social inertia, in which this stagnation becomes accepted as normal and normative, so that subtle sanctions are exercised against deviant individuals: "Reflection is a snare in which one is trapped" (TA, 89). Let us try to see (1) how deliberation can lead to reflection in the second sense; (2) how reflection in this sense causes passionlessness; (3) how reflection in the third sense can grow out of reflection in the second; and (4) how reflection in the third sense can become a support and secondary motive for reflection in the second.

(1) Passions (in the sense of interests) are motivations par excellence—that is, motivations to actions. But actions do not issue directly from passions; typically they are chosen from a pool of possible actions according to their merits, in the view of the agent, as fulfillments of the passion in question. So if I have a passion for tennis, and thus on a particular afternoon a desire to play tennis, and there are five sets of courts within a reasonable distance, I will

choose a course of action by the criterion of how well it satisfies my passion (desire): I reject one court because it is likely to be crowded, another because it has cracks, and so forth until a decision is made. This process of reflecting on options available is deliberation, a necessary background of rational action. (Which is not to say that every rational action must be deliberated.)

If I am passionate, the process of deliberation will be only a necessary *step* towards action. My eye will be fixed on the goal that my passion projects for it, and I will quickly traverse the necessary deliberations on my way. But if my passion is weak I may dally along the way of my deliberations, much as a boy who knows that unpleasant duties await him, dallies on his way home from school. Just as the reluctantly homeward-bound schoolboy may see importance in things to which he usually pays not the slightest heed, so I may become fastidious in my deliberations, checking and rechecking to see that I have entertained all my options, weighing and reweighing the reasons for and against each, calling upon authorities, reading books, chewing the matter over with friends. When Kierkegaard says that his age is devoid of passion and that reflection is partly to blame, he has in mind chiefly ethical (including religious) passions, a fairly rare kind of passion in any age. In most of us our attachment to the kind of ideals that make for ethical passion is sufficiently tenuous that we welcome the sit-tight escape provided by deliberation.

Theological reflection is a case in point. People are typically ambivalent about God. They do yearn to trust and obey, to yield themselves to the Maker in happy love. But they also resist, fearing to let God get too close, anxious concerning changes He may require and concerning the light He may shed on their soul. And so one sometimes runs into a student who went to seminary intent upon learning how better to serve God, but who gets entrapped in theological *reflection* (which can be seen as elaborate deliberations about what to believe and how to carry on one's religious life). Instead of clarifying his thoughts and his life, the theological reflection casts him into a sea of hitherto unimagined theological options in which to swim about more or less aimlessly, and thus provides a high-minded excuse for not settling down into the business of loving and serving God. Theology becomes a device for religious stalling.

It even happens sometimes that a person who was originally attracted to Kierkegaard's writings because of their decisiveness, their edifying quality, their passion—that is, because of their power to foster one's God-relationship—slides imperceptibly from *this* use of them into a concern with "the problems of Kierkegaard's authorship." That is, he starts out with a certain tentative passion for God, but finding an extremely long, challenging, noble, and fascinating deliberative detour, ends up with a passion for Kierkegaard scholarship instead. Persons who are impassioned for their God-relationship are not to be found on this detour.

(2) So passionlessness begets reflection in the sense of the evasive abuse of deliberation. But reflection also deepens passionlessness. The problem is this: human beings live in time, and so, for better or for worse, are constantly developing. There is, from the point of view of the development and maintenance of ethical personality, a natural rhythm between action and deliberation, and so there is what might be called, in any given context, the propitious time for action. Impetuous action is not good for the personality, for it means that the individual has missed one of the opportunities to "soak up" the action mentally, to integrate it into his life view, to cause it to contribute fully to the maturing of the passion within him. Also impetuous actions are sometimes psychologically misconceived in that they entrain consequences that discourage (literally, dishearten—disimpassion?) the individual in respect to the passion that motivated the action. But indecisiveness and prolonged deliberation are just as unhealthy; for the result will be a kind of staleness of the passion after a while, and of course one thing a passion can't abide is being stale. Actions in accordance with a passion have the tendency to keep the passion alive. As Kierkegaard says, "we know clever ways of avoiding decision, and if this keeps on for a time, we are finally captured; we are like girls who have been engaged for too long a time, which is rarely propitious for a marriage" (TA, 76).

A passion is like a momentum, and actions in accordance with it are like thrusts that replenish the momentum: As in bicycle riding, if one goes too long without peddling, so in life if one goes too long without acting. Or one might say that actions are the food of passions; if there is opportunity for acting upon a concern, and adequate deliberation has been taken to convince the individual that he should act, then not to act has the tendency to debilitate the concern. So one of the results of "reflection" in the present sense is that passions (or at least embryonic ones) *starve*.

(3) How does the state of evasive reflection in individuals lead to the "reflection" that is an ethos, a subtle social phenomenon with sanctions of its own? Kierkegaard explains this transition with the help of three concepts—admiration, envy, and characterless envy. The ethically passionate individual is a hero, an outstanding character deserving of admiration. Admiration, which is a frank, cheerful, and humble recognition of excellence, is the most appropriate emotion with which to greet the ethically passionate individual. Indeed, it betokens a sort of reduplication in the admirer of the passion that is at the foundation of the excellence of the admired. The cheerful frankness of admiration is fostered by a social atmosphere in which distinctions among people (rich-poor, talented-untalented, noble-common, and so forth) are frankly acknowledged and willingly accepted. In a democratic society, by contrast, we are taught that all of us are really equally capable of greatness, and so we are less inclined to recognize the distance between us and the hero. And so if, by virtue of our love of excellence, we recognize the hero's excellence, our emotion is more likely to be envy than admiration.

Envy is the unhappy recognition of excellence. The envious person, assuming a basic equality between himself and the ethically impassioned hero, recognizes the hero's excellence but *resents* it because it is not his own. Note that the envious person is still a lover of excellence, though an unhappy one. But envy, being unhappy, is an emotion we tend to avoid. And so in a reflective age, "reflection" in a sense very close to that of the evasive abuse of deliberation, tends to be called in to rescue the sufferer from envy. For the sufferer finds he has plenty of resources for rationalizing away the excellence of the hero: attending a little to his human defects and to the thought that any of us might be as great as he had we been born in the right circumstances, if only our psychological development had been like his, and so forth—and generally, reducing ethics out by a deterministic psychologizing reflection—will cut the hero down to average human size, and thus enable us not to see the excellence in him that is the source of the unhappiness of envy. With this expedient of "reflection," we now have characterless envy.

Characterless envy is but the shadow of real envy, for what it lacks is precisely the ethical passion for excellence that is the basis of real envy's unhappiness. The passion has been dispelled by "reflection" (second sense). Characterless envy has deceitfully convinced itself that there really is no such thing as excellence. But, like all self-deceit, it also believes the denial of what it has deceived itself into believing, and so it is threatened, down deep, by the existence of what it perceives to be real excellence. Thus it is convenient for characterlessly envious people to find *objective* ways to discourage excellence. And when we get a society of people who are interested in preventing excellence from rearing its ugly head, it is understandable that there will develop an "objective spirit" subtlely opposed to excellence: a poisonous mist that floats out upon the social air the message that impassioned persons are not acceptable, that decisive and extraordinary actions in the ethical sphere will be greeted with the condescension deserved by crusaders and juvenile enthusiasts, or with the scorn appropriate to infantile stupidities, impetuousness, and conclusion jumping—that only deliberation, and not action, will be greeted with approval.

> If one person eventually were to surmount his own reflection and act, a thousand reflections from outside would immediately create opposition to him, because only a proposal to consider the matter further is received with rising enthusiasm, and a proposal for action is met with indolence (TA, 104).

So reflection as ethos and social sanctions arises as the result of the self-deceit which is characterless envy; it is the social sanctioning of reflection as the abuse of deliberation, with the purpose of suppressing the excellence that characterlessly envious persons subconsciously fear.

(4) About "reflection" as a sanctioning ethos, Kierkegaard says "The single individual . . . has not fomented enough passion in himself to tear himself out of the web of reflection and the seductive ambiguity of reflection" (TA, 69). Let us consider a little further how "reflection" in this sense works, by thinking about the two metaphors contained in this sentence.

Reflection is like a spider's web. The individual, who in a weak sense would like to act on conscience, and becomes self-conscious enough to realize this, feels like a fly caught in this ethereal trap. Every time he tries to be himself and fly away on his own, to do what he knows to be his duty, he is able to create nothing more than a little motion *in place*: he is bound by the ethos that whispers in his ear, as it were, "Do not act *yet*; you have not yet thoroughly considered the consequences of your proposed action. Consider whom you might hurt by doing such a thing, or what kind of future actions this might encourage persons less wise than yourself to take. Indeed, simply consider the fact that you do not know all the consequences that such a daring action might have." However, most people, like flies that were *born* in a spider's web, are quite unaware that they are even caught in the web of reflection: they can, after all, flutter their wings a bit in deliberation, as well as make minor very domestic and socially acceptable leg movements.

Reflection has "seductive ambiguity." An ambiguous statement is one that may be interpreted in two or more ways, and so cannot be definitely understood. An ambiguous command, analogously, is one to which no single definite act corresponds. In response to an ambiguous command a person does not know what to do. For example, a child is told to do his homework, but not told when to do it. This command has a little ambiguity in it, namely the ambiguity as to when he is to do the job. Now if the child has a passion for doing his homework, or for doing his parents' will, the ambiguity in the command will not matter; he will do the homework. But if he does not want to do the job, he will welcome the ambiguity in the command, and it will seduce him into procrastination. This is something that a less ambiguous command would not have done to him, and so it happens that wise parents, when they find themselves in possession of a child without passion for his homework, issue commands that are not ambiguous, and so not seductive. Then, as the child learns to act decisively, the parents can give their commands again a certain ambiguity, without the result of seducing the child into inaction; and at that point the child is beginning to become an individual.

Ethical action often requires sacrifice, suffering, danger, difficulty, and so a very strong passion for it is a rarity. Like the child,

we do not very much *want* to know what our duty is. So we welcome an ambiguous command, one that leaves it open for us not to
do the ethical thing. Such an ambiguous command is seductive;
that is, it seduces into complacency a person without much ethical
passion. According to Kierkegaard, such ambiguity is to be found
in the social air one breathes in his age, for there people *speak* of
high ideals, but since no one acts on them, sacrifices or suffers for
them, or even *thinks* with decisive clarity about them, the "command" comes across ambiguously. It does not say simply and
clearly "This is your duty." To such an ambiguity a person does not
usually say, "Get thee behind me, Satan; I wish to know clearly
what my ethical duty is." No, this is just what I wanted to hear, I
who really would enjoy the self-esteem attaching to *speaking* ethically while not feeling under pressure to sacrifice something. The
ethos of reflection offers the individual a deceptive substitute for
ethical self-esteem while allowing him to remain inactive. He is
susceptible of this seduction in the first place because he lacks ethical passion; if he had it he would see through the ambiguity and
refuse to be seduced. But once he is seduced he is all the less likely
to develop ethical passion, for he has been rendered quite comfortable with himself. Kierkegaard calls the bluff of such ambiguous
ethical reflection by the presentation of "qualitative disjunctions"
(see next section).

The Subjective Thinker

I remarked earlier that thought is not just an enemy of passion,
but also an essential ingredient of it. Reflection can be used not only
to weaken passion, but also to strengthen it; it can foster characterlessness, but also it can be an element in existential education. I
want now to try to get a little clarity about this positive role of reflection in ethical and Christian character building. My discussion
will have two focuses. First, in the present section, I shall attempt
to say what is essential to Kierkegaard's concept of the subjective
thinker. Then in the final section I shall remark briefly on some of
the things that Kierkegaard is doing in his works. That is, his activity is certainly a case of reflection, and it is also aimed at generating

ethical and Christian seriousness in his reader. What, then, is the character of this reflection in the service of seriousness? In the *Postscript* Climacus has a great deal to say about the subjective thinker. An adequate discussion of his often opaque and paradoxical remarks on this topic, and an adjudication of the question as to when they are to be taken as straightforward conceptual or psychological remarks, and when they are to be taken as some elaborate form of indirect communication, would require a small book. So I shall confine myself here to presenting briefly and without textual argument what I think are the main straightforwardly defensible points that can be derived from Climacus's discussion.

Broadly, there are two points found together in this passage:

> The subjective thinker . . . has the passion of thought requisite for holding fast to the qualitative disjunction. But on the other hand, if the qualitative disjunction is applied in empty isolation . . . . one may risk saying something infinitely decisive and be quite correct in what one says, and yet, ludicrously enough, say nothing at all (CUP, 313).

The two features of subjective thinking to which Climacus refers here belong to different logical categories. One has to do with the *content* of the thinker's thought—the kind of thoughts he thinks, whether he "holds fast to the qualitative disjunction." The other is a matter of what he *does* with whatever thoughts he thinks—how his thoughts are "applied."

The subjective thinker is a dialectician in the sense of a person who is able to hold on to certain distinctions. The distinctions in question are all such that if one confuses what needs to be held apart, the peculiar conceptual lenses of the ethical or Christian life will be lost, and so, consequently, will the possibility of shaping one's interests and emotions in the terms of those concepts. Kiekegaard stresses a number of "either/ors" in his writings, among which are: *either* the commitment of Christian faith, *or* the endless approximation process of historical research; *either* the esthetic life, which does not posit the distinction between good and evil, *or* the ethical life, which does; *either* standing before God as individually responsible to Him, *or* accepting the "crowd" as a substitute for God. I shall dwell now on just two such qualitative disjunctions, that between historical importance and ethical goodness, and that between a Socratic conception of a religious teacher, and the Christian conception of the Saviour.

Roughly, a human figure or action is historically important (see CUP, 119ff.) in proportion to the breadth of explanatory power which reference to it has. Thus Hitler is more important than an obscure grandmother who exemplified moral heroism during the war. But by ethical standards, she is the great one. Further, of her actions the most important ones are by no means the ethically best. It may have been inadvertently, or even with evil intentions, that she did something that led to the survival of someone who after the war became the father of someone who made an indelible mark on the German government. While some other choice, made sacrificially in purity of heart, may have had no ramifications.

But not only does historical significance not make a person ethical; even the goodness of the consequences of his actions does not make him so. To be ethical, the individual must will what is good. No doubt, in willing what is good the individual will often aim to bring about a good state of affairs. But what makes *him* ethical is not that his action brought about a good state of affairs, but that he willed this state of affairs to be brought about (intention), and that he willed it to be brought about because it was good (motive).

When a person gets preoccupied with the magnitude or even the goodness of the consequences of lives and actions, he must be careful not to let the criterion of importance creep into his ethical estimates of his own actions. For to the extent that he does judge himself "in the court of history," his self-understanding will fail to be ethical. If his passion is essentially an enthusiasm for importance (even where he construes "important" as "important because useful to society"), rather than goodness, then his passion, however productive of good it may have been, was not an ethical passion, and he failed to be an ethical person.

The second example of a "qualitative disjunction" is one that is necessary to Christian subjective thinking, and it is one of the main distinctions embodied in Climacus's *Philosophical Fragments*. The distinction is between a Socratic religious teacher, who teaches by causing his "disciple" to come to a religious insight of his own, and Jesus Christ, whose "teaching" consists in his recreating the disciple by establishing the disciple in a certain relationship with Himself called Faith. The contrast between the Socratic religious teacher and Jesus is stark: the identity of the Socratic religious teacher is indifferent to his success as a teacher; the identity of Jesus (namely that He is God) is essential to His role as "teacher." The attachment of the "disciple" to the Socratic teacher must be a loose and passing thing, whereas if the disciple of Jesus Christ ceases in his attachment to the very person of Jesus, the "teaching" (that is, new birth) is necessarily annulled.

If this qualitative disjunction is not held fast, the passional life of the individual will not be a Christian subjectivity. The person's emotions (for example, hope, joy, gratitude, guilt-consciousness) will not be shaped by the Christian concepts of sin and atonement. *Philosophical Fragments* is a masterpiece of literary ingenuity designed to burn this qualitative disjunction into the mind of the reader and to make her, to this extent, a subjective thinker. It might seem to some that this qualitative disjunction is obvious, and hardly worth the enormous communicative ingenuity that Climacus expends on it. But if so, one should take a closer look at the history of Christian thought. Schleiermacher and Bultmann, to take two prominent but typical examples, both agree with Climacus that the logic of Christianity requires that the particular identity of Jesus is essential to his "teaching." But both of them give a fundamentally Socratic account of Jesus' function as Saviour. If Climacus is right, these theologians are in a conceptually untenable position, having attempted to fuse two incompatible spheres of thought. But worse than that, they have become the propagators of an outlook which, subjectively, is not Christianity.

This, then, is the first characteristic of a subjective thinker: he keeps clear certain distinctions fundamental to the ethical or Christian life, so that it is possible for him to have his passions and emotions qualified by these life views. But keeping his thought clear is not enough to make him a subjective thinker, even when the thoughts in question are basic to the ethical or Christian life-views. For these are not just views; they are *life* views—concept clusters whose logic is such that if their user's emotions and passions are not shaped by them, the concepts are violated even if they are impeccably clearly thought. As Climacus says, "if the qualitative disjunction is applied in empty isolation . . . one may risk saying something infinitely decisive . . . and yet . . . say nothing at all" (CUP, 313).

This is a failing to which especially reflective people, such as philosophers, theologians, and theoretical psychologists especially are subject. Such people spend so much energy *just* trying to get clear about certain ideas, that they are extra prone to "forget what it means to exist"—to let their (perhaps quite correct and even profound) thoughts "idle" in empty isolation in their articles, their books, their lectures. Such an eventuality is ludicrous if the thoughts—of ethics and Christianity—are essentially destined for the shaping of people's lives, and if the supposition is that by so shaping one's life, one receives treasures beyond price: human fulfillment, eternity. The "objective thinker" is thus a person who occupies himself with the form of the highest things, but gets so preoccupied with the form that he forgets to seek the highest things. Or he is like a person who buys a priceless jewel and then becomes so fascinated with its box that he never enjoys the jewel itself.

But it's not only professors who let their thoughts "idle." As Kierkegaard shows in *Two Ages*, entire populations are subject to this tendency, and one can even chart, in broad terms, its psychological development. Relatively simple people quickly get the hang of using thinking against their own best interests. So there seems to be something universally human—a taste that doesn't require to be learned—behind people's becoming "reflecting . . . [and] devoid of passion." Though the abstract description of the tendency—using thinking to avoid human fulfillment—sounds like a psychological paradox, the reason for the universality of this tendency is not far to seek. The fulfillments that ethics and Christianity offer are not naturally attractive: they do not appeal to "immediacy," and any effort to make them appeal to it is bound to involve a fundamental distortion of them. *These* forms of fulfillment look like death to the immediate man. So it is not surprising that when people discover that thinking can idle in endless deliberation and that even thought about the highest matters in human life can be dissociated from that life and made into esthetic and intellectual fascinations, they take "advantage" of that fact. Then sets in the dynamic so ably analyzed in *Two Ages*: ethical passionlessness having begotten "reflection" (in the sense of idling thought and a blurring of the qualitative disjunctions), this in turn dulls whatever passion may remain; and this reciprocal pattern of life and consciousness becomes a self-reinforcing ethos, a "spirit of the age."

How can this cunning, humanly self-subverting use of reflection be effectively challenged? It is this question I want to address in the final section of this paper.

Passion-Engendering Thought

I have distinguished two aspects of Climacus's concept of subjective thinking: that involving the keeping *clear* of certain "qualitative disjunctions," and that involving the *application* of one's ethical and religious thought to oneself in such a way that it comes to qualify one's emotions and passions. Much of Kierkegaard's authorship can be seen as an artful effort to foster these two kinds or aspects of subjective thinking in himself and his reader.

As to the enforcing upon his reader of the qualitative disjunctions, I have noted that Kierkegaard makes much use of elaborate indirect communication. The qualitative disjunctions are not very difficult to grasp intellectually, and I suppose that if some scholar were to dig around for a while in Kierkegaard's volumes, looking for qualitative disjunctions, she might find a dozen or so, all of which could be clearly summarized in a monograph of fifty pages or less. Such an essay, if well done, would be a much clearer presentation of these thoughts than Kierkegaard's own rather bumpy and intellectually exasperating presentation in his writings. By "clearer" we would mean here that the reader would be more likely to come away from this essay with a perspicuous view of the qualitative disjunctions in Kierkegaard, and that he would be more readily able to state them (perhaps to burp them forth for a qualifying exam), than if he "just read Kierkegaard." But it would be a complete misunderstanding, if the scholar thought she were thereby fostering subjective thinking better than her author could do. For Kierkegaard is very aware of the human proclivity to thinking that stops when the lecture ends and never makes contact with an individual's passions. So his purpose is not just to make the qualitative disjunctions intellectually clear, but to make them, as far as possible, emotionally unavoidable. He wants to cause the reader to think in terms of the qualitative disjunctions as a matter of second nature, and so to foster what he calls a "double reflection" in which the reader not only thinks passingly about the matter at hand, but begins, dispositionally, to think about *himself* in its terms. I want now to end this paper by sketching very briefly three of the leading ways that Kierkegaard uses reflection against "reflection," to foster subjective thinking.

Intellectual seduction. There is, about the works of Johannes Climacus especially, an air of intellectual artificiality. This is particularly evident in *Philosophical Fragments*, where the first three chapters are in the form of an elaborate mock-Hegelian deduction of the central doctrines of Christianity from a single assumption: the idea of an ethico-religious teacher whose presence and identity is essential to his teaching. Of course Climacus's real purpose here is not to deduce Christianity from this assumption, but to present certain thoughts, among which is the qualitative disjunction between Jesus Christ and any Socratic religious teacher. In other words, this thought is *hidden*, as it were, in a form of discourse that must be taken ironically if it is to be understood. Certain hints of the irony are given, and the reader is thereby invited to resolve the dissonance created by the contrast of the form with the content. It is something like what Anti-Climacus describes when he says,

> An example of such indirect communication is, so to compose jest and earnest that the composition is a dialectical knot. . . . If anyone is to profit by this sort of communication, he must himself undo the knot for himself (TC, 132-33).

Indeed, the dialectical knot of *Fragments* is so elaborate that by the time the reader has occupied himself with it long enough to distinguish the jest from the earnest, the earnest has made a much deeper impression on him than it could ever have done if presented in all its lucid simplicity. This seduction of course works only for intellectuals—people who are initially titillated by such things as deductions of Christian doctrine, and then bright enough to untie the dialectical knot.

Impassioned psychological analysis. Kierkegaard himself is a subjunctive thinker. In practically every sentence he writes it comes across how deeply personally his thoughts affect him. And this characteristic of his writing is one of the most "communicating" features of it. His own ethical and religious passion is infectious, and powerfully draws the reader into an analogous attitude. When this "tone" is combined with Kierkegaard's astute psychological analysis, the effect is strong. The qualitative disjunctions are repeatedly brought before the reader, but against the background of a rich pyschological detail that makes it difficult to sustain a merely intellectual, idling reflection. The discourse not only clarifies such *ideas* as despair and anxiety, but also clarifies the *reader* as an anxious despairer—as one who needs the eternal. The thoughts arouse passion by engendering self-knowledge, by calling the bluff of various devices by which we fog our minds on the subject of who we are. So the reader is drawn, by the persuasiveness of the psychological analysis and the passion of Kierkegaard, to implicate himself by the ethical and religious reflection in which he follows this author. For this reason it takes practice, in reading Kierkegaard, to become able to treat him as just another philosopher presenting theories for classroom discussion. But of course even Kierkegaard's human genuineness and psychological incisiveness do not combine to guarantee subjective thinking in his reader.

Poetically varied repetition. It has often been noted, sometimes reproachfully, how repetitive Kierkegaard's writings are. A handful of ideas come before the reader again and again, in widely varied contexts and diversely dressed up. Such a state of affairs would be embarrassing in a writer whose purpose was "to get his ideas down on paper." For in that case Kierkegaard used more paper than necessary. However, the complaint is not usually couched in paper terms, but in time terms: It takes so much time to read Kierkegaard, and with discernment one just hears the same thing again and again. But Kierkegaard's purpose is not to preserve his ideas for "history," but to transform and humanize the consciousness of individual readers. He is not primarily a theoretician, but primarily a communicator. Or as he himself says, a poet in the service of Christianity. And with this purpose, it is entirely appropriate that he exercises his ingenuity not in thinking up new ideas for those who want to be forever adding to their barns of insight, but in finding ever new ways of impressing upon himself and his reader a few all-important truths. "Poet" is perhaps the best description of Kierkegaard as a purveyor of reflections aimed at transforming the passions (though "dialectician" runs a close second), for in the role of poet is summed up so much of what Kierkegaard's thought is designed to do: by its attractiveness to draw the reader into the thinking of decisive thoughts; by its concreteness to put those thoughts in such a way that their truth and human weight is emotionally unavoidable; by the incessant kaleidoscopic variation of the imagery in which they are dressed to make palatable the repetition needed to etch into consciousness ideas which it is the constant tendency of the human self to forget.

VI

Envy as Personal Phenomenon and as Politics

by Robert L. Perkins

for . . . it was out of envy that they had delivered him up.

Matthew 27:18

A certain miser and a certain envious man went into the temple of Jupiter to pray, and Mercury was sent to tell them that what the one prayed for, the other should receive double. The envious man prayed that he himself might lose one eye in order that the miser might lose both his eyes.

Benvenuto, in his commentary on Dante

Certes, thanne is Envye the worste sinne that is. For soothly, alle othere sinnes been som-tyme only agayns o special vertu; but certes, Envye is agayns alle vertues and and agayns alle good-nesses; for it is sory of alle the bountees of his neighebore; and in this manere it is divers from alle othere sinnes. For wel unnethe is

ther any sinne that it ne hath som delyt in itself, save only Envye,
that evere hath in itself anguish and sorwe.

Chaucer, "Parson's Tale"

. . . and just as *enthusiasm* is the unifying principle in a passionate age, so *envy* becomes the *negatively unifying principle* in a passionless and very reflective age.

Søren Kierkegaard, *Two Ages*

Perhaps the consideration of envy as a philosophic concern today seems strange. My first notice of envy was as a teenager
when I read Matthew 27:18 (above). When I recently read the quotation from *Two Ages* (above) I realized that for all the differences of
context, a phenomenon of considerable philosophic depth in which
inhered an evident political power had largely escaped philosophical notice.[1]

I propose, first, to show envy as a personal phenomenon; second, to examine the source and nature of its political power. Finally, I will briefly compare Kierkegaard's concept of envy with the
concept of resentment with which it has frequently been confused.

Envy as a Personal Phenomenon

Beginning with the showing or description is relatively easy because most of the philosophic concern has been pointed in that direction. The practitioners and theoreticans of the Christian religion
have contributed much to the clarification of the personal dimension of envy, but the classical studies in this tradition did not reach
to the political dimension that was evident in the Gospel account
and in Kierkegaard.

I would not propose to examine all the philosophic and theological treatments of envy, even if I could. One statement is enough,
and to my knowledge no more profound presentation has ever been
offered than that in Dante's *Divine Comedy*. Sometimes it is the task

---

[1]It is of considerable interest (but beyond the scope of this essay) that two recent books in philosophy of politics have contained considerable discussions of
envy. See John Rawl's *A Theory of Justice* (Cambridge: Harvard University Press,
1971) and Robert Nozick's *Anarchy, State, and Utopia* (New York: Basic Books, 1974).

of literature to show what can be said haltingly or imprecisely, if at all.[2]

Dante's *Purgatory* is about the soul's struggle with the seven cardinal (or deadly) sins. Unfortunately, Dante's language game is largely out of style; it is even more deplorable that the phenomena he so clearly and distinctly pictured for all to see have not also gone out of style. Except in a historical essay most would not today speak of the seven cardinal sins; we would talk about dispositions, habits, tendencies, and so forth. Still, perhaps Dante's point would not be entirely lost. ("Cardinal" is from the Latin, *cardo*, "hinge": a lot *turns on* each of the cardinal sins.)[3]

The envious person is one who has a disposition to envy in any of its several forms (jealousy, resentment, or fear). To be sure, an envious person is habitually envious, but we generally make a distinction between a habit and a disposition.[4] For instance, I have a habit of always carrying my car keys in my left front trouser's pocket. Also, we say of a certain professor, "He always coughs before he starts to answer a student's question." A habit is a specific, regularly occurring action. Minimally, dispositions have to do with traits of character, be they vices or virtues, to revert to Dante's language. There is a certain extended sense of disposition argued by St. Thomas to the effect that beliefs are also dispositions. Certainly a belief, in part at least, constitutes a disposition, for on that belief would hinge many actions and consequences. This is true whether the belief is well founded and true or simply false. Furthermore, a belief is not episodic; we come to our beliefs slowly and after considerable intellectual labor or ordinary experience.[5] Neither are we anxious to surrender them.

---

[2]Dante Alighieri, *The Divine Comedy*, Cantica 2, Purgatory, intro. and trans. by Dorothy M. Sayers (Hammondsworth, Middlesex: Penguin Books, 1955). All references are to lines in Cantos in this edition.

[3]See Sayers's introduction to the above-mentioned translation, 65.

[4]St. Thomas Aquinas, *Summa Theologiae*. I refer to the new edition translated by Anthony Kenny (London: Eyre and Spottiswoodie, 1964). This excellent translation is in modern philosophic idiom. See the translator's introduction, volume 22, xix-xxxiv.

[5]Thomas, *Summa*, 1a2ae, q. 49, a3.

To be sure, just as dispositions become, so can they decay. That is, we are not locked into our present condition. Human personality is in the process of becoming. As one could by practice become more tender and caring one also could become less brutal and callous, and vice versa. Human nature is mutable.[6]

It is in this philosophical and conceptual context that Dante's phenomenology of envy is presented in the *Purgatorio*. The dissection of the dispositions in the *Purgatorio* is much more acute than in the *Inferno* where one would have expected it would have had a starring role. The damned are just that and their evil dispositions are confused together. Fine conceptual distinctions of all the dispositional and rational capacities are not possible in hell. On the other hand, in purgatory, if one is to be delivered from the dispositions that separate persons from blessedness, these dispositions must be characterized and categorized. The dispositions must be intellectually known before they can be changed: thus the more analytical care exercised by Dante in the *Purgatorio*.[7]

In the *Purgatorio*, Dante discussed envy (*invìdia*) as a form of perverted love. Envy is the perversion of the proper love of one's own good into the wish to deprive other persons of their own good or well-being.[8] That last sentence, no doubt, is rather tightly packed and requires some unpacking, and that is precisely what Dante does through very singular examples of envy and its opposite.

The love of one's own good is proper; it is even an instinctive good or love (*amor naturale*). The perversion of envy is that we think that by wishing or actually depriving others of their well-being we somehow benefit ourselves. Envy is thus pernicious.

Dante's first example of envy is Sapìa who on some suspicion was banished from her native Siena. She bore an envious grudge against her countrymen for they could still boast of being at home

---

[6]There is a great deal more here (see fn. 5) and in succeeding articles in the *Summa* that is relevant to contemporary discussion of the philosophy of the passions but most must be omitted here.

[7]William Warren Vernon, *Readings on the Purgatorio of Dante, Chiefly Based on the Commentary of Benvenuto da Imola*, 2 vols. (London: Macmillan and Co., 1897) 1:472.

[8]Sayers, introduction to *Purgatory*, 66-67.

in Siena. It is very difficult, if not impossible, for us to appreciate the deep and pervasive patriotism of the citizens of the late medieval and early renaissance Italian city-states. Sapìa's banishment, for whatever reason, justified or unjustified, provoked an envy that made her resentful of her former fellow citizens' well-being, a well-being in this instance of just being at home. In her envy of their well-being she wished evil upon them. In 1269 from a palace near Colle she observed a battle between the Sienese and the Florentines and prayed for the defeat of her native countrymen. She delighted in their rout, defeat, and death. So filling was her perverted joy that she cried against God, "I fear thee now no more" (13:115-21).

The marvelous thing about Dante's poem is that he does not present us a theory about envy. He simply shows it to us in its shocking and dehumanizing character. In the case of Sapìa, envy not only turned her against her native country and perverted a natural love, but also drove her to blasphemous defiance of God.

Dante also refers to the murder of Abel and the story of Aglauros from Ovid where two sisters are set against each other. It seems that Mercury was enamoured with Herse, the sister of Aglauros, and bribed Aglauros to admit him to Herse's presence. However, Aglauros was overcome by envy and refused to let Mercury see Herse whereupon Mercury turned Aglauros into stone. The disposition of Aglauros was not jealousy, for Mercury had not indicated any feeling for Aglauros, and she had no claim upon his affections. Unrequited love, in addition to being bitter, can be the source of both envy and vengeance. These two stories balance each other and show how envy can turn brother against brother as well as sister against sister. This disposition is so dangerous and powerful it can destroy even familial bonds.[9]

There is another character in Dante's picture who complements the above instance. Guido del Duca could not endure the happiness of another, a disposition that is not unknown today. His lament is basic to Dante's view of envy. Only one person can possess a single diamond ring, and to envy another his wealth is all too typical. However, Guido was even more irrationally envious, for he en-

---

[9]Ovid, *Metamorphoses*, ii, 708-832. Many editions.

vied another his happiness. Such a resentment of another's happiness is even more despicable than envying another his goods, for had Guido rejoiced in another's happiness, the amount of happiness and love would have been increased in heaven and earth. But Guido envied and the envy embittered his own life. So the text from Chaucer turns out to be not merely preachment but also true.

We have used some of the examples and language of Dante, and there is no doubt that he has presented a rather despicable human disposition in livid examples. However, Dante also presents examples which show us the opposite of envy: generosity.[10] The three examples of generosity are the Blessed Virgin, Pylades, and Christ. Mary noticed her friends were about to be embarrassed by running out of wine and, not envying them their wealth, their feast, or their happiness, she wished no shadow to fall over the joy of the occasion. She said to her son, "They have no wine" (John 2:3). When Orestes was condemned to death his friend Pylades attempted to substitute himself by claiming that he himself was Orestes. Christ said, "Love your enemies" (Matthew 5:44). Generosity is certainly more fetching than envy. However, we cannot here travel on with those poets. With so little, indeed nothing, to commend it, one is puzzled that envy is such a noticeable human phenomenon and is so widely practiced and cultivated.

However, we notice that Dante's interpretation of envy also has a political dimension. Sapìa's love for Siena had turned to envy. In the *Inferno* Dante named envy (along with pride and avarice) as one of the vices that corrupted his native city.[11] This brings us clearly to envy as a political concept. However, Dante's view of political envy is but an extension, and enlargement, of personal envy. I take him to mean that a city whose leadership and people envy another city's good exercises the disposition of political envy. Political envy is but an extension of personal envy. Political envy is merely the personal envy of rulers and/or citizens expressed as a policy of the body politic. Thus, there is only a difference in quantity between personal and political envy in Dante's view. Sapìa's envy borders on the po-

---

[10]See Sayers's notes to *Purgatory*, 171.

[11]*Inferno*, 6:73-75.

litical in that it was extended to a city, but it was not an envy belonging to a body politic. To find envy in the body politic, that is, as a component of a politics, we must turn to Kierkegaard.

Envy as a Political Power

Kierkegaard's *Two Ages* is a book rich in political and social insight. A whole host of new and old phenomena are set forth in their political relations. Envy, as we have just shown, is an old phenomenon, but Kierkegaard finds it in new contexts and discovers it has far more profound significance than Dante ever dreamed, unfortunately. Kierkegaard finds envy at the depths of the psyche of the present age. Moreover envy is not just a private disposition; it has now gone public and contributes to the form of life in this present age. In the following it will become apparent how this concept is more complex than Dante's.

In a very few pages Kierkegaard sketches the conceptual landscape where envy is located: admiration, passion, reflection, character, inwardness, tension, leveling, the public, the press, and chatter, to name some of the most prominent features. In addition to these categories, he gives us the nearest thing he ever did to a philosophy of history. However, Kierkegaard's effort is not a big, impressive effort like Hegel's *Philosophy of History*. We will attempt in the following to locate the concept of envy in this landscape.

Whereas for Dante the disposition opposite envy is generosity, for Kierkegaard it is admiration. Perhaps there is a family resemblance. Dante shows us generosity through acts, through specific deeds, be they historical or mythological. Kierkegaard develops the concept of admiration, setting forth a morphology.

> But whereas what usually happens where admiration is authentic is that the admirer is inspired by the thought of being a man just like the distinguished person, is humbled by the awareness of not having been able to accomplish this great thing himself, is ethically encouraged by the prototype to follow this exceptional man's example to the best of his ability (TA, 72).

This is precisely the intention underlying Dante's use of examples of generosity. They were shown in order to invoke at least admiration, and preferably imitation.

Envy, on the other hand, is a negative psychological determinant. It causes persons to lose their admiration. The envious person cannot admire another human being, for envy terminates every enthusiastic and appreciative relation to another (TA, 78). Admiration recognizes distinction and greatness and does not denigrate it! It rejoices that there is such greatness, that some excel in some worthy human capacity. This excelling is a labor; the slothful do not attain excellence. The admirer says, "For me also," and in this affirmation he finds purpose, direction, and determination. He buys into what Kierkegaard calls "the idea." What Kierkegaard means by "the idea" (which he occasionally also calls "the third," a term we will not use here) is something like the following (JP, 5: 5100).

"The idea," of course, is and is not all of one kind. It is all of one kind in that its pursuit is, as said above, a labor. It is of one kind in the sense that the labor to attain the idea is the joyful task that fills a life. All labors for the attainment of the idea are one in the sense that in this effort one's life touches at least the outer fringes of the infinite. The labor for the idea is a passion for the infinite that unifies the multiple aspects of life (CUP, 311; CI, 254).

The idea in its several variations is not all of a kind in the sense that one may vocationally be an excellent painter or plumber and one may psychically concentrate his energies in ethical or in religious development. There are infinite overlays and combinations. Kierkegaard uses the term "stages on life's way" to suggest the rich variety of human life. There are three such stages.

The esthetic-sensuous man admires the strange, that which has no relation to himself; the ethical man admires what has an essential likeness to himself—the great, that which can be the prototype of what he himself ought to be; the religious man admires God, who is, of course, absolutely different but still is that with whom he ought to have likeness through the absolute unlikeness (adoration) (JP, 4: 4430; see also CUP, 369; TC, 231ff.; JFY, 207). Aesthetic, ethical, and religious admiration are distinct, but all three save the life from flatness.

There are tremendous differences in the types of persons and objects of achievement referred to here, but Kierkegaard's point is that the life without some pursuit is flat and empty, and such a person is a fit candidate for envy. The pursuit of the idea is an essential passion and the basis for human relations (TA, 62).

Kierkegaard uses the figures of a spring of water and a coiled spring (no pun in either Danish or English) to illustrate the flatness caused by the failure or the drying up of relation to the idea, or as he otherwise calls it, the third.

> If essential passion is taken away, the one motivation, and everything becomes meaningless externality, devoid of character, then the spring of ideality stops flowing and life together becomes stagnant water—this is crudeness (TA, 62).[12]

The coiled springs of live—relationships, which are what they are only because of qualitatively distinguishing passion, lose their resilience; the qualitative expression of difference between opposites is no longer the law for the relation of inwardness to each other in the relation (TA, 78).

Kierkegaard's view of the nature of society is set forth here in a brief quotation:

> Purely dialectically the relations are as follows, and let us think them through dialectically without considering any specific age. When individuals (each one individually) are essentially related to the same idea, the relation is optimal and normative.
> Individually the relation separates them (each one has himself for himself), and ideally it unites them (TA, 62; JP, 3: 1770; 5: 5100).

So the admirers are held together in the ethical relation for each participates in the relation to the idea, a deed or the achievement of moral excellence. This is good glue for a society, but there is even a possibility of an esthetic-sensuous unity in a society. In the novel Kierkegaard is reviewing, the point of view is the aesthetic that tends toward the religious (TA, 14). Even an aesthetic relation can serve as glue for a society, for the esthetic-sensuousness is the third which relates each to each. This could be, for instance, a relation of

---

[12]Kierkegaard may be setting this figure in contrast to John 7:38, following a common punctuation of a less-than-clearly punctuated passage.

sensuous love. Hypothetically and minimally perhaps, the aesthetic sensuousness can be cut even thinner, to "the strange" mentioned above. One thinks of persons who collect dollhouses and miniature furniture for such. Still this quite thin relation to the idea calls forth organizations, magazines, aesthetic judgement (of skill), and so forth. So there is still quite a lot of cohesion even at this level. The individuals are related on the basis of some ideal distance, that is, through some idea, dollhouses in this instance. We are at the edge of parody and triviality. Kierkegaard's own example of the parody of the idea is Don Quixote (CUP, 175).

But the highest relations between persons is that based upon the God-relation. Those who relate to this concept and to each other through this concept are ideally united. The God-relation is not *just* an ethical relation, though it is that. The God-relation is not ordinarily thought of as a sensuous relation, but it involves the sensuous because persons "get high" on God, and there are actual physiological components in worship (singing, kneeling). There is also the sensuousness of the aesthetic in religious music and architecture. In addition there is, for some, the discipline and dedication of the sensuous in celibacy and fasting. So the religious is not something alongside the ethical and the aesthetic; it is the final and highest relation between persons, taking up and uniting the sensuous and the ethical in a higher unity (CUP, 311).

This view of human relations should demolish once and for all the view of Kierkegaard's individualism as locked-in isolationism. Persons ideally relate to each other through the idea. In this way there is both social unity and individuality, for each has his own task, the full development of his relation to the third, and through the third a relation to each other (TA, 69-70). The idea is the link connecting Kierkegaard's views of the individual with his views of society and politics.

This is the very heart of Kierkegaard's thought. If the idea is missing, then persons relate to each other simply *en masse*. The result is violence, anarchy, barbarism, decadence, gossip, rumor, and an apathetic envy that becomes the standard in human relations. Persons have nothing else to look at except each other, and they turn on each other in suspicion and aggression. The wretchedness is caused by the fact that there is nothing more important than their own petty little selves to talk to and think about. There is no passion for anything, including themselves. Social relations become envious; talk becomes chatter; thinking becomes public opinion; right and duty become self-serving prudence; neighbor-love becomes a demand by the neighbor; the aesthetic becomes entertainment (recreational sex or Classic Comics); political thought and policy formation become polls. The only relief from boredom is envy. It would be unbelievable, were it not true, as is noticed every day.

The only deliverance from this mockery of human relations and society is through passion. This prescription by Kierkegaard is surprising and usually an offense to high-minded philosophers. Still, it is seriously intended, for Kierkegaard did not "intend to sanction every uncircumcised immediacy and every unshavened passion" (JP, 3: 3127). Thus, philosophic excitement and expostulation about Kierkegaard's view of passion may indicate rash judgement. Let's look.

First, passion is defined in terms of, and in the search for, the idea, as Kierkegaard expressed it early in his life just as he was coming to himself, "an idea for which I am willing to live and die" (JP, 5: 5100; see also 3: 3125-33).

Second, Kierkegaard most likely never thought—certainly never wrote—that passion in itself and by itself ever justified anything. Passion is equivocal (TCS, 20). He writes about "the ungodly imposition of dark passions" (TCS, 20). He also writes about "the passion of impatience" (TCS, 95). However, the overwhelming use to which the concept is put is to designate religious emotions.

Not only is the concept equivocal, it is related to the stages in such a way that there are passions appropriate to each stage (JP, 3: 852). The highest use of passion is in the realm of the religious and much of the *Postscript* is given to this discussion (CUP, 347, 386ff., 494). We see, therefore, that the concept of passion is not univocal, and that critics should take care to note specifics rather than generalities when they criticize his passionate philosophy.

In *Two Ages* passion is that which motivates character, or in Kierkegaard's language, inwardness (TA, 78). These three words— passion, character, inwardness—delineate that disposition that protects *the person and the society* from envy. Inwardness does not require, and in fact makes it impossible for, individuals to turn away from each other (TA, 63). Inwardness is defined in the highest levels of social intercourse. In the *Postscript* Kierkegaard uses marriage and prayer (both I-Thou relations for Kierkegaard) as examples of what he means by becoming subjective. "Individuals do not in inwardness turn away from each other" (TA, 63). Without religious and ethical passion, persons become devoid of character and a suffocating sameness sets in, a fit field for the growth of envy. With no dedication to an encompassing idea, there is no bond or unanimity in the society at large or between individuals (CUP, 158-64). Envy and suspicion, the very opposites of inwardness, set in.

Speech is changed into gossip and rumor (TA, 63) or into chatter. Words lose their meaning, talkativeness becomes the substitute for considered and reflective language. Silence, on the other hand, is the province of inwardness. (Is it any wonder that today we have Muzak?) The general level of noisiness rises and "the loquacious man can chatter about anything" (TA, 103). When there is no "third," when there is no common passion that shapes issues and delineates the form of thought, when nothing of overriding importance ties things together, when there is no unanimity of convictions to hold things together—then chatter begins (TA, 98-99). The problem about chattering is that there is a lot to chatter about, but nothing to recollect; there is no myth around which either conversation or poetry can gather. That does not mean that poetry or conversation ceases; it means that conversation and poetry are privatized—of interest only to the speaker or poet or at most to a coterie of followers. There is no idea through which persons are related to each other.

In such a situation when language (including poetry) becomes corrupt and emptied of significant and socially cohesive meanings, and where passion has evaporated, persons have nowhere to look but at each other and, voila, persons come too close to each other in the herd sense (TA, 62). Kierkegaard's major critique of the public, numbers, the crowd, the mass, or the herd is that they lack any relation to anything higher than popular prejudice—"they say," or the latest fad. This cluster of concepts (hereafter I will use only "public") is for Kierkegaard to be distinguished from a race or nation that has some specifiable organic (color) or cultural (language) demarcation. The public has no demarcation at all. The public has no character and is for Kierkegaard, "the untruth" (JP, 3: 2932) and the evil (JP, 3: 2936) that feeds on the political and social forms of envy. The language of the passion of admiration is transformed into the language of envy and suspicion.

The envious cannot even enjoy and admire "tricky ice skating." Kierkegaard writes that

> Here again practical common sense would alter the pattern of admiration. Even at the giddy height of the fanfare and the volley of hurrahs, the celebrators at the banquet would have a shrewd and practical understanding that their hero's exploit was not all that good, that when all is said and done the party's being held for him is fortuitous, since anyone of the participants could have done almost the same thing with some practice in tricky turns (TA, 72-3).

It is interesting that the object of admiration in Kierkegaard's example is tricky ice skating, which is almost as trivial an object for admiration as my example of dollhouse collecting was as an example of an aesthetic passion. The point is that society does not demand a high level of admiration to avoid envy, so that the outbreak of envy as a social disease is scarcely excusable even in an age devoid of moral and/or religious heros.

There are three steps in the loss of admiration and the emergence of envy as an institutionalized form of life. These are tension, envy, and leveling (TA, 131-32). Tension arises when the coiled springs of life-relationships lose their resilience. No longer related to the idea, persons are left simply with each other.

> The negative law is: they cannot do without each other and they cannot stay together; the positive law: they can do without each other and they can stay together, or more positively, they cannot do without each other because of the mutual bond. Instead of the relation of inwardness another relation supervenes: the opposites do not relate to each other but stand, as it were, and carefully watch each other, *and this tension is actually the termination of the relation* (TA, 78).

This is very compact writing, again, and requires unpacking. First, we note that Kierkegaard discusses tension in the language of relations, not in terms, such as sin or evil, which are derived from theology. From a theological perspective, such as Dante's, sin cannot be far away. Kierkegaard is not at all adverse to theological language, but he keeps in this instance (as a book reviewer of a book that sets forth no religious claims per se) to the language of relations, and he explains this quotation by several examples. Kierkegaard's example of a (not very happy) passionate relation, is "the father who indignantly concentrates his fatherly authority in one single curse or the son who defies, a rift that would still end in the inwardness of reconciliation" (TA, 79). On the other hand, in a relation of tension the external relation goes on, the niceties are always recited, but there is no father-son relation. There is talk, but the relation has dried up. The father and the son need each other as an object of suspicion or as a participant in some kind of game of supremacy. There even may be verbal avowals of relation, but the father-son relation does not exist. This tension is the only shadow of human relation left to them.

This tension is such that every passion of life is enervated. Fervor, enthusiasm, and inwardness that "makes the child's obedience and the father's authority happy" (TA, 80) have dried up. Officially the relation remains, but the passion—the mutual acceptance of the other as an other—has disappeared.

Kierkegaard also uses the example of the king and the subject in order to observe tension in the explicitly political area. "We do not want to abolish the monarchy, by no means, but if little by little we could get it transformed into make-believe, we would gladly shout, 'Hurrah for the King'" (TA, 80-81). This quotation may come as some surprise to those who think Kierkegaard has no politics, but it should be no surprise to those who think he was an unqualified monarchist. Neither of those considerations are pertinent here. The point is that Kierkegaard thought that tension had created a situation in which governing had become impossible, because governing required authority that is a political form of eminence that is out of place in an age characterized by envy. We now turn to a discussion of that age of envy.

There are two forms of envy that serve as "the negatively unifying principles in a passionless and very reflective age" (TA, 81). Both forms have as their end the frustration of a passionate decision, for a passionate decision even at the level of the erotic would

reassert the individuality so unendurable to the public. Kierkegaard calls both forms "reflection's envy," that is, an envy which
results from reflection's suspicion of decisiveness and action. This
is a strange, new concept and it widens Kierkegaard's critique of reflection decisively. "Reflection's envy" is remarkable also because
it shows the intimacy between reflection and the passions in Kierkegaard's thought. One form of reflection's envy has to do with an
individual's breaking free from the opposition that his own reflection creates to decision, and the second form refers to the vast
amount of reflection one's associates can offer against a decision. A
third form of envy is characterless envy.

What Kierkegaard emphasizes in his discussion of reflection's
envy is the tendency (the academic prejudice) in our age to be long
on analysis, thought, and reflection and very short on decision and
action: reflection does everything in its power to thwart this discernment and maintains the flattering notion that the possibilities
that reflection offers are much more magnificent than a paltry decision (TA, 82). This criticism of reflection is continuous with that
raised against speculation in the *Postscript*. As one instance of the
latter, Kierkegaard argues against the proposition that "possibility
is higher than reality" (CUP, 280). Possibilities can be multiplied ad
infinitum and this quality of possibility bespeaks reflection's disinterestedness. However, even Descartes' *cogito* introduces another
element, in spite of the fact that Descartes wanted to attain disinterested ideas. That element is the existing individual who thinks.
If, however, the individual who thinks introduces a teleology or an
interest into his thought, the disinterestedness and the accompa-
nying multiplicity of possibilities evaporates. The absoluteness of
reflection and the runaway multiplicity of possibilities engendered
by it are bracketed by the existing individual who must choose and
who has interests and is ethically responsible. (Also CUP, 290, 282,
393, 312-22.)

Choice is not a lowly matter, but is the very modus operandi of
the interested individual, and at the level of social and political reality it is no less the task of those whose responsibility it is to govern.
So the envy of reflection that enervates the capacity of choice and
decision has disturbing and profound political ramifications, for it
can incapacitate those whose responsibility it is to govern (as, for

instance, the endless succession of study committees making the same old reports on the same old problem), and make querulous those who are governed by their refusal to acknowledge and submit to the authority that is necessary for government to occur.

In addition to the envy of reflection is the second form, "ethical envy," by which Kierkegaard means "censorious envy." While one is locked up in the tensions caused by the multiple possibilities of reflection, a "meanness comes to the surface" that is caused by the fact that no action emerges from the reflection. Censorious envy turns on the inactive self and engenders self-contempt. Censorious envy is also turned against those who would or do act by those who do not act. They demean the act and/or the interest. The neatest part of the trick is that the envious by their claim to superiority (insured by the disinterest of reflection) escape the attention of reflection itself, which is to say that envy is not self-reflective. Also the vast unreflective majority fail to notice the method of envy in its judgmental and censorious emptiness. Envy has nothing to offer that is superior to the act or the interest. But, again because of its disinterested and superior intellectualism, its emptiness escapes notice.

At this point Kierkegaard has made a very important advance on Dante's concept of envy. Take Sapìa, for instance. Her envy is open and quite visible. It is the expression of a malignant and malevolent passion and disposition. Anyone who knows the story can sight the envy. However, as Kierkegaard has presented the envy of reflection it is hidden by disinterest and intellectual superiority:

> Force can be used against rebellion, punishment awaits demonstrable counterfeiting, but dialectical secretiveness is difficult to root out; it takes relatively more acute ears to track down the muffled steps of reflection stealing down the furtive corridors of ambiguity and equivocation (TA, 80).

Kierkegaard's concept of envy, again in contrast to Dante's, flows out of a certain social situation and infects the individual. It must be resisted for the sake of both the individual and the society, but in Kierkegaard's theory of action, only the individual can resist it.

In an age when reflection has some self-reflective capacity, it is possible for envy to know itself as such and to ironize itself. Kierkegaard mentions ostracism in Greece and the specific incident of the man who told Aristides that he would vote to banish him because he was tired of hearing him referred to as the only just man. The man did not deny Aristides' excellence, but only indicated that he envied Aristides his excellence. in this instance envy ironized itself (TA, 83).

Envy can continue to demolish everything in sight till it does not recognize anything as greatness or excellence. Finally, envy creates characterlessness. It does not recognize itself as even the negation of excellence. It simply degrades and minimizes everything. Its strategies are several: the joke, an insult, a witticism masquerading as ethical satire (TA, 83). So envy is itself without character, and it attempts to form the present and the future in its own image. So personal characterlessness becomes the order of the day and the social form of envy flows back into the individual. Kierkegaard offers his candidate for "the envious man of the year."

> A young man today would scarcely envy another his capacities or his skill or the love of a beautiful girl or his fame, no, but he would envy him his money. Give me money, the young man will say, and I will be all right (TA, 75).

This passage is potent with meaning for the analysis of bourgeois class-consciousness and the capitalist spirit of acquisitiveness (or plain old-fashioned greed). However, it is primarily the puerile and banal object of envy that strikes one. Compared to Sapìa or Guido, this insipid specimen is a mere shadow of a person, for the passion of desire has completely died away. There is no desire for a moral excellence or a happy circumstance. There is simply the whimpering after an external (money) without any inward qualification of character. This is reflective, characterless envy, pale and emaciated. This is in utter contrast to the text from Benvenuto. Further, this low-level, characterless whimperer is a universe removed from even those who *admire* dollhouses, a strange and immediate form of aesthetic admiration.

One of St. Thomas's discussions of envy included the illustration of one person ambitious of eminence envying another who already possessed the eminence.[13] This characterization of the envious person is the more usual in philosophy and in literature (compare *Richard II*), but Kierkegaard's example is by comparison characterless. Thomas also argues that the person who makes no effort to attain the character or excellence in which he is wanting feels no envy when someone else excels him in these.[14] Would that it were so, but Kierkegaard's analysis of characterless envy suggests otherwise, or perhaps Kierkegaard may have found another form of envy.

Characterless envy is the final stage before the phenomenon of leveling. In fact leveling is personal, characterless envy on the political or social scale.

> Envy in the process of *establishing* itself takes the form of *leveling*, and whereas a passionate age *accelerates, raise up* and *overthrows*, elevates and *debases*, a reflective apathetic age does the opposite, it *stifles* and *impedes*, it *levels* (TA, 84).

This language about an "age" is certainly not the expected language from an "individualist" as the stereotype makes Kierkegaard out to be. But Kierkegaard can even indulge in the language of social class.

> Leveling can be caused by one social class, for example, the clergy, the middle class, the farmer class, but this is still nothing more than an analogy to genuine, purely abstract leveling. For that to take place, a phantom must first be produced, a monstrous abstraction which nevertheless is a nonentity—this phantom is the public (TA, 135, unused draft).

The point, if not clear by now, it that envy is a public phenomenon.

Leveling is a quiet enterprise that avoids all agitation. Its motto is "just like the others." As we have seen, the disappearance of the idea means there is nothing with which persons can compare themselves. Therefore the public's only comparison is with itself, each one within the public. The expression "just like the others" is

---

[13]Thomas, *Summa*, 1a2ae, q. 28, a. 4.

[14]Thomas, *Summa*, 2a2ae, q. 158, a. 1.

the indelible mark of our sociality, and it is also the indication of the triumph of social conditioning and the evaporation of individual self-definition and inwardness. Envy arises if any instance of personal inwardness appears. An animal is only a specimen of a species; if man were no more he would not envy. However, the presence of envy is also spirit's despair and refusal to make the final descent into the undifferentiated mass where each person is a specimen—the crowd or the public (JP, 3: 2986). Envy then turns out to be the testimony that the leveling influences of modern society have not entirely triumphed. Yet envy is at the same time the proof of the vigilance the public exerts to insure that all will conform, that leveling will take place, and that finally all will be like each other. Shades of *Brave New World* (JP, 3: 2973). So envy is two-edged: on one hand proof that the levelers have not quite succeeded, and on the other hand the weapon of the public to subdue and blot out any differences or inwardness. (So we now gain additional insight into the first text above.)

With the evaporation of inwardness, of essential individuality, leveling gains an absolute victory. This is equality with a vengeance. The word from the motto of the French revolution has been emptied of all its specific content with regards to the political and *nothing* has replaced it. The term equality now means simply "like all the rest." Equality in this sense is the "idealized positive principle of sociality" that has been turned into a "glittering vice." The religious significance of this is the subsumption of the individual into some sort of homogenized religiosity without reference to Kierkegaard's belief that the individual is "before God in the responsibility of eternity" (TA, 86).

It is in this context that Kierkegaard's concept of number become pertinent. Having denied all inward determinants of religion that really render persons equal, the only possible equality left is equality in the series of numbers. "The majority" is such a term, but it is a class that names no individual, and "the minority" is the same. Yet, the numerical is the only sense of individuality left in the public. (Social Security numbers?)

Leveling is not planned and executed from party headquarters downtown; in fact it is so insinuating that it seems to move by some internal impetus created by some abstract power and beyond the control of any individual. And so once more, the claims for freedom from tradition, from morality, from the past, and so forth end up in creating a new slavery in which none are free, a new legalism in which all are under the law (TA, 86). This new abstraction, the public, has other names, "the superfluous man" of Nietzsche, Unamuno's "no-man" and Heidegger's *Das Man*.

The only recovery from leveling is via the religious through which one can again gain individual separateness (TA, 86) and at the same time acquire "the full sense of equality" (TA, 88).

There is one instrument which Kierkegaard specifies as the instrument and creator of leveling—the press. The press is the actual creator of "the public." He compares the press to a dog "which the public keeps for its own amusement" (TA, 95). Thus the relation of the press and the public is reciprocal. Each serves as the source and product of the other.

These three steps—tension, envy, and leveling—show a public characterlessness of demonic proportions. Kierkegaard has made a gigantic step beyond the descriptions of the disposition of envy offered by Dante. Kierkegaard has shown how envy has spread through his whole society and sapped it of its vitality, individuality, and religious inwardness. The intellectual instrument was reflection and the means of dissemination was the press. Human life has been poisoned in the depths of the individual and the poison has spread to the full number of the public. Human degradation caused by this unholy trio is deep, wide, and pervasive. There is a single cure, but it is radical. This leads us to Kierkegaard's view of history.

Not only does Kierkegaard show the concept of envy in rich detail as a phenomenon of modern life he also uses the concept to sketch a "philosophy of history." That is far too grand an expression, for it conjures up visions of the magnitude of Hegel's efforts. Kierkegaard's effort is miniscule, a molehill compared to Hegel's mountain. Kierkegaard's effort here can be puffed up to a "philosophy of history" only by a resort to humor. Yet near the end of *Two Ages* he construes man's historical experience as a whole.

Both visions are monolinear, but whereas Hegel has four kingdoms, Kierkegaard has only one. Both are Europocentric, but Kierkegaard's is the more so. Though Europocentric, Hegel is concerned with universal history; Kierkegaard, with only the typological history of Europe. Passion and the individual are central to both views of history; central, that is, but in very different ways. Both Hegel and Kierkegaard use their philosophies of history to support or illustrate their wider philosophic views. That is, they both say the same thing in their philosophies of history that they say in their wider philosophic theory, but they say it here in a different medium.

In *Two Ages* Kierkegaard divides history into three periods. The first age is the past age:it is the age when men were passionate, whether that passion was one for truth (Socrates), for God (Moses, the prophets, Jesus, the monastics), or for revolution (the French Revolutionists). Passion, we note, is a very broad concept in Kierkegaard's view of history, as compactly presented in *Two Ages*, but it need not be explored here (TA, 61-68).

The second age is the present age of envy engendered by, and having, the characteristics described above. It is important to note that envy is for Kierkegaard a result of falling away from inwardness and from the Christian religion.

The last age is the future (a consideration entirely and properly omitted by Hegel) in which envy and its resultant reduction of man to the numerical public is overcome. Now is the time of decision:

> They must be lost in the dizziness of abstract infinity or be saved infinitely in the essentiality of the religious life. Then it will be said: "Look, everything is ready; look, the cruelty of abstraction exposes the vanity of the finite in itself; look, the abyss of the infinite is opening up; look, the sharp scythe of leveling permits all, every single one, to leap over the blade—look, God is waiting! Leap then into the embrace of God" (TA, 108).

The leap called for is not according to prudence and it is against the understanding (TA, 111). Again, we face the incommensurable of the religious and the ugly ditch over which Lessing could not leap (CUP, 86-97).

Kierkegaard went beyond his role as reviewer of a novel in this third stage, but he had to do so as a "secret agent" or as an "unrecognizable one" (TA, 107). It is only in this hope and invitation to leap into the arms of God that Kierkegaard's ironic purpose finds

its focus. The possibility of this leap and our need to make it is what
Two Ages is about, its first and final cause.

Kierkegaard's Concept of Envy and Ressentiment

This comment on history suggests a number of reflections, but
the most important of these is the question of the relation Kierkegaard's view of envy bears to the discussion of resent iment. This
discussion will necessarily be very brief. This question is all the
more important because of the focus brought to bear on the concept
by F. Nietzsche and because A. Dru translated Kierkegaard's *mis-
undelse* by "ressentiment" in his truncated edition of *Two Ages* entitled *The Present Age*. This translation led to serious confusion, for
Kierkegaard and Nietzsche were not talking about the same thing.

Nietzsche in the chapter "On Redemption" in *Thus Spake Zarathustra* notes that men often seek revenge on the past, and he links
this search for revenge with his notion of ressentiment. The free
and noble natures are able to externalize their feelings in immediate response, and as a result the emotions are not poisoned. However, those who cannot or do not express their emotions in open
and public deeds have to internalize them. The slave remembers,
and the memory festers. This act of internalization is, for
Nietzsche, the origin of the slave morality. One senses, and
Nietzsche even seems at times to suggest, that he is making a reference to a direct historical event in the past. However, a historical
explanation is not, in the strictest sense, offered in spite of
Nietzsche's reference to Jews and Christians as practitioners of ressentiment. Nietzsche is developing another of his great antitheses
in his discussion of ressentiment, the really big-shot theory of the
master morality and the slave morality. Nietzsche is presenting an-
tithetical models of morality and authority. The historical references are for illustrative purposes.

Now, these two moralities need each other; the development of
a moral philosophy for masters requires a class of slaves. The very
language suggests references to Hegel's *Phenomenology of Spirit*, in
which again historical examples are used only to present a typol-
ogy. Ressentiment, however, is not where the struggle of these two

moralities ends; it is where they begin. In patterns of thought quite reminiscent of Hegel, Nietzsche claims that the slave finally gets the better of it. Civilization is the result. (Shades of Freud too.) Now, however, when the master has been overcome, the tragedy is that the slave morality does not disappear. Formerly, the ressentiment was turned against the ancient enemy, the master; after the defeat of the master the emotion does not disappear. Rather the person turns the sentiment against himself in the form of bad conscience and masochism. For Nietzsche the only hope for salvation is the restoration of the master morality.

Formerly the Christian mythology of the death of Christ allowed repentance and redemption, but now, according to Nietzsche, the death of God has called man himself into question. The death of God deprives man of the only effective relief he ever had from bad conscience, and so again bad conscience and masochism sour the possibilities of human life.[15]

To be sure, now that one looks at the matter, one sees that Nietzsche's theory has really nothing to do with Kierkegaard's description of envy in the present age. Although I have tried (overly hard?) to eliminate the historical dimensions of Nietzsche's analysis, it is hard to make sense of it without some historical orientation. Like Freud, in *Totem and Taboo*, Nietzsche is referring to, or making an explicit appeal to, some primordial historical event. Kierkegaard, on the other hand, is attempting to explain events in the present. The death of God does call into question the "solution" of the problem posed by ressentiment, but the death of God is itself a question. God, on the other hand, is for Kierkegaard the only resolution of the problem of envy. For both, the death of God would call man into question. Nietzsche found ressentiment at the heart of the New Testament; Kierkegaard found its resolution there.

A second author, one who learned much from Nietzsche but who differs from him, is Max Weber. Weber's views of the New Testament are quite different from those of Nietzsche. Weber does not

---

[15]See the section in *Thus Spake Zarathustra*, many editions. This discussion owes much to Tracy B. Strong's *Friedrich Nietzsche and the Politics of Transfiguration* (Berkeley: University of California Press, 1975) 244-50.

find ressentiment in the New Testament.[16] Of perhaps more interest is Weber's appraisal of behavior patterns characteristic of the Protestant ethic. One of Weber's most famous examples of the Protestant ethic is Benjamin Franklin. Franklin is one who cannot live in the present; he is driven ever forward. Never at peace with himself, he always defers gratification to some unspecifiable future. Fulfillment is not possible because the capitalist habit of acquisitiveness is open-ended. Further, the capitalist never comes to himself, but only to the fulfillment of economic and social roles.[17]

Such a brief resume of Weber's thesis at best tells no lie, but it is noteworthy that Weber is in agreement with Nietzsche's rationalism while at the same time he repudiates his view of the New Testament. Nietzsche and Weber are in general agreement with Kierkegaard's view of the displacement of the modern self. Weber finds the hindrance to selfhood more in the rationalization of the economic order in which the envy of possession plays some part. Kierkegaard does not specify the rationalization of economic activity as the source of what he (Kierkegaard) calls envy, but at a more general level both Weber and Kierkegaard understand reflection as a major source of modern man's loss of presence. Further, both lay a rather consistent emphasis upon utility or prudence as a prime element of the modern characterology.

Weber and Nietzsche agree in their naturalistic assumptions that ressentiment is inherent in the human condition whereas for Kierkegaard envy is an aberration to be healed only by the grace of God.

The last writer to be mentioned is Max Scheler, whose treatment is the most extensive of the three thinkers considered in this section. Scheler maintained that though Christian values have been understood as an expression of ressentiment, such is emphatically

---

[16]Max Weber, *The Sociology of Religion*, trans. Ephraim Fishoff (Boston: Beacon Press, 1963) 115-16.

[17]Max Weber, *The Protestant Ethic and the Spirit of Capitalism*, tr. Talcott Parsons (London: G. Allen and Unwin, Ltd., 1930). There has been a storm of criticism of Weber's thesis. See chap. 3 of Joachim Wach's *Sociology of Religion* (Chicago: University of Chicago Press, 1944) and Kurt Samuelson's *Religion and Economic Action* (Stockholm: Svenska Bokforlaget, 1961) 1.

not the case. Rather, it is the erosion of those Christian values that began perhaps as early as the thirteenth century and culminated in the French revolution that is the root of ressentiment. Nietzsche's mistake was to attribute the democratic, utilitarian and socialist philosophies to Christianity, but, on the other hand, he was entirely correct to attack these elements as being the bearers of ressentiment in the modern world.[18]

Of course, it is quite easy to see that Kierkegaard is closer to Scheler than to either Weber or Nietzsche. Had Kierkegaard been writing his own explicit philosophical sociology rather than ostensibly reviewing a book, he might have been even closer to the very vocabulary of Scheler than he is. Yet Kierkegaard's views on envy do suggest specific correlates of some of the terms used by Scheler.

This paper began as a modest proposal to examine the concept of envy in Kierkegaard's *Two Ages*. In pursuing that end we have noted the tremendous advance Kierkegaard made over Dante because he (Kierkegaard) discovered the political and social dimensions of envy in the modern social scene. His critique of his "present age" is devastating, and it is doubtful if our present age would fare as well in his eyes. Finally we have briefly related the fundamentals in Kierkegaard's concept of envy to recent German writers who controverted over what they called ressentiment. The results of the research are disturbing for we have found that what Dante called a cardinal sin has not disappeared with the substitution of Kierkegaard's sociological analysis for Dante's theological analysis. The phenomenon to which Dante referred is even more cardinal than he realized: envy results not only in personal sin, but also in social phenomena of which Dante had no clue. Several thinkers and critics of modernity, among whom Kierkegaard stands as the significant precursor, offer varied analyses of something very like the phenomenon of envy. Only Kierkegaard among the modern analysts saw that hopelessness of man and the "necessity" of grace if man is to recover himself. So, though in his social anal-

---

[18]Max Scheler, *Ressentiment*, tr. Lewis A. Coser (New York: Free Press, 1961).

ysis he makes a great advance beyond Dante, he realized as well as Dante that the cure for envy is radical. The diagnoses discovered and emphasized different manifestations, but the medicine prescribed by Dante and by Kierkegaard is the same.

VII

Kierkegaard's Sociology

by Merold Westphal

Hegel describes philosophy as "its own time comprehended in thought."[1] For all their problems with Hegel, Kierkegaard and his spiritual contemporary, Nietzsche, agree. But whereas for Hegel this meant penetrating the world-historical significance of the French Revolution,[2] Kierkegaard and Nietzsche do not direct their attention primarily to such events as the revolutions of 1848 or the unification of Germany and the Franco-Prussian war. Instead they see their task as interpreting a sociological event, the emergence of mass society, the crowd, the public, the herd. They agree in

---

[1] *Philosophy of Right*, Preface.

[2] See Joachim Ritter, "Hegel und die französische Revolution," in *Metaphysik und Politik* (Frankfurt: Suhrkamp, 1969) 183-255, and Jürgen Habermas, "Hegel's Critique of the French Revolution," in *Theory and Practice*, tr. John Viertel (Boston: Beacon Press, 1973) 121-41.

viewing their own time as engaged in a life or death struggle with this debilitating disease and (against Marx) in viewing the phenomena of mass society as ephiphenomena of a spiritual condition rather than of economic structures.[3] Thus the sociological event is intimately related to a parallel "religious" event, the death of God, or, in Kierkegaard's language, the disappearance of Christianity from Christendom. The massification of society is the flip side of its secularization.

Still, this agreement is anything but total. From Nietzsche's point of view the herd is born of a passion for leveling that has its own origin in a resentment and envy that religion masks as the ideals of justice and equality. This "Christian" morality is all that remains of a religious heritage that the modern world has for the most part disowned. The "herd" is Nietzsche's name for the disease that occurs when people only incompletely break free from Christianity, retaining its morality while repudiating its metaphysics. Health can be achieved only by making the break wholehearted and complete.

Kierkegaard's diagnosis and prescription is equally "spiritual" but quite the converse. The herd—this is a term he also uses to talk about mass society—is the offspring of a passionless age, committed to nothing but self-interest. The envy that generates leveling betrays the increasingly total absence of ideals from social life, though there remains a lot of talk about God. The profession of "Christian" metaphysics is all that remains of a religious heritage that the modern world has for the most part eviscerated. The herd is Kierkegaard's name for the disease that occurs when people only incompletely adhere to Christianity, retaining its metaphysics while repudiating its morality.[4] Health can be achieved only by a wholehearted and complete return to true faith.[5]

---

[3]Implicit here is the suggestion that Marx and Weber have not exhausted the possibilities for a sociology of capitalist society.

[4]Cf. TA, 77, 81. Feuerbach makes a similar observation, describing a modern "believer" as follows: "he denies God practically by his conduct—the world has possession of all his thoughts and inclinations—but he does not deny him theoretically, he does not attack his existence; he lets that rest. But this existence does not affect or incommode him." *The Essence of Christianity*, tr. George Eliot (New York: Harper and Brothers, 1957) 15.

[5]This theme of the necessity of true religion runs throughout TA. See 81-82, 87-88, and 108.

It is his account of mass society that I refer to when speaking of Kierkegaard's sociology, and it is the task of this essay to describe that sociology. It is not only of interest because of its already suggested linkages with the work of Hegel, Marx, and Nietzsche; beyond that is its immediately contemporary bearing on our own times. For Kierkegaard offers us a shoe that fits embarrassingly well. At times it seems as if he knew us better than we know ourselves.

Though Kierkegaard's sociology is to be found throughout his writings, this essay will focus attention primarily on a rather lengthy book review that Kierkegaard published under the title *Two Ages—The Age of Revolution and the Present Age: A Literary Review*, along with materials from the journals on themes central to the review. This little book has had a remarkable, though to my knowledge untraced, history within the existentialist tradition, and the portion of it that most directly sets forth Kierkegaard's sociology has been available to the English-speaking world since 1940 under the title, *The Present Age*.[6]

The novel that Kierkegaard reviews is itself entitled *Two Ages*. His summary of its plot suggests that the soap opera was invented in Denmark, but he keeps insisting that it is a work of genuine literary merit. His primary concern, however, is not literary. In the life and loves of the numerous characters he sees mirrored the essential features of two distinct cultures, the age of the French Revolution and the present age. (The novel was published in 1845, the review in 1846, about a month after *Concluding Unscientific Postscript* appeared.)

It must have seemed providential to Kierkegaard to come across this novel while completing the writing of the *Postscript*; for its characters (at least as he sees them) incarnate his own distinction between subjectivity and objectivity and permit him to restate that

---

[6]The full title is *The Present Age and Two Minor Ethico-Religious Treatises*, tr. Alexander Dru (Oxford: Oxford University Press, 1940). In 1962, Harper and Row replaced one of the "minor" treatises with an introduction by Walter Kaufmann and republished it under the title, *The Present Age*.

distinction as the opposition of passion and reflection. When he says repeatedly that the revolutionary age was an age of passion, while the present age is one of reflection, the point is to describe and evaluate the present age from the perspective of the ethicoreligious subjectivity developed in the pseudonymous authorship that culminated in the *Postscript*.

This is not to say that the revolutionary age was a paradigm of the ethicoreligious subjectivity Kierkegaard sought to evoke. It was not. He cannot, for example, approve of the revolutionary age's disrespect for marriage nor of the affairs that occur outside of its bonds in the first part of the novel. Even so, he sees an essential passion at work, which "is its own guarantee that there is something sacred. . . . But prosiness lacks the concept. Thus when a revolutionary age tolerates a relation to a married woman, it has an idea of propriety despite its false concept . . . [the] propriety that it be concealed" (TA, 64). In the middle of this passage Kierkegaard explicitly evokes a crucial passage from the *Postscript*:

> If one who lives in the midst of Christendom goes up to the house of God, the house of the true God, with the true conception of God in his knowledge, and prays, but prays in a false spirit; and one who lives in an idolatrous community prays with the entire passion of the infinite, although his eyes rest upon the image of an idol: where is there most truth? The one prays in truth to God though he worships an idol; the other prays falsely to the true God, and hence worships in fact an idol (CUP, 179-80).

Kierkegaard's point is to praise neither adultery or idolatry. It is rather to raise the question of inwardness, the question whether outwardly "proper" behavior and "correct" beliefs without the passionate commitment appropriate to them are worth much.

Kierkegaard's praise of passion is no carte blanche to anything that can present itself as an urge. "Let no one interpret all my talk about pathos [*Pathos*] and passion [*Liedenskab*] to mean that I intend to sanction every uncircumcised immediacy, every unshaven passion" (JP, 3: 3127). What then is the "essential passion," the "passion of the infinite" that he admires in the revolutionary age in spite of its adultery and in the pagan in spite of his idolatry? Kierkegaard has already told us. It is the passion that grows out of the conviction "that there is something sacred." The sacred may be misidentified as earthly eros, the "provisional idea" mistaken for the "highest idea." Still, this is better than the "prosiness [which] lacks the concept" and the "fossilized formalism" that presides over human sexuality when nothing at all is any longer sacred (TA, 65-66).[7] The pagan may have a false concept of God but at least "he has the idea that one should fear God" (TA, 64).

Here Kierkegaard links the notions of "the sacred" and "the idea." It is the latter expression that he uses most frequently. It is the clue to the distinction between passion and reflection. An initial indication of what he means by the idea can be found by recalling an oft-quoted passage from the Gilleleie journal of 1835: "the crucial thing is to find a truth which is truth *for me*, to find *the idea for which I am willing to live and die* . . . of what use would it be to me for truth to stand before me, cold and naked, not caring whether or not I acknowledged it. . . . What is truth but to live for an idea?" (JP, 5: 5100). The animal lives out of instinct; man, as spirit, can live for an idea. The animal dies out of necessity; man, as spirit, can give his life because there is something worth dying for. To live, not out of habit but because one knows why life is worth living, and to die, not out of necessity, but because one values something more than life itself—that is to be related to the idea. The idea is a truth that claims me for its own in life and in death and, in claiming me, gives meaning to both life and death.[8]

Passion, then, is the driving force of a life lived in touch with the idea. Reflection is thought's ability to talk its way out of this relation.[9]

---

[7]The distinction between the provisional and highest ideas is a clear reference to the theory of love and beauty in Plato's *Symposium*.

[8]A classical Christian expression of this idea is the opening of the *Heidelberg Catechism*: "What is your only comfort, in life and in death? That I belong—body and soul, in life and in death—not to myself but to my faithful Savior, Jesus Christ."

[9]Reflection, as the thoughtful complement to sheer immediacy and enthusiasm has its proper place (TA, 96, 110-11). It can even be used to help free the self of reflection in the sense described here (JP, 3: 3129). Kierkegaard's complaint is not against reflection as such, but against reflection cut off from passion. Such reflection not only lacks the commitment that passion involves, but serves as a defense against both commitment and passion.

But why would thought want to talk its way free of the idea? We are not talking, of course, about thought in general, for thought is always someone's thought, and the question should more properly be phrased: Why would anyone want to talk his or her way free of the idea? The answer is quite simple if one pays attention to the way in which Kierkegaard uses the term *idea*. It is virtually interchangeable with the term *ideal*, and he views it as providing life's norm, demand, criterion, and requirement. As if to undercut the subtle distinctions of our own moral philosophy, he sees the idea as the individual's telos *and* duty. And he frequently qualifies these normative terms that contextually define "the idea" with the term "infinite" to make it clear that the idea makes unconditional and ultimate demands of our existence. The idea wounds and makes life strenuous; its absence makes life easier. It does not merely demand that I abandon my criminal or immoral ways and conform to the prevailing mores of my society; it subjects social morality itself to the test of an infinite demand and deprives social conformity of an ultimate comfort. It tells me, as it told Socrates of old, that to be a good Athenian one must be more than a good Athenian.[10] So there's not really much mystery about why thought might choose to loosen its links with the idea.

But what has all this to do with Kierkegaard's sociology? The themes of passion, reflection, and the idea provide an elegant restatement of the subjectivity and inwardness motifs of the *Postscript*, and we have just seen that the idea relativizes *every* social morality and socialization process.[11] But the very inclusiveness of that "every" raises the question whether all this has any particular bearing on the phenomena of mass society, a distinctively modern kind of social formation.

Kierkegaard views the individual and society as standing in a relation of dialectical interaction. Though neither unilaterally conditions the other, they are mutually determined by each other.

---

[10]JP, 2: 1770-1825. See also my essay, "Kierkegaard's Politics" in *Thought* 55:218 (1980): 320-32.

[11]This strikes at the heart of the agreement between Aristotle and Hegel on the link between politics and ethics.

There is thus an important isomorphism between them, the one reflecting the character of the other; and the primacy of passion or reflection in the individuals who make up society will be an index of that society's shape. Mass society is the society that is produced by and in turn produces individuals in which reflection predominates and the idea is essentially absent. (Other societies distinguish themselves by the different versions of the idea that underlie their passion.)

Thus the categories we have been exploring are in fact the keys to Kierkegaard's sociology, which he summarizes as follows:

> Purely dialectically the relations are as follows, and let us think them through dialectically without considering any specific age. When individuals (each one individually) are essentially and passionately related to an idea and together are essentially related to the same idea, the relation is optimal and normative. Individually the relation separates them (each one has himself for himself), and ideally it unites them. . . . Thus the individuals never come too close to each other in the herd sense, simply because they are united on the basis of an ideal distance (TA, 62-63).

It is important to notice that Kierkegaard distinguished two ways of deviating from this norm.[12] They invite the labels barbarism and decadence.

> If individuals relate to an idea merely *en masse* (consequently without the individual separation of inwardness), we get violence, anarchy, riotousness; but if there is no idea for the individuals *en masse* and no individually separating essential inwardness, either, then we have crudeness. . . . Remove the relation to oneself, and we have the tumultuous self-relating of the mass to an idea; but remove this as well, and we have crudeness (TA, 63).

A decadent society will inevitably think itself superior to a barbaric society, for it enjoys an orderliness that contrasts sharply with the latter's tumultuous anarchy and riotous violence. Ever the Socratic gadfly, Kierkegaard challenges the self-evidence of this su-

---

[12]In reply to a question about the establishment of this norm, Kierkegaard might well reply in the manner of Hegel in the *Philosophy of History*: that it has already been established, so far as it can be, in the pseudonymous writings, *and* that it will establish itself in use throughout the critical descriptions which follow.

periority. After all, he insists, the barbaric society has at least retained a partial relation to the idea, while the decadent society, beneath its facade of civilization, has lost contact with the idea both individually and collectively. To make the issue concrete and contemporary, Kierkegaard asks the infuriating but carefully grounded question whether civilized Western societies such as our own are perhaps further from being truly civilized than Cambodia under the Khmer Rouge or Iran under the Ayatollah Khomeini.

In any case it is clear that when Kierkegaard speaks of the herd that typifies the modern age it is the decadent society, or in his words, the crude society, which he has in mind. Because of its double loss of contact with the idea, he views it as (1) a subhuman society, (2) an amoral society, (3) a diabolical society, and (4) a society of glittering vices.

A Subhuman Society. The very use of the term "herd" to describe mass society implies the sinking from a genuinely human level of existence to a merely animal level. For Kierkegaard the term "sinking" is especially appropriate, while the term "merely" is not quite right. Man is by nature both animal and spirit. We are not discussing an evolutionary situation in which man has not yet risen or emerged from his animal nature to a truly human nature. Thus to become a herd is to sink, to fall below what one already is. But since man is by nature spirit he cannot become simply or merely animal, and the human herd will always be distinctively human. It presupposes, for example, envy, which the animal herd lacks.

> "Just like the others." This phrase expresses the two characteristic marks of being man in general: (1) sociality, the animal-creature that is linked to the herd: just like the others; (2) envy, which, however, animals do not have.

This envy is very characteristic. To be specific, animals are not envious because each animal is only a copy or specimen [*Examplar*]. Man, on the other hand, is the only animal species in which every specimen . . . is an individuality, intended [*lagt an*] to be spirit. Number or the numerical man, of course, does not become spirit but still retains this feature that distinguishes him from other animal creatures—envy (JP, 3: 2986).[13]

This envy that insists that everyone be just like the others is essential to the leveling process by which the herd is born. It presents itself under the honorific label of equality, but Kierkegaard sees it as a form of escapism. In a revolutionary age, perhaps, talk of equality may well have represented a passion to provide full human dignity to those who had previously been denied it by systems of political and economic domination; but in the present age it serves to soften the spiritual requirements which turn out to be an essential ingredient in that human dignity. Thus the slogans of equality serve not so much to elevate individuals to the dignity of being human as to free them from the responsibility of rising to this vocation.

This escapism is in the direction of a purely animal existence. "The animal's notion of being safe when it is in the flock, that danger consists in being separated from the flock" is all the animal knows, for "the animal creature needs no higher certainty than numbers." Since "man is *by nature* an animal-creation" it follows that "all human effort is therefore in the direction of running together in a herd." But it is not that simple. For man is also spirit and as such he feels "the need for a kind of certainty other than numbers," other than being just like all the others. "Yet the natural man, the animal-man, shrinks from becoming [spirit]," and the reason is clear. "The truth is that in the herd one is free from the criterion of the individual and of the ideal" (JP, 3: 2968, 2970, 2980). Mass society is a flight from spirit. It is the stage on which those who are a polar tension of nature and spirit play the role of the animals they can never be. It is the shared bad faith by which individuals help each other sustain the illusion that they can shirk their spiritual destiny by joining the public.[14] But "the crowd is untruth" just because it is this choice to free itself from the idea.[15]

---

[13]Cf. TA, 81–84.

[14]The theme of self-deception emerges in TA on pages 8, 10, and 77.

[15]This phrase is the constant refrain of the first of two notes on "the individual," written in 1846 and published in PV.

An Amoral Society. It becomes clearer that the herd is an amoral society. For the idea from which it seeks to free itself by huddling together is the ideal, the source of that unconditional claim upon human existence which constitutes the moral life. This is not to say that the herd has no values; rather, a transvaluation of values has occurred in which moral values have been replaced by other values. The categories of the moral life are put out of play and no longer function as the conditions of possible experience.

The revolutionary age is a passionate age, that is, one related to the idea. This means "it has *not nullified the principle of contradiction* and can become either good or evil" (TA, 66). It lives in a framework for which the distinction between good and evil, right and wrong is essential to decision and action. The herd is that society which, by freeing itself from the idea, has freed itself from this opposition or contradiction as well. But this means that from the moral point of view neither the herd nor the individuals who make it up can be said to choose or to act. Instead they remain, like King Agrippa, in "the most enervating state imaginable" (TA, 66).[16]

In his pseudonymous writings Kierkegaard calls this choice not to choose, this freely adopted amorality, the aesthetic stage of existence. Those earlier discussions are brought to mind by a second way in which Kierkegaard refers to the amorality of mass society. Three times on a single page he tells us that "the public is unrepentant" (TA, 95). In a related passage he writes that "a crowd in its very concept is the untruth, by reason of the fact that it renders the individual completely impenitent and irresponsible, or at least weakens his sense of responsibility by reducing it to a fraction" (PV, 112).[17] The amorality of this world in which neither responsibility nor repentance have a place can also be expressed by saying, "The sum and substance of the public life is actually, from first to last, lack of conscience" (JP, 3: 2955).

What especially links this portrayal of mass society to the pseudonymous description of the aesthetic stage is the account of what

---

[16]Kierkegaard's phrase here, "obliged to make a decision," calls for comparison with the argument of William James in "The Will to Believe."

[17]Cf. PV, 116, and JP, 3: 2932.

takes the place of moral seriousness. This unrepentant public is "that gallery public [which] now seeks to be entertained and indulges in the notion that everything anyone does is done so that it may have something to gossip about. . . . If I were to imagine this public as a person . . . I most likely would think of one of the Roman emperors, an imposing, well-fed figure suffering from boredom and, therefore, craving only the sensate titillation of laughter. . . . So this person, more sluggish than he is evil, . . . saunters around looking for variety" (TA, 94). Along with the author of "The Rotation Method," the crowd believes that "boredom is the root of all evil" (EO, 1: 281).[18]

For the amoral herd that fears boredom above all else, everything becomes entertainment. Sex and sports, politics and the arts are transformed into entertainment. Even religion will have to become show business if it is to survive. Nothing is immune from the demand that boredom be relieved (but without personal involvement, for mass society is spectator society). If television does not yet exist it will have to be invented.

The link between an entertainment ethos and the media is perhaps more obvious for us than it was for Kierkegaard. But his discussion of the amorality of the herd gives special attention to "the press," that he views as essential to the creation of "the public" (TA, 90-94). Biographically it is clear that the press becomes an issue for him by virtue of *the Corsair* affair rather than the pseudonymous discussion of boredom and "the interesting." Still, he views it as contributing by means of its impersonality and anonymity to the loss of a sense of responsibility which is the central issue (JP, 2: 2152). Consequently, "the Jesuits in their degeneracy were the most disgraceful attempt to seize control of consciences. The daily press is the most infamous attempt to constitute the lack of conscience as a principle of the state and of humanity" (JP, 2: 2168). The media research that could be generated by taking that last sentence seriously might well be called Socratic sociology, for like Kierkegaard,

---

[18]The last two essays of EO, vol. 1, "The Rotation Method" and "Diary of a Seducer" give special emphasis to the place of boredom and "the interesting" in the pre-ethical stage of existence. Cf. Gabriel Marcel, "The Mystery of the Family," in *Homo Viator*, tr. Emma Craufurd (New York: Harper and Row, 1962) 82-84.

Socrates thought you could understand a society only by examining its commitment to the good.

Kierkegaard views mass society as leaving the distinction between good and evil outside its worldview. One way this happens is through the replacement of such notions as responsibility and repentance with talk about "the boring" and "the interesting." Another way of achieving the same goal comes to expression in the third primary reference of *Two Ages* to the herd's amorality. This is his complaint about its "habitual and excessive relativity" (TA, 70).

Kierkegaard seems to have two things in mind here, a calculative and a comparative mentality. The calculative tendency he links with a procrastinating failure to act, but we should not read this as if nothing ever happened. The calculative habit is one that focuses on the effectiveness of means in relation to ends, and this makes it easy to avoid moral questions about both the ends and the means. In Kantian language the calculative mentality deals only with hypothetical and never with categorical imperatives. In a world where this thinking prevails a great deal may happen, but none of it is worthy of the name of human action from the perspective of the ethicoreligious subjectivity that is Kierkegaard's norm.

The comparative tendency brackets basic moral questions by focusing on another relation, that of my behavior or ours to the behavior of others. "Everyone, everyone is so prone to set his mind at ease in a relativity. Anyone who is a little better than his family and relatives or the others in the provincial town where he lives or among his peers, etc., promptly sets his mind at ease and feels superior" (JP, 3: 2966). "The law of existence for the numerical or for mass men is that they live by comparisons" (JP, 3: 2986).

At the time when the president of Yale University publicly raised the question of whether a Black Panther could get a fair trial in the American courts, I remember discussing the question with a national religious leader. The reply was the solemn assurance that our system was surely to be preferred to the Soviet system. The fact that the answer came from one who loudly asserts the reality of moral absolutes would not persuade Kierkegaard that he had not become brainwashed by the "habitual and excessive relativity" that is an earmark of the amoral herd.

A Diabolical Society. The diabolical character of mass society is grounded in this very amorality. Nietzsche's madman announces, "God is dead. God remains dead. And we have killed him. How shall we comfort ourselves, the murderers of all murderers? . . . Must we ourselves not become gods simply to appear worthy of it?"[19] Nietzsche sees the herd as unable to comfort itself in this way because it remains too tied to the morality of good and evil. By contrast, Kierkegaard sees the very amorality of the herd to be the ground of its own eventually demonic self-deification.[20] The first step can be described as follows: "Therefore mankind felt an unspeakable relief when it got Christianity turned around in such a way that it got rid of God and Christianity came to mean there is no duty toward God. Man thinks he will have the easiest time of all when there is no God at all—then man can play the lord. After that God becomes at most a handsome ornament, a luxury item—for there is no duty toward God" (JP, 2: 1808).

This religious implication of the herd's amorality can be described as *atheism*—"But from an ethicoreligious point of view, to recognize the 'crowd' as the court of last resort is to deny God" (PV, 118); or as *pantheism*—"all doubt has ultimately its stronghold in the illusion of temporal existence that we are a lot of us, pretty much the whole of humanity, which in the end can jolly well overawe God and be itself the Christ. And pantheism is an accoustic illusion that confounds *vox populi* with *vox dei*" (PV, 135);[21] or as *idolatry*—"The idol, the tyrant, of our age is 'the many,' 'the crowd,' statistics" (JP, 3: 2951).

In *Two Ages* the language of idolatry prevails. We have already seen Kierkegaard compare mass society unfavorably with paganism, and now a slightly different aspect of that comparison emerges. "When passion is essentially present in the pagan, [es-

---

[19]*The Gay Science,* paragraph 125, Walter Kaufmann translation (several editions).

[20]This is the central theme of my essay, "Kierkegaard's Politics." See fn. 10 above.

[21]In JP, 3: 2942, Kierkegaard notes that it is from this *vox populi* that the cry goes up: "Crucify! Crucify!" He calls this pantheism because the divine has become wholly immanent, not in nature but in society.

sential passion = living before the Idea] even his idolatry is not devoid of devoutness; although he has a false concept, he has the idea that one should fear God" (TA, 64). In other pagan idolatry Kierkegaard has in mind falls short of self-deification and preserves an understanding of God as morally transcendent to both the individual and society. The implicit comparison, that the present age has lost even this sense that "one should fear God," is made explicit in the *Journals*. By virtue of becoming the crowd, Christendom has become "a far more serious battle against God than man's battle against God in paganism ever was" (JP, 3: 2992).

It is not surprising that self-deification should be seen as a particularly pernicious form of idolatry. The Christian tradition (with special help from Milton) has identified the serpent of Genesis 3 and the King of Babylon whose fall is described in Isaiah 14 as Satan. The fall of Satan and the fall of man represent the entry of evil into the universe and into human history. In both cases the story of origin is also a story of essence, and the secret of sin is exposed as the rebellious pride that insists on one's becoming like God, obliterating the difference between creature and Creator. Since Kierkegaard sees the crowd that is Christendom as practicing precisely this pride, we might expect him to see the idolatry of the present age as demonic. He does not disappoint us. (Remember in reading the following quotation that reflection here signifies the attempt of thought to free itself from the idea.)

> The idolized positive principle of sociality in our age is the consuming, demoralizing principle that in the thralldom of reflection transforms even virtues into *vitia splendida* [glittering vices]. And what is the basis of this other than a disregard for the separation of the religious individual before God in the responsibility of eternity. When dismay commences at this point, one seeks comfort in company, and thus reflection captures the individual for his whole life. . . . Leveling is not the action of one individual, but a reflection-game in the hand of an abstract power. . . . While the individual egotistically thinks he knows what he is doing, it must be said that they all know not what they do, for just as inspired enthusiastic unanimity results in a something more that is not the individuals', a something more emerges here also. A demon that no individual can control is conjured up (TA, 86).

That the present age is one of reflection is the constant refrain of *Two Ages*. By now there is nothing especially surprising in the triple reference to reflection in this passage so far as it (a) moves effortlessly between individual and society (since Kierkegaard views them as dialectically interdependent), (b) identifies reflection with a loss of responsibility, and (c) views this loss as idolatry. What is of note in this passage is the triple reference to reflection as bondage. Modern society is "in the thralldom of reflection." "Reflection captures the individual for life." And the leveling process that belongs essentially to the herd is "a reflection-game in the hand of an abstract power," rather than any genuinely human action.[22]

Living in a godless society the individual "seeks comfort in company." This company is "a something more" than the individuals who make it up. But it is not a human *We* that transcends the human *I*'s who make it up. It is no voluntary association as Locke would have it, nor a moral commonwealth as Rousseau and Kant would have it, nor the incarnate spirit of a nation as Fichte and Hegel would have it. It is an "abstract power," that, though not human, holds human beings in bondage. It is "a demon." Through satanic pride a demonic power has been conjured up, and modern mass society is itself this demonic power.[23]

This network of thoughts may throw some light on a rather puzzling passage in the Introduction to *Two Ages*. There Kierkegaard describes the youth who speaks *"in the name of the age* concerning the demands of the times," as giving the impression "that an intoxicated divinity is speaking, least of all an individual human being" (TA, 9). The image of the intoxicated divinity suggests something from a Dionysiac revel. The following journal entry from 1850 might well be taken as a commentary on press secretaries for the present age as drunken deities.

---

[22]Cf. TA, 81 where reflection is described as a "vast penitentiary."

[23]Cf. JP, 2: 2152, 2164-65. Kierkegaard's sociological analysis of demonic powers relates directly to a number of contemporary discussions of the "principalities and powers" in Pauline theology. See John Howard Yoder, *The Politics of Jesus* (Grand Rapids: Eerdmans, 1972) chap. 8, and, for a partial bibliography, fn. 4 on page 142.

In contrast to what was said about possession in the Middle Ages and times like that, that there were individuals who sold themselves to the devil, I have an urge to write a book, *Possession and Obsession in Modern Times*, and show how people *en masse* abandon themselves to it, how it is now carried on *en masse*. This is why people run together in flocks—so that natural and animal rage will grip a person, so that he feels stimulated, inflamed, and *ausser sich*. The scenes on Bloksberg are utterly pedantic compared to this demonic lust, a lust to lose oneself in order to evaporate in a potentiation, so that a person is outside of himself, does not really know what he is doing or what he is saying or who it is or what it is speaking through him, while the blood rushes faster, the eyes glitter and stare fixedly, the passions boil, lusts seethe (JP, 4: 4178).

Kierkegaard is not complaining here about the sexual revolution. Sex is clearly but a metaphor for people running together in flocks in order to lose themselves in a distinctively modern kind of possession. Mass society is not only demonic because of the superhuman but godless power it holds over people; it is demonic as the metaphysical *Walpurgisnacht* that enables them to give themselves over to this power and be possessed by it. Just as decent, civilized people are to be shocked and offended by Goethe's essentially medieval portrayal of demonic revelry, Kierkegaard intends those who are ethicoreligiously serious to be horrified at this picture of their modern world. He might well have used the words of Marx, "The people must be put in *terror* of themselves in order to give them *courage*."[24]

What features of the modern world are to be interpreted by these images? We must not too hastily think of German masses whipped to a frenzy by Hitler's rhetoric, nor American youth screaming "Hell no! We won't go!" to the Vietnam war, nor Iranian throngs shaking their fists and chanting against the Shah and the Americans. These scenes fit the imagery of Walpurgis Night, and Kierkegaard's analysis surely applies to them. But they are examples of what was previously called the barbaric society, in which individuals relate *en masse* to the idea in some form, whereas the

---

[24]"A Contribution to the Critique of Hegel's *Philosophy of Right*. Introduction," in *Karl Marx: Early Writings*, tr. Rodney Livingstone and Gregor Benton (New York: Random House, 1975) 247.

prime focus of *Two Ages* is the decadent society he calls crude, the terribly civilized society in which he and we live.

We need to remember that whatever delight Mephistopheles takes in escorting Faust to the Bloksberg, his normal pose is that of a suave and debonair man of the world. Similarly, in the New Testament the Devil is a "roaring lion, looking for someone to devour," but he is more frequently described as a clever trickster who "disguises himself as an angel of light."[25] We should therefore not be surprised if the forms of possession that Kierkegaard invites us to examine will have the appearance of civilized respectability rather than Dionysian revelry. This only means, in the light of his analysis, that we will have to look harder to see the demonic aspect. He calls our attention to the marketing executive intoxicated with market shares, and the TV mogul intoxicated with Nielsen ratings; the economist who has sold his soul to the theory of growth, and the conglomerate chairman who has sold his soul to its practice; the philosopher who defines rationality as the effective calculation of means toward ends, and the scientist who practices this rationality; the educator who confuses ignorance reduction with education, and the religious leader who confuses church growth with evangelism. The passions that underlie all this civilized dedication may be viewed as seething lust just to the degree that reflection has freed them from the service of the idea. It is the best and the brightest who reveal most clearly the demonic nature of the present age.

A Society of Glittering Vices. A fourth and final conceptual weapon that Kierkegaard wields against modern mass society is in the notion of virtues as glittering vices. We have already noted the crucial passage. "The idolized positive principle of sociality in our age is the consuming, demoralizing principle that in the thralldom of reflection transforms even virtues into *vitia splendida* [glittering vices]" (TA, 86). Kierkegaard had already used this idea in the *Philosophical Fragments* and would use it again in *Works of Love*.[26]

---

[25] Peter 5:8 and 2 Cor. 11:14. Cf. Eph. 6:11, 1 Tim. 3:7, 2 Tim. 2:26, and Rev. 20:10.

[26]PF, 66-67. WL, 66.

Though it originates with the church fathers' (Lactantius and Augustine) critique of paganism, it is the point at which Kierkegaard's critique is most Nietzschean. Just as when the virtuous say "I am just" [*Ich bin gerecht*], Nietzsche hears "I am revenged" [*Ich bin gerächt*], so Kierkegaard is sensitive to the less-than-noble reality that often underlies the self-proclaimed virtues of his society.[27]

Among these numerous unmaskings, which deserve a separate essay, I shall mention but two. Though the present age is proud of its commitment to equality and to prudence, Kierkegaard finds these phenomena at least open to a very different interpretation than would make their bearers proud.

While Nietzsche finds resentment and revenge where people talk a lot about justice, Kierkegaard finds envy barely hidden behind the praise of equality (TA, 84). His polemic against equality is often so shrill as to be dismissed without being examined. In other writings he makes it clear that there is an equality that he affirms, grounded in the command of neighbor love.[28] And in *Two Ages* he praises the Moravian Brethren for their religiously motivated pursuit of equality (TA, 66). But he sees something entirely different in the leveling process by which mass society is constituted. Though this process is justified with the rhetoric of equality we have already seen him (in the discussion of the herd as a subhuman society) suspect it of being the envy that demands that each be just like the others.[29]

That earlier discussion of envy interpreted it in terms of the ontological difference between animal and spiritual existence. The particular animal is a specimen rather than an individual with a unique responsibility and destiny. As a printed reproduction is to an original painting, so is a particular animal to an individual human being. Envy is a hostility directed against those who take their

---

[27]*Thus Spake Zarathustra*, from "On the Virtuous." Cf. "On the Tarantulas." Both sections are from part 2. At this point Kierkegaard's method is more nearly *ad hominem* than before, like Hegel's in the *Phenomenology* rather than in the *Philosophy of History*. See fn. 12 above.

[28]PV, 118. WL, 70-72, 80-83.

[29]Cf. the citation of JP, 3:986 above in relation to 2: 2166.

spiritual nature seriously enough to be anything but just like the others, anything but a social specimen. As such it is both a form of metaphysical rebellion, the flight from a spiritual vocation, and a form of intersubjectivity, "the *negatively unifying principle* in a passionless and very reflective age" (TA, 81).

A negatively unifying principle is one that brings people together on the basis of what they are against rather than what they are for. The term envy suggests that what they are against is a person's being different. Kierkegaard gives a profound interpretation of this antipathy toward difference by noting the increasing willingness or inability to *admire* another (TA, 78-87). Since, as Marcel has noted, it is "the function of admiration to tear us away from ourselves and from the thoughts we have of ourselves,"[30] the envy that will not or can not admire is essentially egocentric. Kierkegaard sees the same connection and in the midst of his commentary on the demise of admiration he bluntly calls the leveling that springs from envy, "selfishness" (TA, 81-82, 87). While both the love of the ideal and the love of the neighbor put constraints on self-love, there is a love that does not and that can easily be put in the service of pure self-interest. It is the love of the crowd (JP, 2: 1789, 1799; PV, 118).

The crucial test of this suggestion that the egalitarian sentiments of the modern age are instruments of self-interest (will to power) rather than commitments to the ideal of justice or compassion for the needy neighbor would be to examine what happens to those sentiments when they lead in directions costly to the bearer. How does a union treat the individual who refuses to break the no strike clause of a contract or public law? How does a bureaucracy respond to the individual who dares to blow the whistle on corruption or incompetence? What explanations are to be given of changing public attitudes toward social welfare and foreign aid legislation? What happens to lofty statements about human rights and the folly of the arms race in the face of appeals to national interest and security? In short, is "liberty and justice for all" anything

---

[30]*Creative Fidelity*, tr. Robert Rosthal (New York: Farrar, Strauss, and Giroux, 1964) 47-48.

but a slogan? Once again Kierkegaard's critique suggests research projects for a Socratic sociology.[31]

Finally we come to the unmasking of prudence. In this case it is laziness and even cowardice that Kierkegaard finds disguised as virtue. While the present age is proud of the calculating carefulness with which it weighs all the alternatives and avoids making a "big stupid blunder," he finds them to be "prudentially relaxing in indolence" and "strangled by calculation" (TA, 68). Though the age has great power at its disposal, and great skills of management, communication, transport, finance, and publicity, they are for the most part wasted, producing little that could be called action (TA, 66-67, 70). This sluggishness is closely related to the previously noted boredom-entertainment syndrome (TA, 94). In sum: "Exhausted by its chimerical exertions, the present age then relaxes temporarily in complete indolence. Its condition is like that of the stay-abed in the morning who has big dreams, then torpor, followed by a witty or ingenious inspiration to excuse staying in bed. . . . Vis inertiae [the force of inertia] is at the bottom on the age's tergiversation" (TA, 69).

But it is cowardice as well as laziness that parades as prudence. It takes no courage to side with the crowd against an individual. It may well be a cowardly act, as when the crowd spit on Jesus,

---

[31]It is clear that Kierkegaard's "Socratic Sociology" intends to be a critical theory of society. It thus invites comparison with the "critical theory" of the Frankfurt School, and of Jürgen Habermas in particular. It seems to me that the strongest affinity between the two lies in the centrality for both of what the contemporary project calls Ideologiekritik, the attempt to unmask the false consciousness that emerges as society seeks to legitimate itself. The two primary differences I see are these. First, Kierkegaard operates from explicitly normative premises (ethicoreligious) that he does not expect everyone to share and that he does not seek to derive from some unavoidable human interest. He would not be intimidated by the charge that his is a "moralizing" critique, a charge Habermas would consider devastating. Second, without denying the presence of coercion and unequal power in the contexts that generate false consciousness, Kierkegaard emphasizes the eager participation of the members of the herd in mass society and their willing acceptance of the self-deceptions necessary to validate their membership. Thus his kinship is more with Nietzsche than with Marx, though the difference between the socially weak and strong is even less important for him than for Nietzsche. See Raymond Geuss, The Idea of Critical Theory: Habermas and the Frankfurt School (New York: Cambridge University Press, 1981) and Thomas McCarthy, The Critical Theory of Jürgen Habermas (Cambridge: MIT Press, 1981).

though perhaps no one in the crowd would take personal responsibility for the act (JP, 3: 2926, 2932; PV, 113). But the very essence of moral courage "is one person holding out alone, as a single individual, against the opposition of the numerical" (JP, 3: 2987). Here, as elsewhere, the question of courage is a question of fear. Moral courage is to fear God or to fear error more than one fears men, their laughter, or standing alone against them (JP, 2: 2162, 2166, 2171; 3: 2941, 2976, 2988). Moral cowardice is opposite.

There are two ways of describing this cowardice. On the one hand, it is the easy way. Going the way of the group "makes life easier and more comfortable" (JP, 4: 4186). But just because this path is "the coziest and most convenient, it is hypocritically prettied up to be true moral earnestness" (JP, 3: 2973). The path of least resistance must be made to seem something better. Sometimes it masquerades as loyalty (JP, 3: 2978). In *Two Ages*, it is the pose of prudence that Kierkegaard seeks to expose with help once again from Socrates. Because Socrates feared God and error more than being alone against the crowd he chose the right way instead of the easy way. Because his courage was matched by insight, he knew, and he helped us to see, that the easy way is sometimes the cowardly way posing as prudence (TA, 111).

Traditionally, prudence (self-control, temperance) was the rational control of the subrational. Kierkegaard and Socrates see that the rationalizing (legitimizing) of subrational behavior (laziness, cowardice) can also pass itself off as prudence. In this case the crucial test of whether prudence is rationality or rationalization can be formulated by two questions: Does prudence ever demand a strenuousness other than that of the rat race, in which I do my best to keep up with the crowd and climb a rung or two higher on its ladder? Does it ever call for the courage that says, as Socrates, in substance, said to Athens: Because of my loyalty to you I cannot but challenge the most basic assumptions of your lifeworld? The implication of these questions is that in the present age true prudence would show itself in radically countercultural behavior. At issue is not the counterculture of self-interest, which quietly folds its tents and evaporates as soon as the draft is gone and drug laws are no longer strictly enforced. What is envisaged is rather the counterculture that springs from passionate commitment to the Idea and is willing to subject both personal and social life to its critical scrutiny. To put it a bit more concretely: the issue is between the prudence caused by the working principles of our world's military-industrial complex; and the prudence that causes us to question our definition of what constitutes the most advanced civilization.

VIII

Marx and Kierkegaard on Alienation

by James L. Marsh

An initial response to the title of this paper might be to question its usefulness. Are not Marx and Kierkegaard so dissimilar in orientation that any attempt to relate them would be a useless, scholarly tour de force, interesting perhaps to the writer but of little value to the reader? Do not Marx's emphases on the economic and social dimensions of human life render him fundamentally opposed to Kierkegaard's stress on the spiritual and individual? What common ground or even interesting disagreements can arise between one who despises religion as an opiate and one who commends it as man's salvation?

Nonetheless such objections may be premature and misdirected. For Marx and Kierkegaard, simply because they have common roots in Hegel, may have more in common than first meets the eye. Also, juxtaposing two such different thinkers' viewpoints can reveal the limits of each and the extent to which each complements the other. In an age seething with a welter of conflicting methodologies, such reflections can be very useful indeed.

The project of this paper will be, then, first to outline Marx's theory of alienation by focusing primarily, but not exclusively, on *The Economic and Philosophical Manuscripts of 1844*. Second, I will discuss Kierkegaard's notion of alienation as developed in *Two Ages*. Third, I will compare and contrast the two thinkers, and finally conclude with a few reflections concerning the complementarity and contemporary relevance of each.

Is not talking about the common ground between Marx and Kierkegaard in terms of "alienation" already favoring Marx too much insofar as Marx uses the term more than Kierkegaard in a way that is central to Marx's analysis? First, Kierkegaard does use the term or grammatical variants of it in *Two Ages* (TA, 91-92), although much less than Marx does in the *Manuscripts*. Second, as I will argue in the third part of this essay, the term "alienation" indicates a deep structural homology between Marx's description of the loss of self and the division from self taking place in the economy and Kierkegaard's description of the same tendencies in the sociocultural sphere. Third, such a structural homology can be useful insofar as both accounts mutually illumine, qualify, and correct one another.

Marx's Theory of Alienation

For Marx, alienation in a general sense means that people are at odds with themselves, nature, and other people. Alienation in capitalism takes four forms: alienation from the object, from work, from species life, and from other people.[1]

The experience of the worker in capitalism is that his product is alien to him. Not only does the product exist outside the worker, but it is hostile and enslaving to him. The more energy and time he puts into the object produced, the poorer he becomes. The more the worker appropriates nature by working on it, the more he is de-

---

[1]Karl Marx, *The Economic and Philosophical Manuscripts of 1844*, ed. Dirk J. Struik, tr. Martin Mulligan (New York: International Publishers, 1964) 106-27.

prived of the means of life in a double sense: as material on which to work and as means of subsistance. Thus he becomes enslaved to this object in that he has to receive work and also means of subsistence.

The worker is exploited in that he works more time than he is paid for. Abstract labor or value, the average, socially necessary labor time for making the product, divides into that used to pay the worker and that extracted by the capitalist, surplus value. The tendency of capital is to increase the latter as much as possible and to decrease wages relatively or absolutely. The more surplus value there is, the higher is the profit, which is the overriding goal of capital.[2]

Alienation from the object implies alienation from the process of work itself. The labor remains external to the worker rather than expressive of his being. Because his labor is forced, he is not at home with work and works only in order to make a living. Such labor also is alienating because it is directed by someone else. Finally because the measure of wealth is value, labor becomes increasingly abstract and undifferentiated. Division of labor contributes to this process, for the worker is gradually deprived of his skill, which is then transferred to the machine. The worker is thus made qualitatively indistinguishable from other workers and made a mere appendage to the machine.

> As a result, therefore, man (the worker) only feels himself freely active in his animal functions—eating, drinking, procreating, or at most in his dwelling and in dressing up, ect.; and in his human functions he no longer feels himself to be anything but an animal. What is animal becomes human and what is human becomes animal.[3]

For Marx, "use value" is the qualitative relation of the product to human need, and "exchange value" is the value of the product

---

[2]Marx, *Manuscripts*, 108-10; *Capital*, tr. Samuel Moore and Edward Aveling, ed. Frederick Engels, 3 vols. (New York: International Publishers, 1967) 1:35-46, 146-230; 3:25-40.

[3]Marx, *Manuscripts*, 110-11; Karl Marx and Frederick Engels, *The German Ideology*, ed. R. Pascal (New York: International Publishers, 1947) 19-27; *Capital*, 1:312-507.

measured in money. In capitalism the latter rules over the former. All the work is subjugated by capital, quantified, robbed of all intrinsic satisfaction, and used as a mere means of profit. This instrumentalizing of work Marx describes as alienation from species life. People as sensuous, intelligent, free, and conscious beings can and should make themselves in community the end of their labor—labor can express and realize their rationality and freedom. Instead, this rationality and freedom are transformed into mere means for profit. Work itself becomes a way of keeping body and soul together a little longer. That which should be an end becomes a means, and the means becomes the end. "Life itself appears only as a means to life."[4] A commodity fetishism develops in which relationships between men appear as relationships between things. Men forget that it is their own labor that is the source of the value of products and instead ascribe that value to the commodity and money. Money, even more than clothes, makes the man.[5]

Such alienation is increasingly abstract, homogeneous, and quantitative. Because the value of the commodity is more important than its use value, and the value-producing aspect of labor more important than the quality of that labor, money as the expression and measure of that value is the true need of capitalist society. As man becomes ever poorer, his need for money becomes greater in order to protect himself from a hostile, competitive society. Because there is no genuine community in capitalism, money becomes the true community that allows men to exchange their products. Everything is ordered around it, and for it, everything is sacrificed. The real needs of people for dignity, happiness, and love are continually preyed upon and manipulated for the sake of profit.

> No eunuch flatters his despot more basely or uses more despicable means to stimulate his dulled capacity for pleasure in order to sneak a favor for himself than does the industrial eunuch—the producer—in order to sneak for himself a few pennies—in order to

---

[4]Marx, *Manuscripts*, 112-15.

[5]Marx, *Capital*, 1:71-83.

charm the golden birds out of the pockets of his dearly beloved neighbors in Christ.[6]

The dominance of money in capitalism leads to a curious inversion. Rather than the natural excellence of particular spheres of endeavor ruling in those spheres, money holds sway. Not the most loving man wins the woman but the most wealthy. Not the most intellectually talented person goes to Harvard or Yale but the sons of corporate executives. Not the most politically talented person gets into office but the person with the most money or the most wealthy friends.

> Thus, what I am and am capable of is by no means determined by individuality. I am ugly, but I can buy for myself the most beautiful of women. Therefore I am not ugly, for the effect of ugliness—its deterrent power—is nullified by money. I, as an individual, am lame, but money furnishes me with twenty-four feet. Therefore, I am not lame. I am bad, dishonest, unscrupulous, stupid; but money is honored, and hence its possessor. Money is the supreme good, therefore its possessor is good.[7]

The economic sphere spills over into the social, cultural, and political spheres and subordinates them.

Implied in the first three forms of alienation is alienation from other men, the capitalists who own the means of production, seize the product, and control the work. Thus, for the capitalist, a worker is not an individual person but simply an object or commodity who can make money for him. Capitalism, by so impoverishing the worker that he has nothing to lose but his chains, educates him to transcend capitalism through theoretical understanding of his situation and organized resistance. Such transcendence means overcoming private property, the capitalist ownership of the means of production. Communism, in the sense of collective ownership of the means of production, democratic participation in decisions concerning the use of these means, and an aesthetic environment re-

---

[6]Marx, *Manuscripts*, 147-48. *See Capital*, 1:47-83, 94 145; *Grundrisse*, tr. Martin Nicolaus (Baltimore: Penguin Books, 1973) 136 72, 186-238, for discussions of money as the real community in capitalism.

[7]Marx, *Manuscripts*, 167.

flecting the species life of human persons, is the rational solution to the problem of alienation. With such a solution, the abstract, fetishistic quality of social life is transcended, and a rich, many-sided individuality emerges. Such a solution is dialectical in that opposites initially opposed in capitalism, such as mind and body, individual and society, subjectivity and objectivity, now intersect and interact in a complementary way.[8]

Kierkegaard's Theory of Alienation

Kierkegaard's discussion of alienation arises in his reflections upon the contrast between the present age and the revolutionary age of the French Revolution in the novel *Two Ages*. Unlike the passionate, revolutionary age, the people of the present age are merely prudent in a reflective, indolent manner. Rather than take the risk of decision and action, the people of the present age prefer merely to beguile themselves with possibilities in a grandiose manner. Rather than enthusiasm and commitment, there is mere publicity and loquacity (TA, 68-71).

Because the present age has been given over to such abstract reflection, one living in such an age is unable to make the choices that educate and form him as an individual. Reflection itself is not the problem, a point that some of Kierkegaard's critics have missed; it is the use of reflection as an evasion, as an excuse for avoiding choice that is the problem. Reflection is necessary if one is to leave mere immediacy behind. But the state of reflection in which one wallows without choosing is an evil. In thus refusing to commit himself to a choice, a person remains in the realm of infinite possibilities; but such richness is illusory. Whereas in a revolutionary age the crowd applauds a skater willing to go out on thin ice and take audacious risks, in the present age the crowd applauds the ac-

---

[8]Marx, *Manuscripts*, 132-46. See *Grundrisse*, 324-25, for a discussion of the rich, many-sided individual in communism. See G. W. F. Hegel, *The Logic of Hegel*, tr. William Wallace, *The Encyclopedia of the Philosophical Sciences*, 2nd. ed., vol. 1 (London: Oxford University Press, 1965) 143-55, for a definition of dialectic. See Shlomo Avineri, *The Social and Political Thought of Karl Marx* (London: Cambridge University, 1968) 124-48, on the importance of theory for revolutionary praxis.

robatics of a skater willing to go to the very edge of the safe ice but
no further—to go any further would be mere foolishness and im-
prudence. In a revolutionary age, a person watching the skater taking risks is inspired to imitate him and is humbled when he does
not measure up; in the present age there is only empty applause at
a theatrical joke. Indolence and passivity masquerade as energy
and creativity (TA, 71-73, 96).

To live in the present age is thus to be satisfied with false, not
true coin; with paper money, not real money; with mere talk of action rather than the genuine deed; with opinions held at second
hand rather than those won through personal insight and experience. Kierkegaard reminds us that the lack of such paper money
caused Ferdinand, one of the characters in *Two Ages*, to refuse marriage to the woman he loves. This timid prudence is the opposite of
a love that risks all, sacrifices all, hopes for all. "A young man today
would scarcely envy another his capacities or his skill or the love of
a beautiful girl or his fame, no, but he would envy him his money"
(TA, 74-76). Such are the depths to which the present age has sunk.

A passionate, revolutionary age strives to overthrow everything, but the present age, revolutionary only in reflection, leaves
everything as it is. A person typical of such an age is neither passionately good or evil, but ambivalent and prudent in his ambivalence. He is a Polonius who publicly approves the good and secretly
violates it. In contrast to the revolutionary age's admiration of excellence, envy permeates the present age. Too timid to aspire to excellence and too passionless to admire great deeds, people are
reduced by envy to the least common denominator. Confronted by
the possibly upsetting implications of his own remarks, an envious
persons says, "That is not what I meant at all / That is not it, at all."[9]
Confronted with the either/or of a real choice, he or she does not
oppose it but only turns it into make-believe. When he hears the
Christian message, he does not wholeheartedly commit himself to
it or reject it, but only tolerates it or ignores it. When he meets a
beautiful woman, he does not marry her or engage in a passionate
affair but merely philanders (TA, 76-81).

---

[9]T. S. Eliot, "The Love Song of J. Alfred Prufrock," *The Waste Land and Other
Poems* (New York: Harcourt, Brace and World, 1962) 7.

Envy is present both in the individual, who refuses to sacrifice himself or devote himself to anything higher than himself, and in his associates, who resist fiercely any aspirations towards such goals on his part. Both the individual and his associates are imprisoned by reflection, from which one can escape only through a solitary leap of religious faith. "In our age, the principle of association (which at best can have validity with respect to material interests) is not affirmative, but negative; it is an evasion, a dissipation, an 'illusion'" (TA, 106). Passages such as this indicate the priority of the ethicoreligious not only in order of importance but also in order of time and logic. Not only is the ethicoreligious more important than the principle of association, but the spiritual transformation of the individual must precede any transformation of the socioeconomic order.

Nevertheless, we should not read into such comments a hostility to the social on Kierkegaard's part, a mistake that some critics have made. In his thought there is an aspiration towards a community of authentic individuals, but the age is so engulfed in reflection and anonymity that no genuine community is possible, only mass society. For true community to exist, its members would have to be related to an idea.

> When individuals (each one individually) are essentially and passionately related to an idea and together are essentially related to the same idea, the relation is optimal and normative. Individually the relation separates them (each one has himself for himself) and ideally it unites them. When there is essential inwardness, there is a decent modesty between man and man that prevents crude aggressiveness; in the relation of unanimity to the idea there is the elevation that again in consideration of the whole forgets the accidentality of details. Thus the individuals never come too close to each other in the herd sense, simply because they are united on the basis of an ideal distance (TA, 62-63).

Nonetheless Kierkegaard's confining of the principle of association even at its best to the sphere of material interests does indicate that this principle can never be ultimate for him. In the last analysis it is the ethical and religious individual, related to his own more selective kinds of philosophical, moral, and religious community, who is primary. Whether there is a tension in Kierkegaard about this primacy and the apparent ethical significance of public, sociocultural community or its lack in *Two Ages* remains an open question.

With envy there is leveling, the reduction of all to the least common denominator. In ancient times the category of the "individual" reigned supreme; "generation" rules today. In ancient times there was tension between the crowd and the great individual; majority rule is the practice today. Since quantity is more important than quality today, no one ventures anything, because reflection tells him the efforts of one individual would make no difference. Excellence has given way to mediocrity, distinctiveness to abstract, mathematical equality (TA, 84-88).

Leveling is not the action of one individual on another but a reflection game in the hand of an abstract power, the public. The public is a mirage, a phantom possible only in an age bereft of passion and originality. Because the public is so powerful an abstraction, it alienates the individual from his own real powers of reflection, choice, and social life. "The abstraction that individuals paralogistically form alienates individuals instead of helping them." Only when there is no strong communal life present does the press and reflection create the public, made up of unsubstantial individuals who are never united at one time and place in any situation and yet who claim to be a whole. Though I am not enough of an individual to have my own opinions, I can watch the evening news or read *The New York Times*. Because an age devoid of individuality can produce few real leaders, the public becomes the leader through such devices as Gallup polls, Nielson ratings, and the Top Ten. We cannot act together or communicate with one another, but we can watch the Super Bowl together (TA, 90-104).

When the public takes over a person's life, he or she inevitably becomes passive, sensate, decadent, degenerate, interested only in being entertained.

> If I were to imagine this public as a person . . . I most likely would think of one of the Roman emperors, an imposing, well-fed figure suffering from boredom and therefore craving only the sensate titillation of laughter, for the divine gift of wit is not worldly enough. So this person, more sluggish than he is evil, but negatively domineering, saunters around looking for variety (TA, 94).

On account of the leveling, omnivorous action of the public leaving nothing outside of itself untouched and allowing nothing personal or original, crucial distinctions between being silent and speaking, hiddenness and revelation are obliterated. Chattering is the annulled distinction between speaking and being silent, and superficiality the annulled distinction between hiddenness and revelation. People mired in the present age forget that silence and inwardness are the conditions for saying anything essential. The result is a one-dimensional, quantitative sameness in which everything is like everything else, and everyone spouts the current majority opinion. Talking to a person of the present age is to have the impression that his opinions and sentiments are not original, that we have heard it all before. No one risks anything, and consequently no one becomes anybody. All is ambiguity, mediocrity, tepidity, sloth. Every activity, even lovemaking, turns into an anonymous technique that anyone can learn. The most individual is the most universal, and the most private is the most public. Not having any personal lives of their own, people gossip and are insatiably curious about the private lives of celebrities.

Kierkegaard's solution to the problem is not a sociopolitical revolution like Marx's, but the leap of religious faith. A solution on the sociopolitical level is impossible, as I have already indicated, because such a solution presupposes the genuine individuality and community that are so lacking. What is possible, however, is that the individual, reflecting on his own alienation in the public sphere, can recover himself before God. The public, by making the individual so unhappy that he turns to God, educates the individual. By forsaking the abstract, mathematical equality of the public, he achieves genuine equality with other men. By renouncing the specious universality of the public, he realizes the essentially, universally human in himself. Through faith the individual unites opposites such as being silent and speaking, inwardness and revelation, form and content, subjectivity and objectivity in such a way that both the distinction and union between such opposites is maintained (TA, 88-92, 96-106, 108).

Comparison and Contrast

Here the stress will be on comparison rather than contrast, on the common ground rather than what separates the two thinkers. Differences will be mentioned only insofar as it is necessary to qualify certain comparisons. The common ground lies in the norms governing the analysis and critique of alienation, the method used in such analysis and critique, the structure and content of that alienation, and the solutions to the problem of alienation.

What becomes clear first in any comparison of Marx with Kierkegaard is their common interest in autonomous individuality, community, and the mutual relationship between the two—these function as norms for critique. For Marx the community is the condition for the flowering of the rich, free, many-sided individual who would "hunt in the morning, fish in the afternoon, rear cattle in the evening, criticize after dinner."[10] Even an apparently very private activity such as scientific or philosophical thinking is performed with a common language and is oriented towards communication.[11]

For Kierkegaard as well the fully autonomous individual, at one with himself and the world, makes genuine community possible and vice versa. Genuine community in mass society is impossible because of the lack of individuality; on the other hand, the dominance of the public sphere discourages the emergence of individuality. Because authentic community is absent, the public can function as a specious substitute. In times past when men could act together politically, there was a more ideal reciprocity of individual and community. In the light of that ideal Kierkegaard measures the present age and finds it wanting. An important difference between Marx and Kierkegaard here is that Marx gives more weight to the economic and social, and Kierkegaard at times gives more weight to the spiritual and individual. In *Two Ages* there is at least a suggestion that Kierkegaard regards concern for material interest and

---

[10]Marx and Engels, *German Ideology*, 22.

[11]Marx, *Manuscripts*, 137-38.

the principle of association as at best a secondary matter, in contrast to the task of ethical living and religious faith. Such a relegation to secondary status may not be consistent with the ethical significance of material interests and the principle of association, a significance which also seems to be present in *Two Ages*. As an expression of inwardness, and as a hindrance or help to it, the social realm seems to be anything but trivial and unimportant.

Second, there is a common method—dialectic—a movement in which opposites initially opposed to one another come to interact and complement one another. Dialectic is both subjective and objective, it concerns the way we think about things and the way things are. Also the relationship between mind and world is dialectical in that subject and object are not reducible to one another and yet they interact with one another. Marx has been misinterpreted in a positivistic, reductionistic way on this point; recent scholarship has corrected this misinterpretation. More specifically, in Marx, dialectic is present in the contradiction between labor and capital in capitalism, a contradiction that will be overcome in communism. In this society the false oppositions of mind and body, individual and society, and subject and object will be transcended. Such transcendence will not occur automatically, but requires that workers take charge of their own destiny, become conscious of their alienation, organize, and revolt.[12]

Kierkegaard uses "dialectic" and "dialectical" to describe his method in *Two Ages*. Contemporary mass society, which is alienated and one-sidedly mediated, points back to antiquity, in which there was an immediate relation of men to one another and to their leader; and points forward to faith, in which alienation is overcome and there is true reconciliation between such opposites as silence and speech, inwardness and revelation, individual and community (TA, 84-91). In contrast to the present age's false reconciliation of opposites, creating the public and crushing the individual, the religious individual is no longer totally isolated but reaches out to other men and encourages them to become themselves.

---

[12]G. W. F. Hegel, *The Logic of Hegel*, 143-55. See George Lukács, *History and Class Consciousness*, tr. Rodney Livingstone (Cambridge: MIT Press, 1968) 83-222, for a nonreductionistic interpretation of Marx's dialectic.

But through the leap out into the depths one learns to help himself, learns to love all others as much as himself even though he is accused of arrogance and pride—for not accepting help—or of selfishness—for being unwilling to deceive others by helping them, that is, by helping them miss what is highest of all (TA, 89-90).

There is thus a movement in Kierkegaard'a thought from a stage of immediacy through one-sided mediation to true mediation.

Third, alienation for both Marx and Kierkegaard has a common content and structure. Here the differences are more apparent than the common ground, because Marx emphasizes the economic and Kierkegaard the sociocultural aspects of alienation. Nonetheless there is an affinity that is easily missed. Both capital and the public are infinite in aspiration; capital allows nothing outside of itself that is not subject to the norms of profitability, and the public tolerates no disagreement. As a result there is a loss of autonomy, individuality, and community, as the worker becomes enslaved to capital and the citizen to the public. Individual skill gives way to division of labor and the machine, and individual, critical thinking to the whims of the media. All that remains is a multitude of self-interested, competitive individuals, interested only in profit and totally uninterested in reciprocal sharing and giving.

For both men also, alienation is abstract, anonymous, quantitative, and fetishized. In the economic sphere described by Marx labor is reduced to abstract labor time measured in dollars and cents in which the qualitative difference between different kinds of work is less important than their profitability. The worker is increasingly indifferent to the specificity of his labor and only interested in the money he can make.[13] Use-value is completely overshadowed by exchange-value as all spheres of human endeavor come under the rule of money. "Universal prostitution appears as a necessary phase in the development of the social character of personal talents, capacities, abilities, activities."[14] Work is progressively commodified and the worker progressively impoverished, passively subject to the dull sameness of the machine and the anxieties of possible unem-

---

[13]Marx, *Grundrisse*, 297.

[14]Marx, *Grundrisse*, 163.

ployment and poverty. Being is less important than having; being human is less important than being rich. A fetishism of commodities develops in which relations between men are interpreted as relations between things. The power and promise that men should find in their own communal activities are ascribed to money. The decisive question about a man is not "What kind of man is he?" but "How much does he make?"

In the sociocultural sphere described by Kierkegaard the public causes an alienation that is abstract and homogeneous. Because all men are simply numerical units of a quantitative mass, quality has been shoved out by quantity, excellence by mediocrity, and originality by fashion. No person forms his own opinions or makes his own decisions. Like Marx's worker, Kierkegaard's citizen is passive and "distracted from distraction by distraction,"[15] easily manipulated by the media, and willingly seduced by the latest entertainment fad. The public becomes a fetish supplying the community, thought, security, and authority that men are unable to supply for themselves.

Not only is there a complementarity of structure and content between Marx's economy and Kierkegaard's public, but also each understands a relationship between the economic and the sociopolitical domains. For Marx the dominance of the economic implies universal relations of utility and exploitation in social life, an abstract, bureaucratic state alienated from the individuals it rules, and the continual growth of capital.[16] Consequently capital attempts to expand existing consumption, to create new needs by propagating existing ones in a wider circle, and to produce those new needs. The omnivorous hunger of capital for ever more and more profit leads it to continually extend its sway.

> Thus, just as production founded on capital creates universal industriousness on one side—i.e. surplus labor, value-creating labor—so does it create on the other side a system of general exploitation of the natural and human qualities, a system of general

---

[15]T. S. Eliot, "The Four Quartets," *The Complete Poems and Plays* (New York: Harcourt, Brace, and World, 1952) 120.

[16]Marx, *Grundrisse*, 90-94, 163, 407-10. *The 18th Brumaire of Louis Bonaparte* (New York: International Publishers, 1963) 62, 120-23.

utility, utilizing science itself just as much as all the physical and
mental qualities, while there appears nothing higher in itself, nothing legitimate for itself, outside this circle of higher production and
exchange. . . . For the first time, nature becomes purely an object
for humankind, purely a matter of utility; ceases to be recognized
as a power for itself; and the theoretical discovery of its autonomous laws appears merely as a ruse so as to subjugate it under human needs, whether as an object of consumption or as a means of
production.[17]

For Kierkegaard as well, the sociopolitical domain is related to
the economy. We have already discussed his emphasis on the ab-
stractness of money and the love of money above all else in the present age. Just as paper money more and more takes the place of real
money, so also human relationships have become abstract and deprived of all primitivity (TA, 74-75).

And eventually human speech will become just like the public:
pure abstraction—there will no longer be someone who speaks,
but an objective reflection will gradually deposit a kind of atmosphere, an abstract noise that will render human speech superfluous, just as machines make workers superfluous (TA, 104).[18]

Like paper money, ideas, opinions and witticisms circulate at
second hand, divorced from personal passion, thought, and responsibility. Such abstract reflection buys everything at second
hand prices. Because thought has become a commodity, a dog the
public keeps for its own amusement and a technique that anyone
can learn, the only way thought can be redeemed is through the
leap of religious faith (TA 74-76, 88-89, 94-95, 104-105).

Of course one should not overstate the parallelism here. For
Marx the economy is dominant, not in any one-sidedly deterministic sense, but in the way the heart is dominant in a human being
over the hands, legs, and feet. Like the hands, legs, and feet, social,
cultural, and political spheres are relatively autonomous and exer-

---

[17]Marx, *Grundrisse*, 408-10.

[18]I am indebted to a student colleague of mine, Russell Hittinger, for suggesting
that such references to production and commerce are not unusual in Kiekegaard's
work. For instance, see FT, 22-25, 129-32; EO, 2:100-103, 280-97.

cise a causality of their own.[19] For Kierkegaard, on the other hand, the public is emphasized, whose causes are not economic but social: reflection and the press (TA, 90-93). The economic is conceived as an instance and reflection of the public. Nonetheless, that both thinkers perceive a relationship between the economic and the sociopolitical spheres and a homology of structure and content between these spheres is important.

The solutions of Marx and Kierkegaard to alienation are obviously quite different, but even here there are some common traits. For both, alienation can be educative, motivating Marx's workers to become conscious of their collective plight, organize, and resist; and motivating Kierkegaard's citizen to recover his individuality before God. For both thinkers the overcoming of alienation is a matter of practice, collective for Marx and individual for Kierkegaard, in which reflection is a necessary condition. For both thinkers, however, practice moves beyond a false reflection, which plays an ideological role in the capitalism described by Marx and functions as an excuse for inaction and indecision in the individual described by Kierkegaard. For both a component of the solution is the rich, many-sided individual who has replaced passivity with activity, self-estrangement with integrity, and abject dependence with autonomy.

Implications

The discussion here will necessarily be tentative, hypothetical, and exploratory, avoiding any facile syntheses. I propose to reflect upon the Marx-Kierkegaard relationship first from a Marxist, then from a Kiekegaardian perspective. Needless to say, such reflections are only one possible interpretation and do not claim to represent all varieties of Marxism or Kierkegaardism.

For a Marxist, what first emerges is the complementarity of the economic alienation described by Marx and the sociocultural alienation described by Kierkegaard. The homogeneous, abstract nature

---

[19]Helvin Rader, *Marx's Interpretation of History* (New York: Oxford University Press, 1979) 56-81.

of economic alienation is mirrored in and partially determined by cultural and political alienation. For some twentieth-century Marxists this neat fit is no accident.[20] Late capitalism, in order to meet problems of accumulation and legitimation, requires increasing control over the cultural and political spheres and thus imposes its own properties on them. To the alienated worker, we have to add the alienated consumer, mindlessly absorbed in advertising, enthusiastically buying the latest car to keep up with his neighbors, and anxious about his deodorant lest he be a social outcast; and the alienated voter, manipulated by political image makers, ignorant of the political issues of the day, and uninvolved in the political process.

Advertising, mindless entertainment on such media as television, and public relations approaches in politics, then, represent an expansion of Kierkegaard's public sphere. The preoccupations with entertainment, technique and media, of which Kierkegaard is so critical, have now become essential for capitalism: the public has actually become the Roman emperor of his parable, constantly looking for titillation and amusement. If capitalism is to avoid depressions, it needs to insure demand for goods through advertising and government spending. If revolution is to be avoided at home and abroad, strong welfare and defense programs are necessary. If capital is to keep men politically and socially subservient, they must be objects of technique. Not only cars but the president must be sold.[21]

In some types of twentieth-century Marxism, the so-called "superstructure" of culture and politics becomes increasingly important in relation to the economic "base," not only reflecting but, in turn, influencing it. The economy still remains dominant, but other

---

[20]Theodor Adorno, *Negative Dialectics*, tr. E. B. Ashton (New York: The Seabury Press, 1973); Herbert Marcuse, *One Dimensional Man* (Boston: Beacon Press, 1964); Jurgen Habermas, *Towards A Rational Society*, tr. Jeremy Shapiro (Boston: Beacon Press, 1971); *Legitimation Crisis*, tr. Thomas McCarthy (Boston: Beacon Press, 1975).

[21]TA, 94-95. See Stuart Ewen, *Captains of Consciousness* (New York: McGraw Hill, 1976) and Alan Wolfe, *The Limits of Legitimacy* (New York: The Macmillan Company, 1977) for a development of these themes in an American context. On the problem of technique, see Habermas, *Towards A Rational Society*, 81-122.

spheres have a relative autonomy in relationship to it, like the hands in relationship to the heart.[22] The homologous relationship between the economic and sociopolitical realms, already noted in an incomplete, indeterminate way by both Marx and Kierkegaard, is fully realized in the twentieth century. In such a context Kierkegaard's reflections on the public acquire increasing importance and cogency.

Second, Kierkegaard's claim that individuality is disappearing is confirmed in twentieth-century developments of late capitalism. Marxist thinkers such as Adorno, Jacoby, and Lasch have pointed out that the expressed concern about individuality, self-fulfillment, and narcissism indicate a decline of the individual.[23] Like a car owner who locks his garage when it is already empty, we are talking about individuality so much because it has already been lost. The conformism and extroversion described by Kierkegaard have become even more prevalent in the era of the organization man, public opinion polls, and Madison Avenue. There is a pressure to conform even down to the underwear one wears and the deodorant one buys. In such a milieu Kierkegaardian inwardness becomes a radical stance; existential, dialectical thinking becomes a radical act. The movement to inwardness away from the pressures of mass society, even though such inwardness is not a fully adequate solution because community is lacking, nonetheless can be the first step towards such a solution. The individual refusal to consume, to think and to act in ways prescribed by technocratic mass society is an essential, minimal way of keeping alive the possibility of revolution.[24]

----

[22]For the distinction between base and superstructure, see Karl Marx, *A Contribution to the Critique of Political Economy*, ed. Maurice Dobb, tr. S. W. Ryazanskaya (London: Lawrence & Wishart, 1970) 20-21. On the relative autonomy of the social, cultural, and political realms in late capitalism, see Nicos Poulantzas, *Political Power and Social Class*, tr. Timothy O'Hagan (London: NLB, 1975) 25-33, 284-85, 294, 263-74, 294-303.

[23]Adorno, *Negative Dialectics*, 312-14, 344-50. *Minima Moralia*, tr. E. F. N. Jephcott (London: New Left Books, 1974) 148-50, 152-54; Russell Jacoby, *Social Amnesia: A Critique of Conformist Psychology From Adler To Laing* (Boston: Beacon Press, 1975); Christopher Lasch, *The Culture of Narcissism* (New York: W. W. Norton & Co., 1978) 3-30.

[24]Adorno, *Negative Dialectics*, 3-5, 204-207, 244-45; *Minima Moralia*, 15-18, 24-28.

Finally from a Kierkegaardian perspective, there are certain questions one can ask about the history of Marxism as a political movement. One can ask, as even some Marxists have asked,[25] why the revolution has not occurred in western capitalist countries and why it has simply led to another form of alienation and capitalism—state capitalism—in such nations as Russia and China. What appears to be confirmed, first, is Kierkegaard's pessimism, in contrast to the more sanguine hopes of Marx, about the possibility of social revolution without the prior spiritual transformation of the individual. Conformism is so deep and individuality and community so lacking that either working people cannot see what their true interests are and consequently worship what enslaves them, as they do in such countries as the United States, or become subject to another kind of alienation and another kind of mass society, as they do in such nations as Russia.

Second, it is true that without community and communal action on a social, economic, and political level there is no complete overcoming of alienation, and here Marx is correct in taking a stance against a simple reliance on nothing but inwardness and faith. To the extent that Kierkegaard relies simply on those qualities, he is one-sided.[26] But it is equally true that there is no community and no satisfactory overcoming of alienation without the subjective, psychological domain that some twentieth century Marxists have rediscovered.[27] The further step that Kierkegaard would insist upon is that inwardness is impossible without religious faith. The atheistic character of such experiments as Russia and China insures that the revolution will be an aborted revolution—objectivis-

---

[25]Michael Harrington, *Socialism* (New York: Bantam Books, 1972); Marcuse, *One Dimensional Man*, 1-120; *Soviet Marxism* (New York: Vintage Books, 1961); Habermas, *Legitimation Crisis*. *Towards A Rational Society*, 81-122.

[26]See Mark C. Taylor, *Kierkegaard's Pseudonymous Authorship: A Study of Time and The Self* (Princeton: Princeton University Press, 1975) 343-56; for a critique of this tendency in Kierkegaard, of which we only get hints and intimations in *Two Ages*, and which seems to be in tension with other central claims in *Two Ages* affirming or implying the ethicoreligious significance of the social realm.

[27]Lukács, *History and Class Consciousness*, 83-222; Karl Korsch, *Marxism and Philosophy*, tr. Fred Halliday (New York: Monthly Review Press, 1970); Trent Shroyer, *Critique of Domination* (Boston: Beacon Press, 1973) 132-68; Herbert Marcuse, *Eros and Civilization* (New York: Vintage Books, 1955).

tic, economistic, totalitarian. Moreover if the religious impulse present in the striving for community is denied proper expression, such striving easily becomes fanatical and repressive, demanding from the economic and social arena a total salvation that it cannot give. A successful revolution would have to respect a totality that is both objective and subjective, economic and cultural, social and individual, secular and sacred. Religious faith without social praxis is empty and escapist; praxis without faith is technocratic and enslaving.

IX

Two Ages:
A Story of Søren Kierkegaard and Isak Dinesen

by Jackie Kleinman

In his article, "Isak Dinesen, Søren Kierkegaard and The Present Age," published in *Books Abroad*[1] a generation ago, Eric Johannesson got it right, I think, when he compared Dinesen and Kierkegaard, two writers united in a point of view, separated by a century of time. Now the complete text of Kierkegaard's *Two Ages, The Age of Revolution and The Present Age, A Literary Review*, to which Johannesson referred in his article, has made an appearance in English translation, and I should like to take a second look at it in relationship to these two unique figures in Danish arts and letters.

The point that Johannesson makes in his article is that Dinesen and Kierkegaard—two figures dissimilar in many respects on the face of it—are really more alike than one might at first suppose.

---

[1]Eric Johannesson, "Isak Dinesen, Søren Kierkegaard and The Present Age," *Books Abroad* 36 (Winter 1962): 20-24.

They do, in fact, have affinities at the very heart of their respective authorship. The affinities he found were in their religious point of view and in what he took to be their shared advocacy of a vanished or vanishing age.

Johannesson's choice of two writers to compare could not have been more apt, and much of what he has to say is illuminated by the text on which he focused his essay, Kierkegaard's review of a novella written anonymously by a woman contemporary whose stories he had read and enjoyed for twenty years. Her name was Thomasine Gyllembourg, but she was known on the literary scene of nineteenth-century Denmark, and to Kierkegaard, as "the author of *A Story of Everyday Life*." The stories in this collection (which takes its name from one of them) had appeared individually from time to time in a popular Danish weekly edited by her son—poet, philosopher, and literary critic, as well as editor—J. L. Heiberg.

In the century following—between the two world wars, essentially, and just into the sixties—the Danish Baroness, Karen Blixen, wrote under the pseudonym Isak Dinesen. She read and admired Kierkegaard, referred to him sometimes in her own writing, and even penned a playful rejoinder to his *Diary of a Seducer*, which she first proposed entitling *The Seducer's Diary* for its abbreviated appearance in *The Ladies' Home Journal*. The story eventually appeared in the December 1962 issue as "The Secret of Rosenbad." In its complete form, *Ehrengard*, Dinesen brings to bear her gift of turning things around, and Ehrengard, the seducer's intended victim, ends by having the laugh on *her* side.

Contemporary interpreters have called Dinesen's gift for turning things about "irony," and consider her a master of it. (Kierkegaard, it might be noted, was of the opinion that women haven't the strength for irony.) Although both writers were masters of irony—which, according to Kierkegaard, qualifies them both as "philosophers" ("existentialists" according to contemporary labeling of them)—neither was interested essentially in irony or in the strictly philosophical as a form of expression in literature or in life. For each, the humorous, the comic, was the more interesting form, the incognito form of the religious, and the story was its vehicle. In addition, Dinesen and Kierkegaard agreed, in general, about the role of the male/female image in the nature of things, and both used the classical interlocking, interdependent image of that relationship as paradigmatic of the essential relationship in all things, and of the relationship between the individual and God. Both agreed that "feminine" submissiveness, of the freely chosen variety, was a superior form of strength (Dinesen called it the "price" and the "pride" of life). In their writing, each displayed another sort of strength that both considered essential to their artistry, and that was the strength required to remain faithful to, consistent with one's point of view in the story. (Logical consistency in the expression of a point of view was something else which Kierkegaard did not think women had the strength for.)

In his article for *Books Abroad* Johannesson puts his finger on the key elements in any comparative analysis of the relationship between the writing of Dinesen and Kierkegaard. A good case can be made that the fulcrum of both authorships was indeed a religious point of view, and, in addition, the interested reader knows that in a curious way neither writer seems quite fitted to the century into which he/she was born.

Concerning the latter point, Johannesson seems to get the notion that Kierkegaard is partly engaged in the task of advocating the values of a former age from Kierkegaard's review of *Two Ages*. It does seem in that review—despite the fact that both reviewer and author have denied any comparative evaluation of the two ages— that those qualities characterizing the Age of Revolution come off as the more desirable ones. In the same vein, contemporary interpretation of Dinesen seems agreed that during the golden age of her life in Africa she experienced a kind of civilization she valued, but one that was vanishing there, and was already lost in Europe. One interpreter has noted that Dinesen linked the natural aristocrat, the native, with the official aristocracy of European tradition, and saw them both as out-of-place in modern life, cut off from their roots in nature.[2]

In the face of what seems to be a shared alienation from the dominant values of their respective ages, one might be tempted to search for the clue to their eccentricity in the past—some historical

---

[2]Robert W. Langbaum, *The Gayety of Vision: A Study of Isak Dinesen's Art* (New York: Random House, 1965, 1964) 5.

era. Johannesson directs our attention to the "Romantic Age" precisely because in art and literature it exemplified the noble values that Kierkegaard and Dinesen seemed to favor in the expression of their point of view—the part of pride and passion, courage and humor, of suffering and acceptance in the recognition of one's identity and destiny.

To take a wholly different tack, however, one may stick with the text, *Two Ages*, and search out the noble standard in the essential criterion for evaluating an authorship that Kierkegaard presented in the introduction to that text. Here the noble standard resides in how true the author has remained to his point of view, in any particular piece, of course, but more importantly, in the whole body of his work to be measured over a span of decades.

According to Kierkegaard's analysis there, the antithesis of the writer who has "won something eternal" in a point of view, and remains true to himself in the expression of that point of view, is the writer whose stimulus is primarily that of meeting "the demands of the age," any age. Kierkegaard makes it clear that any writer who seriously tries to please the fickle, soulless, mindless, artless "public" will only produce a piece equally fickle, soulless, mindless, and artless. Kierkegaard judged Thomasine Gyllembourg (whom he thought to be a man) to be an author time-tested and "twice-matured," consistent in a point of view and the expression of it—in short, "a guide." Kierkegaard would doubtless have made the same judgment of Isak Dinesen, had he been privileged to read her.

In elaboration of the principle offered in his review of *Two Ages* as governing the evaluation and analysis of an authorship, Kierkegaard introduces a theory of "story." In brief outline, Kierkegaard's theory runs like this:

(1) every story knows a "way out", and is known by the "way out" it knows.
(2) every story is informed by a point-of-view that knows "a way out."
(3) every story-teller is a guide whose point-of-view is the "way out" informing the stories he tells.

In illustration of this aspect of his theory, Kierkegaard points out that "actuality" was the life view which informed Gyllembourg's *Stories of Everyday Life* and *Two Ages*, and the principles of "common sense" and "persuasion" controlled its passageways. Kierkegaard respects Gyllembourg as a guide of the commonsense point of view, and he respects the strength of that point of view, persuasiveness, which she exhibits in a consistent fashion. "Whether or not we can come to rest in the identical life view," he writes, "there nevertheless is peace here and the incorruptibility of a quiet spirit" (TA, 16). In Gyllembourg's stories Kierkegaard finds a storyteller "twice-matured" whose "work is, if anything, the reward that God gave the author since he, twice-matured, won something eternal in a life view. Because he is not a self-seeking author, but one who found himself before he became an author, he can be a guide" (TA, 15).

Kierkegaard would have recognized in the life-view that informed Dinesen's stories and memoirs, on the other hand, a *religious* way out akin to his own—not a return to an historically vanished past—not a movement through time at all—but, rather, a point of view transformed, a "metamorphosis," "a more and more intensive return to the original condition." In an identical expression of means and end, Kierkegaard and Dinesen both tell us that the end of any proper education (Kierkegaard considered his writing to be his education) is "naiveté regained." And how shall one attain his goal? "Be loyal to the story," Dinesen tells us. "Where the storyteller is loyal, eternally and unswervingly loyal, there, in the end, silence will speak." Johannes de Silentio is the pseudonym of a similar message.

To put the point in the context of the philosophically interested interpreter, there has emerged some agreement, if not consensus, concerning their task. Consider, for example, the interpretations of Louis Mackey and Gregor Malantschuk.[3] Approaching the authorship from fundamentally different points of view, these two interpreters nevertheless agree with most contemporary interpretation that, although one will not find a *system* presented in the authorship, consistency is to be found in the authorship, and revealing

---

[3]Louis Mackey, *Kierkegaard: A Kind of Poet* (Philadelphia: University of Pennsylvania Press, 1971); Gregor Malantschuk, *Kierkegaard's Thought* (Princeton: Princeton University Press, 1971).

consistency is an important part of the job of interpretation.[4] I agree that if there is to be a common ground for philosophically interested interpreters of Kierkegaard, it is to be found in the task of revealing consistency in the authorship.

The consistency or unity that Malantschuk and Mackey argue is a central feature of the authorship is envisioned by both interpreters to be a methodological consistency, and for both the interpretive process involves imitating that method which each sees to be central to the structure of the authorship.[5] For Malantschuk, "consistency is the nerve of the method" and the method is dialectical.[6] For Mackey, "the unity and consistency of his [Kierkegaard's] thought . . . is a metaphoric unity", and the method is maieutic.[7] In the dialectical method, progress in understanding is made through straightforward rational progression, whereas in the maieutic method progress in understanding is made through a process of indirectly induced recognition. By stripping away an illusion—a feature of the maieutic—one takes a step back, a progress in understanding that, if understood "directionally," is the opposite of a dialectical movement.

The interpreter's focus in the last decade has gradually shifted from a preoccupation with discovering the real Kierkegaard and what made him tick to an even more sophisticated regard, or disregard—as the case may be—for Kierkegaard's method. Although investigation and interpretation via method has traditionally fallen into either one of the two main categories considered indigenous to Kierkegaard's works—the maieutic or the dialectic—there is always the possibility of investigations consciously borrowing a popular philosophical method in an attempt to make Kierkegaard's insights

---

[4]A notable exception to the view that there is no system presented in the authorship is John Elrod's *Being and Existence in Kierkegaard's Pseudonymous Works* (Princeton: Princeton University Press, 1975). Entries pertaining to "system" in the authorship: Malantschuk, *Kierkegaard's Thought*, 359; Mackey, *Kierkegaard: A Kind of Poet*, 7.

[5]Mackey, *Kierkegaard: A Kind of Poet*, xii; Malantschuk, *Kierkegaard's Thought*, 7.

[6]Malantschuk, *Kierkegaard's Thought*, 182.

[7]Mackey, *Kierkegaard: A Kind of Poet*, 259.

relevant to current philosophical trends. Such an approach would have the considerable virtue of facilitating communication within the philosophical community, but it suffers from the equally considerable defect of fostering obtuseness to Kierkegaard's oft-repeated statements that the content and form (method) of his work are two sides of the same coin—the form reflects the content, and the content reflects the form. It may be tempting to appropriate the day's fashionable models of interpretation—justified perhaps by the notion that each age has its own idiom to which the communicator should be sensitive—but I would suggest that the interpreters of Kierkegaard must resist that temptation in favor of what Kierkegaard clearly recognized as the more difficult task: that of coming to an understanding about the form, the method which is in fact at work in the authorship. If Climacus' remarks on the subject can be applied to an interpretation of the whole, it seems that the traditional focus has been too narrow.

> The subjective thinker has a form, a form for his communication with other men, and this form constitutes his style. It must be as manifold as the opposites he holds in combination. . . . As he is not himself either poet or ethicist, or dialectician, his form cannot be that of either directly. His form must first and last relate itself to existence, and in this connection he will have at his disposal the poetic, the ethical, the dialectical, and the religious (CUP, 319).

The interpreter who ignores the difficult task of coming to terms with Kierkegaard's style and how that style shapes content, does so at the peril of his analysis. Take the philosopher, for instance. If, in the course of his interpretation of Kierkegaard, he engages in a typical philosophical analysis of a traditional concept (like truth) using traditional distinctions (subject/object) he will more than likely violate some simple rule of form in the process, but think instead that he has found a contradiction in content.

If a borrowed method is the wrong way to go, and if the focus of those who *are* doing the job of excavating the extant method is too narrow, where does one turn next? I have suggested here that an interesting possibility for interpreting method is presented by Kierkegaard in his introduction to *Two Ages* in which he gives us a theory-of-story as method. It is in the introduction to this review that

Kierkegaard first publishes a formulation of this theory, but—as with every really important, germinal idea that gets developed through the course of his authorship—Kierkegaard's theory-of-story was present from the very beginning in an early, unpublished, unfinished essay—*Johannes Climacus or De Omnibus Dubitandum Est* where he focuses on "the story" as the most appropriate vehicle for the communication of truth. In a provocative statement he there gives us our first hint of a central feature for the understanding and interpretation of his authorship.

> He who supposes that philosophy has never in the world been so near solving its problem (which is the revealing of all secrets) as now, may well feel it odd, affected, offensive that I choose this method of storytelling, and do not, in my humble way, lend a hand with putting the coping-stone on the System. On the other hand, he who is convinced that philosophy has never been so perverted as now, so confused, in spite of all its definitions, so entirely to be likened to the weather last winter when we heard what had never been heard before, men crying mussels and prawns in such a way that he who attended to a particular cry might at one time think it was winter, at another time spring, at another midsummer; while he who paid attention to all these cries at once might think that Nature had become all muddled up, and the world could not continue till Easter—he will certainly think it right that I should try by means of this story-telling method, to counteract the abominable falsity which is the mark of modern philosophy; a philosophy which is speedily distinguished from older philosophy by the discovery of the ridiculousness of doing what one said one did or had done—he I say will find this storytelling method appropriate, and will only be sorry, as I am, that the person who begins this task has not greater authority than I have (JC, 102).

It is no exaggeration to say that one is left—if one is reading chronologically—to wonder over that first provocative statement that, like a strangely shaped but familiarly colored piece of jigsaw, clearly belongs to the puzzle, but belongs as the piece one continuously pushes to the periphery with the other recalcitrant pieces. Kierkegaard does not pick it up again until *Two Ages*.

In speaking of method, the maieutic and the dialectical have been the more easily recognized and manageable forms, and whereas they definitely have their place in interpretation procedure, they also clearly exhibit their limits. They harmonize the broad outlines, but somehow they don't quite manage to incorporate that recalcitrant periphery. Despite the demonstrated value of both methods, I would argue that each one, separately or in combination, will ultimately contribute to, or fall short of, a resolution to the most persistent dilemma in Kierkegaard interpretation that is how, within the content of the authorship, to maintain a philosophical basis for the interpretation of the skeptical crisis that one author has maintained is the recalcitrant feature common to all existential thought.[8]

Traditionally, in Kierkegaard interpretation, the problem with resting one's interpretation on the maieutic and all of its devices—irony, parody, humor, self-concealment, and so forth—has been that of deciding whether, in the last analysis, one is interpreting the work of a kind of skeptic, or the work of a kind of moral and intellectual nihilist. From the pessimism of Henry Allison's "Christianity and Nonsense" to the optimistic inconclusiveness of Bernard Dauenhauer's "On Kierkegaard's Alleged Nihilism" the interpreter moves between the poles of this dilemma.[9] If one does not care to become entangled in the intricacies involved in approaching the authorship through the maieutic, one may choose with Malantschuk and others to interpret the authorship on the basis of some kind of dialectic where the emphasis is, as Malantschuk puts it, on "converting everything into direct communication." Excur-

---

[8]William Shearson, "The Common Assumptions of Existentialist Philosophy," *International Philosophical Quarterly* 15:2 (June 1975): 131-47.

[9]Henry Allison, "Christianity and Nonsense," *Essays on Kierkegaard* (Minneapolis: Burgess Publishing Co., 1969); Bernard Dauenhauer, "On Kierkegaard's Alleged Nihilism," *Southern Journal of Philosophy* 12:2 (1974). In his article Henry Allison attempts to demonstrate that *Concluding Unscientific Postscript* is *intentional* nonsense for the purpose of preventing the philosopher "from theorizing, even in an 'existential' sense about Christianity. . . . Thus, far from being a contribution, good, bad, or indifferent, to a philosophy of existence, the *Postscript* emerges as Kierkegaard's attempt at a *reductio ad absurdum* of any such enterprise." In his article, Bernard Dauenhauer argues that *in existence* the nihilistic charge against Kierkegaard's religious point of view cannot be maintained (he distinguishes between practical and conceptual problems). He does not argue, however, that the charge of nihilism can be definitively laid to rest. "There are, on Kierkegaard's own grounds, no such arguments. All that can be done is to show of each charge of nihilism that it fails to prove its claim conclusively."

sions along this line have produced a dialectic of existential stages, a dialectic of value, a dialectic of the prophetic and deluded imagination. (The latter employ aspects of the maieutic as well as the dialectical method.) In this tradition, Malantschuk proceeds by way of method "imitating" method to elucidate two equally decisive ordering principles—the dialectic of thought and the dialectic of communication. But alas, the dialectical method—no less than the maieutic—generates, again, the skeptical crisis. Malantschuk outlines for us its path of self-stultification.

"Christianity is the orienting principle in the longitudinal structuring of the dialectical method." The philosopher moves, via the pseudonymous existents, through the dialectic of existential levels toward Christianity. He is met at the border by the "theory of the leap." "The most important boundary line for him [Kierkegaard] comes between the purely human life-sphere and Christianity. . . . Kierkegaard uses the term 'the despairing leap' to denote the transition from the human to the Christian and the cleft between."[10]

At this point one might well use the term "the despairing philosopher" to denote the transition from the purely human life-sphere to the Christian and the cleft between for it has generally been recognized by both critics and defenders that the dialectical method is essentially a rational procedure, and "the leap," whatever it may be, does not fit the category of a rational transition. Perhaps the Christian succeeds in his leap, but the philosopher is always left behind and speechless as the dialectical method comes to its abrupt end as a philosophically useful tool. The Christian philosopher cannot but feel divided.

> "Existence," Climacus explains, "involves a tremendous contradiction, from which the subjective thinker does not have to abstract, though he can if he will, but in which it is his business to remain" (CUP, 313).

How then does the philosopher of existence conduct the business he must be about? Every interpreter of the philosophically significant in Kierkegaard eventually comes knocking at this door.

---

[10]Malantschuk, *Kierkegaard's Thought*, 131-32.

The fundamental problem with the dialectical and maieutic methods in interpreting the religious point of view as exemplified in Kierkegaard's works has been in those methods' failure to adequately relate that point of view to the skeptical crisis that the manner of communication inherent in each method generates. Neither the direct, rational method of the dialectic, nor the indirect, ambiguous method of the maieutic provide a philosophical basis for an interpretation of the skeptical crisis inherent in Kierkegaard's religious point of view. Each method does, in fact, contribute to an illumination of that crisis—an important and necessary function for those methods to perform. It becomes far too easy in each case, however, for the critic to dismiss Kierkegaard's point of view, and the style of its communication, as too "private," and thus unintelligible, to be worth the effort of rational inquiry. Kierkegaard's religious point of view becomes defined as unintelligible because it appears to be either (1) "beyond" rational apprehension, and thus private, (2) ambiguous without recourse, and thus private, or (3) ineffable, and thus private.

Enter the breach—Kierkegaard's theory-of-story as method. Kierkegaard's theory-of-story becomes a theory-of-story as method for his entire authorship, and in the context of the ultimate skeptical crisis which lies at the very heart of his religious point of view it is the "way out" of the strictly "private" and ineffable. It offers a means of communicating the eternal in a religious point of view, a means of making "silence speak." Kierkegaard engages the method in his stories of Abraham, of Job, of the prince who loved a common maiden, of the teacher who would be different from Socrates, and of others. He tells us that stories have an internal consistency, and he tells us, moreover, that the best of completed authorships have an internal consistency. Finally, he tells us that the consistency internal to his stories provides a clue to the consistency internal to his authorship as a whole.

I do not think that philosophical analysis of the authorship lies in imitating Kierkegaard's storytelling method, but, rather, that it lies in doing more fully that which Kierkegaard did only briefly when he focused on the nature of the method he used. The philosopher has focused on the nature of the method he used. The philosopher has the completed authorship and its stories before him.

He does not need to reproduce the authorship or even to retrace the steps of that production. That creative task has been completed. The philosopher may use his time and perspective to view the authorship as a whole, to analyze the storytelling method itself, its potential for making "silence speak," its function in unifying the authorship, and in giving the authorship a consistent point of view.

In short, the philosopher may use the clue that Kierkegaard provided—when he singled out his theory-of-story as method for attention—in responding to one of the most familiar and widely quoted statements that the secondary literature on Kierkegaard has ever produced, from Aage Henriksen's award-winning paper on the subject of the methods and results of Kierkegaard studies in Scandinavia,

> A point of view which neither violates the totality nor the separate parts does not seem to have been attained by anybody. The core of the authorship has not been penetrated.[11]

In *Two Ages* one sees Kierkegaard's major philosophical categories, those that have subsequently acquired currency in an existential philosophy, brought to bear for the first time to achieve a special, practical purpose—to review a story—and in this simple exercise the old material becomes illuminated for us in a new and interesting way, through being put into the context of a theory-of-story as method. Understandably, philosophically interested interpreters have looked for a model of method in the methods of other philosophers. But it seems they have looked in vain. Kierkegaard has rejected "Kant's honest way out"—the transcendental deduction or critical method. Hegel's dialectical method and the Socratic maieutic reveal the Pyrrhonian skeptic in Kierkegaard, and perhaps that is revelation sufficient for the philosophically interested interpreter. On the other hand, it might prove useful to look for a moment to another discipline for a model of method. Look to literature; look to Isak Dinesen; look to the story. "The story knows the way out," Kierkegaard tells us, "and the storyteller is the guide."

---

[11]Aage Henriksen, *Methods and Results of Kierkegaard Studies in Scandinavia* (Copenhagen: Munksgaard, 1951).

As one sensitive to the clue in a pseudonym, Kierkegaard would have recognized Dinesen by her mask. He also—if we are to judge from experience and his predispositions—doubtless would have swallowed the red herring that is there. For both Kierkegaard's and Dinesen's humor graces the passageway to the Eternal and Dinesen tells us that she chose the masculine proper name "Isak" because it means, literally, "laughter." Kierkegaard's pseudonym of the more nearly philosophical portions of his authorship, Johannes Climacus, refers to himself as "a humorist in private practice." Both pseudonyms were about the business of telling stories, love stories usually.

In philosophical circles Kierkegaard has not been made much of as a storyteller, except for the purpose of dismissing him as a philosopher. It is surely not that philosophers have been ignorant of the fact that he is a master of the art of storytelling, but rather that they have not seen the art for what it was in Kierkegaard's authorship—a method suited to his existential purposes, a method that communicates beyond the skeptical crisis, that invades the "private" sphere of the religious in communication and interpretation. The publication of *Kierkegaard's Parables*,[12] edited by theologian Thomas Oden, who notes that storytelling was a preoccupation of Kierkegaard, even in his most closely reasoned philosophical dialectic, would be a most welcome addition to the ways in which philosophers have chosen to focus on Kierkegaard's philosophical contribution. So much of the attempt to extract his thought from his art, the philosophical essence from the literary form, has made it appear that one really can do that, and ought to. Kierkegaard's theory-of-story as method informed everything he wrote, but he did not focus on it as a method until he wrote the review of *Two Ages*. This little book, which was a very long review, opens the door to an avenue of Kierkegaard interpretation that philosophy has not yet explored. It gives the interpreter who has tried for too long to fit Kierkegaard's philosophical contribution into the more familiar, broad outlines, the chance to begin again, and to begin this time with what I would identify as a recalcitrant piece, Kierkegaard's theory-of-story as method.

---

[12]Thomas C. Oden, ed., *Parables of Kierkegaard* (Princeton: Princeton University Press, 1978).

X

Haecker, Kierkegaard and the Early Brenner: A Contribution to the History of the Reception of Two Ages in the German-speaking World

by Allan Janik

The enormity of Kierkegaard's impact upon twentieth-century German philosophers can scarcely be overestimated despite the fact that his writings remained unread by philosophers for more than fifty years after his death. This poses a problem, one that historians of philosophy have by and large failed to recognize, the question of the circumstances under which the Dane's works were rediscovered. If he had to be rediscovered, who, we may ask, made that rediscovery? How did the circumstances under which his writings reappeared affect the way Kierkegaard was perceived? These are but two of a host of interesting and important questions that remained to be asked about this subject.

The list of German thinkers who were profoundly impressed by Kierkegaard is long and distinguished to say the least. It includes: philosophers of dialogue like Martin Buber, who felt obliged to devote a major essay to what he took to be the shortcomings of Kierkegaardian individualism[1] "analytic" philosophers like Ludwig Wittgenstein, for whom the Dane was the most important philosopher of the nineteenth century[2] Marxists like T.W. Adorno, whose habilitation dissertation treated the construction of the aesthetic level of existence,[3] yet, Kierkegaard's influence was most profoundly felt by "existentialists" like Martin Heidegger, whose concept of idle talk (Gerede) in *Sein und Zeit* has its roots in Kierkegaard,[4] and Karl Jaspers who found Kierkegaard's critique of society as relevant "as if it had been written yesterday."[5] Though only the latter two thinkers drew directly upon the text of *Two Ages*, all of these figures were sharply critical of the modern mores and recognized in Kierkegaard's assault upon his society something deeply significant for their own. Moreover, it is significant that none of the figures I have mentioned read Kierkegaard in the original; so, it ought to be of interest to locate the avenues through which Kierkegaard, who wrote only in Danish, entered the German-speaking world. In the following essay I shall be concerned with the influential translator and expositor of Kierkegaard who first rendered into German that part of *Two Ages*, which the English reading public is familiar with as *The Present Age* (in German it was known as the *Kritik der Gegenwart*), Theodor Haecker.[6]

---

[1]Martin Buber, "The Question of the Individual," *Between Man and Man*, trans. R. G. Smith (New York: Macmillan, 1965) 48-82.

[2]See Maurice Drury's contribution to the BBC series "Ludwig Wittgenstein: A Symposium," ed. Erich Heller, reprinted in K. T. Fann's collection *Ludwig Wittgenstein: The Man and His Philosophy* (New York: Dell, 1967) 70.

[3]Theodor Wiesengrund-Adorno, *Kierkegaard: Konstruktion des aesthetischen*, 3d ed. (Frankfurt am Main: Suhrkamp, 1966).

[4]This was brought to my attention by Professor Caputo of Villanova University.

[5]Karl Jaspers, *Man in the Modern Age*, trans. Eden and Cedar Paul (Garden City: Doubleday, 1957) 10.

[6]Søren Kierkegaard, "Kritik der Gegenwart," uebersetzt und mit einem Nachwort versehen von Theodor Haecker, *Der Brenner* IV (1914) 815-49; 869-908. Further references to this journal will be simply to "B" with the appropriate number and page. See also Søren Kierkegaard, *The Present Age*, trans. Alexander Dru (London: Fontana; New York: Harper & Row, 1962). Though the translation is the same in

Haecker, for several reasons, is particularly important for understanding the reception of *Two Ages*. To begin with, his translation, which appeared almost on the eve of World War I was among the first reliable translations of a major work of Kierkegaard and, thus, helped to set the tone for the reception of Kierkegaard's *oeuvre* generally.[7] Second, he only translated part of *Two Ages*. The major portion of part three, *The Present Age*, became important because it set a precedent followed by Alexander Dru, who also translated Haecker's wartime *pensées*, *Tag- und Nachtbuecher*, along with an appreciation of the relevance of Haecker's brand of Catholicism for the modern spiritual crisis.[8] Third, Haecker published his selection from *Two Ages* in a polemical context that did much to fix the image of Kierkegaard in the sense of associating him with certain individuals and movements and dissociating him from others. The point is that *The Present Age* (and the German *Kritik der Gegenwart*) is in a sense Haecker's creation. To the extent that it has colored the interpretation of Kierkegaard's social criticism, Haecker's rendering of it, above all, the context into which Haecker transported it, is of vital importance to our grasp of the Kierkegaard reception. Moreover, in his otherwise laudable efforts to expound and extend Kierkegaard's work, Haecker's close association with Kierkegaard may well have saddled the Dane with prejudices and misunderstandings foreign to his texts. For these reasons, it is essential to establish just who this important mediator of Kierkegaardian thought was and just what he wrote. In addition it will be of equal value to determine the nature of the journal through which he published his translations and commentaries, the Innsbruck periodical *Der Brenner*, and its adjunct Brenner Press, to ascertain its philosophical readership as well as the impact that Kierkegaard's critique of society made upon it.

---

the English and American editions the introductions are not. They were written respectively by Alexander Dru and Walter Kaufmann and themselves represent two different modes of viewing *Two Ages*.

[7] I owe this information concerning the bowdlerization in the Schrempf translations of Kierkegaard to Dr. Marcel Faust.

[8] Theodor Haecker, *Journal in the Night*, trans. Alexander Dru (London: Pantheon, 1950) xi-xlvi.

With that in mind, my aim is threefold. First, I want to provide an account of Haecker's concept of philosophy. Second, I hope to explain how Haecker's editions and studies of Kierkegaard were aspects of a revisionist program for intellectual life that was entailed by that concept of philosophy. Finally, I propose to write an important chapter in the history of the periodical that Karl Kraus called "The only honest review in Austria"[9] by tracing some of the principal effects that Kierkegaard's critique of society had upon *Der Brenner*.

Der Brenner is perhaps best known as the first periodical to publish the superb lyrics of Georg Trakl, but it was no less important for its social criticism than its championing of avant-garde literature. The journal was founded in Innsbruck in 1910 by a self-styled Nietzschean poet-turned-social-critic, Carl Dallago; a gifted caricaturist and art critic, Max von Esterle; and its editor and guiding spirit, Ludwig von Ficker[10]. *Der Brenner* was modeled upon the satirical and polemical journal, *Die Fackel*, which Karl Kraus founded eleven years earlier for the purposes of castigating Viennese philistinism and hypocrisy. Like *Die Fackel*, *Der Brenner* placed itself outside of the journalistic establishment and esteemed satire as a purgative for the overly inflated egos of the self-appointed protectors of public morality, German nationalists, pretentious artists, and *soi-disant* critics.

Der Brenner was founded principally as a vehicle for Carl Dallago to express his non-conformist world view. Dallago provided the journal with a steady stream of poetry, aphorisms, soliloquies and, above all, polemics against the dehumanizing forces of materialism and against all forms of institutionalized morality from liberal nationalism to Catholic theology. Dallago celebrated life close to the

---

[9]Die einzige ehrliche Revue Oesterreichs, Karl Kraus, *Die Fackel* 368-369, 32. Unless otherwise specified all translations are my own.

[10]On *Der Brenner* see Gerald Stieg, "Der Brenner und Die Fackel," *Brenner Studien*, Vol. 3 (Salzburg: Otto Mueller, 1976). Walter Methlagl's unpublished dissertation treats the philosophical themes in the early *Brenner*. See Walter Methlagl, *"Der Brenner": Weltanschauliche Wandlungen vor dem ersten Weltkrieg* (Innsbruck University, 1966). Also, Walter Methlagl, "Ludwig von Ficker," *Neue Oesterreichische Biographie* (Vienna: Amalthea, 1968) and Allan Janik, "Carl Dallago and the Early Brenner," *Modern Austrian Literature* Vol. 11 (1978) 1-17.

Alpine landscape of his native South Tyrol; while he excoriated the decadence of urban life. He was distinguished less by the depth of his thought than for the way in which he practiced what he preached. Dallago exhorted his readers to emulate his heros, Walt Whitman, Jean-Francois Millet, Nietzsche and the Tyrolese painter Giovanni Segantini. Like Nietzsche, Dallago esteemed Jesus at the same time that he excoriated institutional Christianity. His encounter with Kierkegaard in Haecker's early writings both deepened and altered this attitude.

Late in 1913 Ficker received a slim volume, *Søren Kierkegaard und die Philosophie der Innerlichkeit,* from the Munich publisher Ferdinand Schreiber. The book's author was, Theodor Haecker, an employee and protege of Schreiber's. Ficker forwarded the book to Dallago, who read it with enthusiasm and suggested that Ficker invite Haecker to contribute to their journal. Haecker accepted but informed Ficker that his need to support himself by working for Schreiber might make it difficult for him to be a regular contributor. Born in Swabia in 1879, Haecker was reared in the best tradition of Swabian Pietist Protestantism.[11] He attended the Universitites of Munich and Berlin. At Berlin he heard the lectures of such luminaries as Dilthey, Wilamowitz, Virchow, and Vahlen. In the six years between 1905 and 1911 he regularly attended Max Scheler's Munich seminars.[12] He remained both fascinated by, and critical of, Scheler's efforts to create a philosophical anthropology. There can be little doubt that Scheler's insistence that Nietzsche had failed to understand the true nature of Christian love in the latter's concept of *Ressentiment* had a profound effect upon Haecker's view that Kierkegaard was the Christian response to Nietzsche.

Haecker's writings divide into three groups: satires and polemics closely modeled upon those of Karl Kraus, translations and expositions of Kierkegaard, Cardinal Newman, Virgil and others and, finally, "little books" containing metaphysical reflections on aesthetics, history, philosophical anthropology, and Christian cul-

---

[11]On Theodor Haecker see Eugen Blessing, *Theodor Haecker: Gestalt und Werk* (Nuernberg: Glock und Lutz, 1959).

[12]Ibid., 264-65.

ture. His studies of Virgil and Christian culture influenced T.S. Eliot's thinking about classics and culture.[13] These groups of writings roughly (but only very roughly) correspond to the stages of his intellectual development. His career as a writer can be divided into his Krausian phase, 1913-1921, the period from his conversion to Catholicism (after encountering Newman's works)to the Nazi seizure of power, 1921-1933, and the last twelve years of his life under the Nazis, 1933-1945. Throughout the whole of his life Haecker was deeply concerned with Kierkegaard's significance for the modern spiritual malaise. I shall be concerned primarily with his first period as the background against which his edition of *The Present Age* must be set.

What, then, did Haecker contribute to *Der Brenner* in its early phase (that is, the period between its founding and the publication of the *Brenner Yearbook* of 1915) in addition to the selection he translated and commented upon from *Two Ages*? A complete listing of his contributions to *Der Brenner* in this period includes:

> —a translation with prefatory remarks on Kierkegaard's "Prefaces,"[14]
> —a translation with preface of the discourse, "The Thorn in the Flesh,"[15]
> —a polemic against Franz Blei, who questioned whether the man Haecker described in *Søren Kierkegaard und die Philosophie der Innerlichkeit* could possibly be a Christian,[16]
> —a polemic against Richard M. Mayer, who alleged that Dostoevski was some sort of wild man,[17]
> —a translation of the discourse "The Decisiveness of Death,"

---

[13]Eliot mentions Haecker in a footnote to "Religion and Literature," *Selected Essays* (London: Faber and Faber, 1951) 388.

[14]Søren Kierkegaard, *Vorworte*, uebersetzt mit einer Vorbemerkung versehen von Theodor Haecker, B, 1:666-83.

[15]Søren Kierkegaard, "Der Pfahl im Fleisch," uebersetzt mit einem Vorwort versehen von Theodor Haecker, B, 4:691-712; 798-814.

[16]Theodor Haecker, "Franz Blei und Kierkegaard," 4:457-65.

[17]Haecker, "Die muede Nazerenerseele," B, 4:611-14.

one of Kierkegaard's three *Thoughts on Crucial Situations in Human Life*,[18]
—the satirical polemic, "The Leading Intellectuals and the War,"[19];

The latter two pieces appeared in the antiwar *Yearbook* of 1915. The last mentioned piece is arguably the most vitriolic indictment of the chauvinistic element of the German intelligentsia written by a German during the war. In 1914 Ficker's Brenner Verlag reissued *Søren Kierkegaard und die Philosophie der Innerlichkeit* (which Schreiber had only published as a favor to Haecker in the first place) and also published Haecker's selection from *Two Ages* with his *Afterword* as a separate volume. Carl Dallago's two responses to his encounter with Kierkegaard should also be mentioned here along with Haecker's editions and commentaries, for they represent the most immediate reaction to Haecker's presentation of Kierkegaard and *Two Ages* in *Der Brenner*. They were: *Ueber ein Werk, Søren Kierkegaard und die Philosophie der Innerlichkeit*, which originally had been serialized in *Der Brenner* in March and April 1914[20] and in *Der Christ Kierkegaards*, which was written in 1914 but only printed by the Brenner Verlag in 1922.[21]

These, then, are the works that contain what, for want of a better term I have called Haecker's philosophy of inwardness. The term itself has its roots in the simple religiosity and reverent attitude toward the universe that pervades pietism.[22] The philosophy of inwardness revolves around three central themes: critique of contemporary philosophy (and the society that nourishes it), exposition of the nature of inwardness and the practice of inwardness. It must be emphasized that these three elements are only

---

[18]Søren Kierkegaard, "Vom Tode,"übersetzt von Theodor Haecker, B, 5:15-55.

[19]Haecker, "Der Krieg und die Fuehrer des Geistes," B, 5:130-87.

[20]Carl Dallago, "Ueber eine Schrift, *Søren Kierkegaard und die Philosophie der Innerlichkeit*," B, 4:467-78; 515-31; 565-78.

[21]Dallago, *Der Christ Kierkegaards* (Innsbruck: Brenner Verlag, 1922).

[22]See I. Weilner, "Innerlichkeit," *Lexikon fuer Theologie und Kirche*, eds. Hoefer and Rahner (Freiburg: Herder, 1960) vol. V, col. 684.

distinguishable for convenience sake. They are hardly ever present without one another and certainly do not follow from one another. A note is also necessary here with regard to the role of style in Haecker's philosophy of inwardness. For Haecker, there is an absolute unity of style and content. Haecker takes it that all authentically philosophical arguments will be passionately polemical. Thus, all of Haecker's works are unsystematic sometimes almost to the point of being expressionistic in character.

Haecker's critique of philosophy proceeds from his efforts to stave off degeneration of a crucial element in intellectual life, its embeddedness in spirituality. German intellectual life, he believed, was becoming increasingly sterile as instrumental reason lost its rootedness in spiritual values. *Ratio* had been divorced from *intellectus*, to use the language of the scholastics or to put the matter in German terms (the two are by no means identically related) *Vernunft* had been divorced from *Geist*. The philosophy of inwardness was a strategy for returning *Geist* to intellectual life.[23] This is Haecker's point of departure and the point of reference that brings Haecker's various cultural concerns into focus.

Haecker believed that contemporary philosophers, unwittingly or not, had lost sight of the subordination of the intellectual to the spiritual; for they had rejected, or ignored, methaphysics, and allowed ethics to degenerate into questions of abstract theory, thus neglecting the demand that theory be internalized in personal commitment. Had he chosen, Haecker could have aligned contemporary philosophers along a spectrum according to their concern with *Geist*. At one extreme we would discover the charlatans who claimed to speak in the name of *Geist* but were actually opposed to everything for which it stands. At the other extreme we would find its actual defenders, the foremost of whom will be Kierkegaard. However, lest the image of such a spectrum prove misleading, it should be emphasized that there is a chasm, stylistically as well as substantively, between the defenders and the enemies of *Geist*. Nevertheless, the idea of a spectrum is a helpful tool for distinguishing Haecker's perspective from that of his enemies.

---

[23]See Roy Pascal, *From Naturalism to Expressionism* (New York: Basic Books, 1973) 238.

Ernst Haeckel (with whom Haecker is perennially confused despite the utter disparity of their positions) and his Monist League exemplified the conscious assault of rationalist scientism upon the spiritual bases of human existence.[24] The Monists possessed a messianic faith in science's ability to solve all problems once it could be freed from the fetters of religion and metaphysics. As ardent supporters of Bismarck in the *Kulturkampf* they ridiculed religion as the enemy of progress. They acrimoniously attacked metaphysics, which, in their view, opened the door to dualism and ultimately led to the justification of religious belief. They took religion to be essentially superstitious and repressive. Their enthusiasm for science was ironically little more than a secularized religion. In their eyes the scientist became the priest. His was not only the right but the duty to manipulate the masses for their own good—to force them to be free in Rousseau's infamous phase. The Monists' views were warmly received by both Communists and National Socialist ideologues. For Haecker, they were the full antithesis of everything philosophers should be.

Fritz Mauthner's critique of languages ran a close second to the Monist League on Haecker's scale.[25] To be sure, Mauthner was not the rabid nationalist that Haeckel was. Indeed, his whole program aimed at deflating the claims of fanatical nationalists (with their quasi-mystical jargon of *Volk, Deutschtum, Rasse*, and other phrases), not through a counter dogmatism, but by means of a skepticism based upon the empiricist view of language descended from Locke through Mill to Wundt. In Mauthner's view, the height of superstition was to believe that these nouns—and others such as *Geist*—referred to entities. He construed the vocabulary of nationalism—and religion—as reified throughout and sought to examine the psychological and grammatical sources of our tendency to reify. Paradoxically, Haecker tended to share some of these views. However, he insisted that these terms refer to lived realities that cannot

---

[24]On Haeckel and Monism see Daniel Gasman's *The Scientific Origins of National Socialism* (London: MacDonald, 1971).

[25]On Mauthner see Gershon Weiler's definitive, *Mauthner's Critique of Language* (Cambridge: Cambridge University Press, 1972). See also, Allan Janik and Stephen Toulmin, *Wittgenstein's Vienna* (New York: Simon and Schuster, 1973).

be abstracted from the concrete individuals who embodied them. They could not be apprehended merely by intellectual abstraction. Mauthner was no less an opponent of organized religion than the Monists. In its place, he substituted a curious *Ersatz* language-mysticism drawn from sources as disparate as Maeterlinck and Meister Eckhart. Mauthner's journalistic activities as theater critic for the *Berliner Tageblatt* were no less obnoxious to Hacker than his theories. They were further evidence that Mauthner was not serious about philosophy.

Georg Simmel was another object of Haecker's wrath, though Haecker failed to explain just what it was about Simmel's thought that he found so "dishonorable."[26] This failure would surely have been evident to his readers. It is most likely that Haecker found unacceptable Simmel's equation of *Geist* with sexual self-expression and with that capacity that enables us to cope with the stress of modern city life. Haecker, like his fellow Schwabian, Martin Heidegger, and a host of German thinkers of the period, was no lover of the values of modern urban civilization. To be fair, it must be emphasized in the case of Simmel and Mauthner that Haecker's opinions tell far more about him than they do about his opponents. Both Mauthner and Simmel were vastly more talented and surely more upstanding than he gave them credit for being. Haecker's religious and moral perspective blinded him to their talents.

Toward the center of Haecker's spectrum we find the contemporary Neo-Kantians. Haecker was rather ambivalent about Kant himself. While he admired Kant's moral seriousness and his concern with the paradoxes and antinomies at the limits of human experience, he deplored Kant's penchant for abstract epistemology.[27] Among contemporary Neo-Kantians he considered the Marburg School the most respectable. Yet, even they were mere *epigoni*, more preoccupied with the analytic and logical aspects of Kant than they

---

[26]Unehrlich, Haecker, "Nachwort," B, 4:897. On Simmel's concept of Geist see Pascal, *From Naturalism*, 298-99.

[27]Like many German thinkers of the period, Haecker seems to proceed from Kant's notion that science is only phenomenal; whereas ethical action puts us into contact with the noumenal.

were with the moral center of Kant's thought.[28] Haecker had the impression that they were incapable of concerning themselves with anything more concrete than the construction of the circle. Hermann Cohen's treatment of ethics seemed to bear this out, for he ended up reducing questions about life to questions about moral theory, which in turn became resolved into an ethical system when 'scientifically' dealt with.[29]

All of the enemies of *Geist*, then, are fundamentally reductionists who fail to take some crucial area of human experience for what it is in the concrete.[30] The first step toward redressing the lost balance in intellectual life had to be a metaphysical assault upon reductionism, which would expose the vanity of Monism and the irrelevance of Neo-Kantianism. In Haecker's eyes Henri Bergson's vitalism, which subordinated knowledge to life totally, provided the requisite basis for a negative critique of contemporary thought.

While Haecker was always fascinated, sometimes morbidly, by the insights of his profound, if intellectually rootless, mentor, Max Scheler[31] it was Bergson, "the complete metaphysician, the poet to learning,"[32] who supplied the epistemological critique that exposed the emptiness of so much of contemporary thought. His description of Bergson is revealing, for we can perceive in the conjunction of metaphysician and poet, Haecker's endorsement of the venerable Romantic coalition of *Dichter und Denker* against the inroads of rationalism into spiritual life. In this context it should be mentioned that Haecker admired Schopenhauer for his insight into the metaphysical significance of art.[33] With Bergson we begin to discover the task of philosophy in the service of *Geist*. His meta-

---

[28]Haecker, "Nachwort," B, 4:897.

[29]Haecker, "Der Krieg," B, 5:182-86.

[30]This is a point that would have been sufficiently clear to his readers without Haecker mentioning it explicitly.

[31]Haecker, "Nachwort," B, 4:897.

[32]Der vollkommenste Metaphysiker, der Dichter nach der Wissenschaft, Haecker, *Kierkegaard*, 15.

[33]Ibid., 49.

physics is no longer a parody of natural science but an effort to demonstrate the radical limitations inherent in scientific methodology. These limitations make it impossible for scientifically-minded philosophers to study human beings reductionistically. Haecker takes it that Bergson turned positivism on its head by showing why it is impossible for physical concepts and mechanical explanations to be employed in the study of living phenomena and, *a-fortiori*, man.[34] Once Bergson had established the qualitative difference between the inorganic and the organic, the door was open for drawing a further distinction between the living and the spiritual. Presumably, the terms that were appropriate for the one were inappropriate for the other.

One of Bergson's greatest achievements, according to Haecker, consisted in drawing out the hidden implications in positivism's instrumental theory of knowledge, namely, the notion that language conceals as much as it reveals about the nature of the things we describe with it. Bergson discovered that language, "refers mostly to the spatial intuition of matter and, consequently, obscures, veils and prevents the bursting forth of the spiritual, which is no less real than the material."[35] Haecker also found Bergson's emphasis upon the role of risk as the key to successful adaptation of species to be a metaphysical antidote to the ubiquitous social pressures toward conformity. Nevertheless, Bergson's philosophy was wanting in one crucial area, ethics. This was the gap that Kierkegaard filled on our spectrum. The Dane's ethics of becoming was the perfect complement to Bergson's metaphysics of becoming. To Haecker, the two positions together constituted the philosophy of inwardness.

Inwardness is the recognition in practice: in concrete ethical action, that intelligence is fundamentally spiritual. As we have seen, the philosophy of inwardness proceeds from a curious critique of reason and entails a subordination of the intellectual (science and technology) to the spiritual (religious). There are three basic as-

---

[34]Ibid., 15.

[35]"Dass sie die meisten Beziehungen zur raeumlichen Anschauung der Materie hat und deshalb die geistigen phaenome, die nicht minder wirklich sind, als die materiallen, verdunkelt, verschleiert und nicht zum Durchbruch kommenlaesst," Haecker, ibid., 928.

pects of inwardness; they are only distinguishable for purposes of analysis. They are ethical individualism, radical adherence to Christianity, and virulent opposition to aestheticism. So intense is the inward man's commitment to his beliefs that they can neither be understood nor evaluated apart from his personality. Thus, it is not difficult to see why Kierkegaard should become the paragon of inwardness for Haecker. Interestingly, Haecker was aware that Kierkegaard's concept of the Christian may have been completely novel and, therefore, that his (Haecker's) philosophy of inwardness was something more than a mere renewal of the traditional notion of *Geist*.

Yet, Haecker's very choice of the word *inwardness* to describe Kierkegaard echos Augustine's admonition, "Do not go outside but turn into thyself. The truth abides inwardly in men."[36] Further, the theme of the inward nature of the spiritual life has specifically German sources in Meister Eckhart, for whom the inner-outer antithesis is fundamental[37] and is, as we have seen, found in pietism.[38] Thus, in the mind of the twentieth century's first "existentialist"— there can be little doubt that Haecker deserves that title—is at one time innovative and traditional.

Haecker's philosophy of inwardness is a kind of inversion of the Platonic world picture. Where Plato insists that reason can and does grasp the world of permanence and Being with certitude in cleaving to the universal, the abstract Idea, Haecker radically denies that we can know what is really real except existentially because only the everchanging, ineffable individual really exists. Thus, Bergsonian nominalism implies skepticism about the possibility of scientific certainty; such certainty as we can possess arises in the individual's immediate experience of the lived world around him.

---

[36]Cited from Augustine's *De Vera Religione* in Richard Kroner's *Speculation and Revelation in the Age of Christian Philosophy* (Philadelphia: Westminster, 1959) 111.

[37]See Meister Eckhart, "Reden der Unterweisung," in *Meister Eckhart: Deutsche Predigten und Traktate*, ed. Josef Quint (Munich: Hanser, 1955) 53-100; "Von der Abgeschiedenheit," *Vom Wunder der Seele*, ed. Friedrich Alfred Schmid Noerr (Stuttgart: Reklam, 1966) 19-25. Kroner traces Eckhart's mysticism to Augustine but insists that his concept of God is not that of Israel, *Speculation*, 233.

[38]See fn. 23, above.

However, it is of a different order than rational knowledge; in fact skepticism regarding the intellect's ability to know with certitude implies the need for faith as the mooring for science and philosophy.[39] Those things concerning which we can have objective knowledge are at best morally indifferent,[40] for they tell us nothing about the supremely important issues, God and the Self.

"For Kierkegaard," Haecker asserts, "nothing is so unutterably real, so eternal and indestructible as the spiritual self of the individual man, the Ego that is here the highest reality and the opposite of an abstraction."[41] Just as for Kierkegaard there is a dialectical continuity between the stages of human growth, by which the passionate hedonist comes to realize the futility of hedonism and the necessity for the rational regulation of his life, while the ethical man comes to realize that the fulfillment of the demands that reason makes upon nature only comes through an unreasonable leap into the absurdity of faith; so Haecker maintains that our efforts to grasp human reality are all part of one undertaking. Psychology, ethics, and religion not only form a continuum but permeate each other such that we are unable to understand one of these without the others. However, it cannot be overemphasized that they can only be comprehended existentially, that is, from the depths of the individual's own interior experience. The stringent requirements of the inward life as Haecker conceives it insure that genuine inwardness will only be accessible to a few: "The subjective thinker is aesthetic enough to give substance to his life, ethical enough to regulate his life and dialectical enough to master it reflectively."[42] At first glance it might seem contradictory to speak of passionate com-

---

[39]See Richard Popkin, "Kierkegaard and Skepticism," *Kierkegaard: A Collection of Critical Essays*, ed. Josiah Thompson (Garden City: Doubleday, 1972) 342-72.

[40]See fn. 28, above.

[41]"Fuer Kierkegaard ist nichts so unsagbar wirklich, so ewig und so unzerstoerbar, wie das geistige Selbst des einzelnen Menschen, das Ich das hier aber das Gegenteil einer Abstraktion und die hoechste Konkretion ist." Haecker, *Kierkegaard*, 15.

[42]Der subjective Denker ist aesthetisch genug, um seinem Leben einen Inhalt zu geben, ethisch genug, um es zu regulieren, dialektisch genug, um se denkend zu beherrschen, Haecker, *Kierkegaard*, 20.

mitment and reflection in the same breath; yet, it is essential that the inward man be sufficiently detached to be capable of conveying his experience of inwardness to others. Depth of feeling is necessary but it is not sufficient to this task. Haecker, then, is less an irrationalist than a thinker whose primary proccupation is the fear of reason running amok at the expense of human dignity. His ultimate fear was that psychology, ethics, and religion would come under the sway of rationalism.

Haecker attacked contemporary psychology as superficial because it emphasized the external and quantifiable to the exclusion of the inner life. This "French" mechanistic psychology (that is, deriving from Descartes and reflected in the classical tragedians but including the psychology of Nietzsche and, ironically, the German chauvinist Wundt)[43] fails to grasp man as he is, in the uniqueness of his individuality. This external approach had no place for the most typically individuating experience that human persons have, such as doubt, despair, lust and anger, to name a few. These states are the real subject matter of psychology. The authentic psychologist understands the psyche of others principally because he understands himself.[44] He understands himself because he has faced and transcended suffering. Ultimately, he understands life because he has looked death in the face.[45] His individuality results from his awareness of his finitude. The real task of psychology is not to measure the intensity of sensations but to make us aware of the depths of human experience. To be capable of this the psychologist must be an artist. In this respect Dostoevski and Kierkegaard help fill the void in the study of human nature. They are prime examples of the kinds of men who understand the human soul because they understand themselves.[46] To have learned this is to be aware of the extent to which crisis and ambiguity are part and parcel of the human condition.

---

[43]Haecker, *Kierkegaard*, 31-32.

[44]Haecker, *Kierkegaard*; of "Vorwart," B, 4:694-95.

[45]Cf. Kierkegaard, "Vom Tode," B, 5:15-55.

[46]Haecker, *Kierkegaard*, 32.

Transcending the depths of despair and loneliness, one acquires inwardness and with it the authority to communicate that experience.[47] But how do we recognize who has moral authority? This was a question that profoundly disturbed Haecker (and ultimately led him to embrace Catholicism in the early twenties). Gurus were everywhere. How could one distinguish the true from the false prophet? The best that he could say at this point was, "inwardness is only known from inwardness."[48] It is clear from his subsequent development that he was both dissatisfied with this view and deeply proccupied with this problem, for he devoted a great deal of effort throughout his life to the elucidation of the psychology, epistemology, logic, and rationality of Christian belief.[49] It is equally clear that he wanted to resist the temptation to equate inwardness with a particular style or set of tastes.[50] He insists that there is never a commensurability between the outer and the inner manifestations of inwardness—he criticized modern art for failing to grasp this.[51] Indeed, the problem arises because inwardness is a property of an individual personality. As such it always involves ambiguity, but more than that, it entails transcendence of the external, that is, disciplined mastery of style and gesture, which becomes the basis of the inward person's knack for turning the very superficiality of the external against itself.[52]

---

[47]Ibid., 21. These are Kierkegaard's central concerns in "Der Pfahl im Fleisch" and "Vom Tode."

[48]Innerlichkeit wird nur von Innerlichkeit erkannt, Haecker, *Kierkegaard*, 25.

[49]This is more obvious in the books he chose to translate than in his own writings. These include Kierkegaard's *Book on Adler*, which treats the question of how we distinguish genuinely inspired individuals from those who have not had the experience of God, selections from Kierkegaard's religious discourses (the centrality of which in Kierkegaard's *oeuvre* Haecker was among the very first to appreciate) which aim at leading their reader to an awareness of their own spiritual life by being read aloud to oneself and Cardinal Newman's *Grammar of Assent*. Together they constitute a guide to the theory and practice of religious rationality.

[50]Haecker, *Kierkegaard*, 25.

[51]Ibid. Haecker thinks that modern sculpture especially illustrates this point but he gives no examples.

[52]This is also foreshadowed in Bergson. See his "Laughter," ed. Wylie Sypher (Garden City: Doubleday, 1956).

Kierkegaard's aesthetic writings—and their contemporary counterpart, Krausian satire—are cases in point. To the man lacking a spiritual center, these writings appear frivolous, arbitrary, and perverse. The seriousness of the inward author is only observable to those who understand him from the inside. Christian faith is the essential prerequisite for that understanding. Thus, the philosophy of inwardness culminates in a deeply Protestant critique of secular efforts to create a science of man, in which Haecker claims to find a program for the radical revision of psychology, ethics, and even epistemology.

Haecker, like Wilhelm Dilthey and Otto Weininger before him,[53] takes the basic problems of psychology to be those associated with loneliness and despair. In short, those are the kinds of problems more often associated with psychoanalysis than with psychology. It is not as difficult to regard faith as an alternative to psychotherapy in this context as it might seem, for Kierkegaard's individual is precisely that person who has come to grips with himself emotionally. Madness, for example, is impossible for him because he has faced and transcended the crises of sexuality, loneliness, and despair.[54] Kierkegaardian Christianity, as opposed to the degenerate Christianity of the Church, provides a program for the resolution of ethical dilemmas inasmuch as it allows us to perceive those dilemmas as enmeshed in our very relation to ourselves—a fact that mere systematic analysis, with its objectified perspective, obscures. Finally, the certitude that philosophers have traditionally sought through reason is achieved in the decision to make the leap into the absurd. The moral authority of the inward man proceeds from that certitude. It entails the imperative to attack those relative institutions—whether the Church, the state, the *Volk*, or the family—which would usurp the individual's claim to be an absolute

---

[53]For Dilthey's conception of psychology see his "Ideen ueber eine beschreibende und zergliedegende Psychologie," *Gesammelte Schriften*, 17 vols. (1-12, Stuttgart: Teubner; 13-17, Goettingen: Vandenhoeck und Ruprecht, 1914-1974) 139-237. Weininger's *Geschlecht und Charakter*, the great philosophical *sucess de scandale* of the Viennese *fin de siècle* endeavored *inter alia* to reorient psychology along Diltheyan lines. Some Brenner thinkers considered Kierkegaard to be the answer to Weininger's view of life.

[54]Haecker, *Kierkegaard*, 46-47.

value in and of himself.[55] Let us complete the discussion of the philosophy of inwardness with an account of its expression in social critique. This will reveal the centrality of Kierkegaard's *Two Ages* to Haecker's philosophy of inwardness as well as Haecker's means of understanding and extending Kierkegaard's social criticism.

It should be clear from the preceding discussion that any effort at communicating inwardness is going to be difficult, for to do so will have to involve employing words and symbols, which are "objects" inwardly. How, then, can a critique of society take on inwardness? Clearly, objective reasoning, deduction and demonstration are merely formal and external and, therefore, incapable of moving anyone to act. What is required is a mode of exposing the shallowness of material things. Since the corruption we encounter in society is due precisely to its inverted priorities, we need a medium that will stand accepted values on their heads. Haecker took his cue from the only living individual he found worthy of comparison with Kierkegaard, Karl Kraus.[56]

Kraus was the only figure who could confront the corruption of a whole society. His satire devastated the emptiness of Viennese mores in much the same way that Kierkegaard assaulted those of Copenhagen seventy years earlier. According to Haecker, Kraus was the living embodiment of the Kierkegaardian indictment of society in *Two Ages*—something Kraus found both flattering and challenging.[57] Kraus exposed the fatuousness and posturing of the Viennese by simply quoting advertisements, editorials, speeches, cliches, and so forth, verbatim. He was living proof of the possibility that reflective thought and imaginative writing were capable of turning the double standard of the Viennese public against itself. Eugen Blessing has succinctly expressed the characteristics that distinguishes genuine Krausian satire from its counterfeit, mere ridicule. "Satire," Blessing asserts, "is the unmasking of the inward nothingness behind the ostentatious facade of exteriority by

---

[55]Ibid., 63.

[56]Ibid., 57.

[57]Stieg, in *Brenner Studien*, vol. 3, 182-90.

means of comedy, motivated by disappointed love."[58] This, then, was the strategy and the motivation; we must now turn to the substance of Haecker's social criticism.

Haecker continued the project that Kierkegaard originated in *Two Ages* (and Kraus sustained in *Die Fackel*) in a series of satires and polemics revolving around the following four themes: a revision of the common understanding, a battle against "spiritless liberalism,"[59] an assault upon the corruption of the press, and a campaign against rootless aestheticism.

Søren Kierkegaard und die Philosophie der Innerlichkeit opens with the allegation that there does not seem to be a single Christian, in Kierkegaard's sense, among the sixty-five million residents of Imperial Germany.[60] Germans are Christians from conformity rather than conviction. Haecker sees his task as providing these pseudo-Christians with a model of genuine Christian living as well as admonishing them against false prophets. In his first contribution to *Der Brenner* Haecker went to great lengths to dissociate himself—and Kierkegaard—from Franz Blei and the aesthete Catholicism of *Die weissen Blaetter*. Blei alleged that Kierkegaard was not really a Christian but something entirely novel on the spiritual scene. It was this attack that confirmed Haecker's belief that Kierkegaard was indeed a Christian in the traditional sense. Haecker's response came in the form of a tirade against what he called "literary-Jewish Neo-Catholicism."[61]

Blei and Paul Claudel (whose *Tidings Brought to Mary* Blei translated into German) represented the degeneration of religion into mere spectacle, substanceless pomp and circumstance. So he attacked them savagely in the name of simple, committed religiosity. For Haecker, only Kraus—and possibly Gerhart Hauptmann, whose *Emanuel Quint, A Fool in Christ* Haecker greatly admired—

---

[58]Satire ist die Entlarvung des Nichts der Innerlichkeit hinter der Prunkfassade der Aeusserlichkeit durch das Mittel der Komit auf Grund entaeuschter Liebe, Blessing, *Theodor Haecker*, 20.

[59]Geistlose Liberalismus, Haecker, *Kierkegaard*, 11.

[60]Ibid., 5.

[61]Literarisch-juedischen Neo-Katholicismus, Haecker, "F. Blei," B, 4:461-62.

could legitimately be associated with the mission of the Dane. It is important to note that this polemic has a typical feature of Haecker's work in the genre: His insistence that an opponent who is mistaken on a fundamental issue is somehow decadent and, therefore, wrong in everything he asserts. Truth, for Haecker, is all of one piece. Blindness to the possibility of finding even isolated insights from another world view is a permanent feature of his thinking. This blindness is a serious shortcoming in Haecker's world view, for it determined that his intolerance toward corruption was much closer to intolerance pure and simple than he ever realized.

Although Haecker did not devote any single essay to the evils of "spiritless liberalism," it is clearly to blame in his eyes for all of the evils in the modern world. His deep-seated opposition to liberalism is very important for the antimodern tinge it lent to the interpretation of Kierkegaard's social criticism in *Two Ages*. For Haecker, modern society's concern for money and, generally, its preference for the quantitative rather than the qualitative is attributable to liberalism's baneful influence. In the liberal's world picture the whole world is a huge department store (an institution that epitomized modern society in the eyes of most German fin de siècle social critics) in which everything, even religion, is for sale.[62] The liberal clergy, epitomized by Friedrich Naumann, fatally mixed their faith with politics and science. In the end they were little better than the Monist "clergy." Both fell prey to the illusion of equating civilization with material progress.

While Haecker viewed the state as a necessary evil, and, therefore, considered its form immaterial so long as it did not interfere with the individual's spiritual life, he did consider the liberal state a threat to Christian belief. He believed that liberal parliamentary democracy was less conducive to the life of the spirit than princely authoritarianism. His belief apparently stemmed from the morally dubious notion that politics itself is something liberal in origin: "Everything in this world that belongs to politics, and also happens in politics, is, in a negative case, distant from *Geist*, in the neutral

---

[62]Haecker, "Vorwort," B, 4:703.

case, appearance of movement, and in the positive, only an approximation."[63]

Haecker hated liberal democracy because he believed it manipulated the individual in the name of individualism. Since these attitudes became closely associated with Kierkegaard's views in *Two Ages* and since they are at best a hideous caricature of the way liberal democracy works, it will be worthwhile examining the sources of the misapprehension of liberalism Haecker shared with so many of his contemporaries.

Bismarck's adroit maneuverings left Germany with the trappings of parliamentary democracy without actually altering the authoritarian power structure.[64] On the surface there was a flurry of party politics in the Second Reich, but the constitution left all power in the hands of the Emperor and his Prime Minister. Bismarck successfully managed to reduce political parties to mere interest groups. John Boyer has recently shown that this sham democracy was also in evidence in Vienna in the last quarter of the nineteenth century.[65] This had the effect of contradicting the universalistic claims of liberal rhetoric with its particularistic day-to-day politics. In short, it transformed liberalism into a phenomenon begging to be satirized.

Moreover, liberalism was associated with industrialization, which was fast and furious in Germany (at least as compared, say, with England). The result was that two values systems coexisted in

---

[63]Alles was sich in dieser Welt, die Politik gehoert, ereignet, ist im schlimmen Fall Entfernung vom Geist, im neutralen Schein bewegung, und im guten nur Annaehrung, Haecker, "F. Blei," B, 4:463.

[64]I am painfully aware of the inadequacy of any brief description of the complex sociopolitical situation that I have caricatured in this paragraph. Various salient features of the situation I have sketched can be found in the following works: Ralf Dahrendorf, *Society and Democracy in Germany* (Garden City: Doubleday, 1967). Kenneth Barkin, *The Controversy Over German Industrialization* (Chicago: University of Chicago Press, 1969). Erich Eyck, *Bismarck and the German Empire* (New York: Norton, 1950). Arthur Mitzman, *Sociology and Estrangement* (New York: Knopf, 1973). Mitzman, *The Iron Cage* (New York: Knopf, 1970). Hans Rosenberg, *Grosse Depression und Bismarckzeit* (Berlin: de Cryter, 1967).

[65]John Boyer, *Political Radicalism in Imperial Vienna* (Chicago: University of Chicago Press, 1981) 7.

Germany, a traditional one in the pre-industrial countryside and a modern competitive one in the cities. To Schwabian country boys like Haecker these were simply two antagonistic ways of life. The former seemed natural; whereas it was difficult to conceive of the latter as anything but artificial. The artificiality and perverseness of liberal values seemed borne out in the wake of the Viennese stock market crash of 1873. The scandals unearthed in its wake marked the rise of both antiliberalism and its ugly twin, anti-Semitism. (Haecker detested anti-Semitism as yet another abstract world view but nevertheless shared the views of some anti-Semites that Jews were prominent in those circles that represented the greatest threats to inwardness).[66] Utilitarianism became equated with opportunism of the crassest sort such that it never succeeded in regaining its good name in Central Europe as a result of these scandals.

Finally, in some circles there was a tendency to identify liberalism with the militant atheism of the Monists in the wake of the *Kulturkampf*. Thus, it was by no means impossible to be deceived about both the nature and reality of liberalism in Germany and Austria at the time when Haecker was writing. This, combined with Haecker's penchant for seeing everything in black and white terms (another characteristic of the Central European outsider at this time) goes a long way toward explaining Haecker's lifelong preference for authoritarian forms of government. In any case, Haecker lost no opportunity to castigate liberalism and the institution that most embodied its evil, the press.

In Haecker's eyes the newspapers represented "the comic unity of talented smuttiness" because "the feuilleton is contained in politics and politics in the feuilleton."[67] The feuilleton, a favorite target

---

[66]Boyer and Eva Reichmann have emphasized that not all animosity toward Jews was fanatical or irrational in the period before World War I. See Boyer, *Political Radicalism*, 51 et passim. Cf. Reichmann, *Hostages of Civilization* (Westport: Greenwood, 1970). Haecker's comments on Judaism in "Nachwort," B, 4:902, illuminate his position on this topic.

[67]Die komische Einheit der talentertierten Schmierigkeit ist da, denn das Feuilleton ist in der Politik und die Politik im Feuilleton erhalten, Haecker, "Nachwort," 895.

for Kraus's barbs, concentrated all of the obnoxious characteristics of liberal journalism. Born in France as a form of political commentary, it was adapted as a form of cultural commentary in the German-speaking world, where political commentary was *streng verboten*. It combined subjective reflection about a locality with its description in an effort to determine its significance. Hence, it combined hard facts and personal conjecture in a highly whimsical manner.[68] The feuilleton invited the writer to indulge his narcissistic inclinations as well as to express them in ponderously complex descriptions, which in turn opened the door to grammatical chaos. A master of language like Karl Kraus could produce hilarious parodies of feuilletonist like Hermann Bahr, which pilloried the writer on his own sentence constructions. For Haecker, the fueilleton was the primary example of the modern tendency to confuse subjective and objective accounts of situations. The result was that all sense of distinction between facts and values was lost; the resulting situation utterly confused the relation of man to language. Understanding the roots of this debasement of language will take us to the very core of Haecker's philosophy of inwardness and further expose the centrality of *Two Ages* to his project.

The debasement of language stems primarily from failing to distinguish the profane, which can be discussed, from the sacred, which cannot. The ultimate source of the impiety and the decadence in the modern world, in the eyes of Haecker, and also Kraus and even Wittgenstein[69], consists in chattering on about spiritual matters (which is self, God, love, fear, and so forth), as though they were commonplaces and conversely, treating commonplaces (which are matters of fashion) as though they were the highest spiritual truths. Chatter, babble, and talkativeness are all ways of avoiding the ethical imperative to inwardness:

> What is it to chatter? It is the annulment of the passionate disjunction between remaining silent and speaking. Only the person who can remain essentially silent can speak essentially, can act es-

---

[68]On the feuilleton see Carl Schorske, "Politics and the Psyche in *fin de siècle* Vienna," American Historical Review, Vol. 66 (1961) 935.

[69]See Janik and Toulmin, *Wittgenstein's Vienna*, 67-201.

sentially. Silence is inwardness. Chattering gets ahead of essential speaking, and giving utterance to reflection has a weakening effect on action by getting ahead of it . . . chattering dreads the moment of silence, which would reveal the emptiness. (TA 97-98)

Ultimately, chatter debases faith into heathen triviality. It is exactly at this point that the person of inwardness is compelled to respond with a devastating critique of the encroachments of the human upon the divine, of the immoral and unthinking—upon the committed individual. His language, like that of Kierkegaard and Kraus becomes the very embodiment of his inwardness. He reveals the moral bankruptcy of the philistine by attacking him with the vacuousness of his own phrases. "Whatever creates and produces," Kierkegaard wrote in *Two Ages*, "is always latently polemical, because it must have room for itself" (TA, 95). Satire and polemic, then, clothe the inward person's spirituality. His relation to language is, therefore, the exact opposite of the feuilletonist. Mauthner was a prime example. His activity as a feuilletonist blatantly contradicted his skepticism, for, as a feuilletonist, he simply had to take his own impressions and conjectures as definitive on a given topic. What was this, if not the ultimate form of chatter? "Ah! All words pass through Mauthner's gigantic word eater and are made into a mush,"[70] he lamented. But this kind of confusion is just what we ought to expect from the press.

The evil wrought by the press is not limited to that which is done by individual journalists. It is much deeper than that, for it lies ultimately in the irreparable damage done to the very notion of individual responsibility by an institution that can accuse without facing counter-accusation. Hacker wholeheartedly endorses Kierkegaard's view of the press in *Two Ages*

Together with the passionlessness and reflectiveness of the age, the abstraction for "the press" (for a newspaper, a periodical, is not a political concretion and is individual only in an abstract sense) gives rise to the abstraction's phantom, "the public," which is the real leveler (TA 87).

---

[70]Ach! alle Worte, Begriffe, und Gefuehle gehen ein in Mauthners Riesenwoertermaul und werden dort zu Blei, Haecker, "Nachwort," B, IV, 901.

The press has the power to coerce and depersonalize through its ability to create mass sentiment in the form of "public opinion." Haecker construes the faceless irresponsibility of the press as the ultimate betrayal of the classical concept of moral action to the extent that moral judgment depends upon responsibility. Haecker was utterly appalled that university professors should participate in this irrational process of opinion formation. In this respect they were no better than the aesthetes who dominated the German and Austrian literary scene.

Haecker considered the literary artist on a par with the moral philosopher and metaphysician to the point that the three ultimately merge in the inward man. Consequently, the attitude of modern writers professing the "art for art's sake" creed was the height of irreverence and irresponsibility in his eyes. The notion that art should "shock the bourgeoisie" by presenting sexuality frankly and openly particularly disturbed him. While Haecker only discussed these themes occasionally, there can be no doubt that they were central concerns of his—as they were generally in the early *Brenner*. It is not suggested here that Haecker was a prude. In his first book, he praised Ibsen and Strindberg, along with Tolstoi, as the first writers to treat marriage seriously in a thousand years of western literature. Their opposite numbers among aesthetes, according to Haecker, were Wagner and Thomas Mann, whose *Death in Venice* was taken to be the very epitome of aestheticism by the members of the *Brenner* circle in the years before World War I. Mann and Wagner, in Haecker's eyes, spawned a brood of followers and imitators who wrote about human sexuality as though they had just discovered that sex is something men share with lower animals.[71] Haecker agreed with Kraus that such portrayals of sexuality were, like psychoanalysis, the disease, not the therapy. Both Kraus and Haecker found more depth in the overt whimsicality of Offenbach's treatment of sexuality in operettas such as *La Périchole* (which Kraus rendered into German). The immense immorality that was the First World War simply brought to the surface aestheticism's latent immorality.

---

[71]Haecker, "Vorbemerkung," B, IV, 669.

The reactions of German intellectuals to the Great War was the provocation for Haecker's most rancorous polemic, "The Leading Intellectuals and the War," a work that could not but be associated with what Haecker had already presented to the *Brenner's* readers from *Two Ages*. Kraus described prewar Vienna as a "proving-ground" for world destruction"[72] but even he was astounded when he became aware of the extent of the horrors wrought by the war. His response was to assemble in the pages of *Die Fackel* —and later under separate cover as *The Last Days of Mankind*—a vast array of public statements by military men, civil servants, writers, journalists and the like, which reflected their crass insensitivity and hypocritical stupidity. *Der Brenner's* response was the 1915 yearbook dedicated to themes surrounding the horror of war. The volume contained Rilke's plaintive "Verse," Dallago's "The Connection to the Law," which was his effort to render the *Tao Te Ching* into German, the last poems of Georg Trakl with their horrific vision of death, Haecker's translation of Kierkegaard's "The Decisiveness of Death", and his own polemic against the intellectuals.

The title of Haecker's diatribe once more reflects his preoccupation with *Geist* and its degeneration at the hands of German intellectuals. The focus of Haecker's attack was the *Neue Rundschau*, which referred to itself as "Germany's leading intellectual monthly."[73] Its impressive list of contributors certainly suggested that the journal had a claim to that title. Indeed, the catalogue of distinguished figures who contributed to the journal is such that one might be tempted to question Haecker's judgment in pressing such an acrimonious assault upon them. The list includes Carl and Gerhardt Hauptmann, Wilhelm Wundt, Rudolf Eucken, Hugo von Hofmannsthal, Alred Kerr, Maximilian Harden, Karl Lamprecht, Friedrich Naumann, Hermann Cohen, Mauthner (here referred to as "pithicanthropus scepticus"),[74] and numerous others.

---

[72]Versuchstation fuer Weltuntergang, Kraus, *Untergang der Welt durch Schwarze Magie* (Munich: Koesel, 1960) 418.

[73]Der Fuehrenden geistigen Monatschrift Deutschlands, Haecker, "Der Krieg," B, V, 130.

[74]Ibid., 155.

Mauthner's shallowness is betrayed by his rapid conversion from skepticism to blind nationalism. Franz Blei is castigated along with Haecker's erstwhile hero, Gerhardt Hauptmann, for belittling the philosophical achievements of Henri Bergson simply because he was French. Wundt is pilloried for trotting out Fichte's patriotic utterances of 1813 with blatant disregard for differences between the circumstances under which they were written and those of 1914. Eucken is taken to task for enlisting Meister Eckhart into the war effort and for making "inwardness" into a war slogan. The following illustrates the sort of thing Haecker finds objectionable in Eucken: "The struggle for the Fatherland appears also as a struggle for the ideal good of mankind, for preservation of a higher world in our midst; thus the fighters as well as the sufferers appear as enlargers of the realm of spirit."[75]

The critics, Harden, Kerr, and Herzog, men weaned on Nietzsche's demand for an ethic "beyond good and evil," nevertheless transformed the war into a moral crusade. For Haecker, who had previously written of Nietzsche with a respect verging upon enthusiasm, this implied that there was something radically wrong with the master: "What was blindness and delusion in Nietzsche becomes idiocy and insolence in these 'intellectual leaders' and 'new ethicians.' "[76] The need for a Christian response to Nietzsche's assault upon bourgeois society was yet another truth for which the war provided more than ample corroboration.

Perhaps the best way to see the war from Haecker's standpoint is to reproduce some of the many texts he quotes to establish his view that the war has become an occasion for word orgies in the press. Wilhelm Herzog, editor of the *Forum*, wrote, "We friends of peace and heralds of a new ethics announce that we are volunteer-

---

[75]Denn der Kampf fuer das Vaterland erscheint dann zugleich als ein Kampf fuer die idealen Gueter der Menschheit, fuer einer hoeheren Welt in unserem Bereich; Kaempfende sowohl als Leidende erscheinen dann als Mehrer des Reiches des Geistes, Rudolf Eucken, *Die Traeger des Deutschen Idealismus* (Berlin: Reuther und Reichard, 1915) 247-48.

[76]Was bei Nietzsche Blindheit und Verblendung war, das wird bei diesen "Fuehrer des Geistes" und "neuen Ethikern" Idiotismus und Frechheit, Haecker, "Der Krieg," B, 5:146-47.

ing for the war. We want to kill like the others."[77] Haecker responds to this jingoism by inquiring who Herzog intends to kill in press-rooms and beer halls. Blei takes the prize for sheer fatuous pomposity: "What people call peace is only the appellation of the condition antagonistic to the utterly other condition, which is war."[78] It seemed that the press was the one sure winner of the war: "The power of the phrase has established itself over all other powers."[79] Thus, the obligation of the philosophers of inwardness to turn the very emptiness of these phrases against themselves, to let the moral depravity masquerading as duty to the Fatherland unmask itself.

This completes our picture of Haecker's philosophy of inwardness. It will be worthwhile to summarize its main points briefly. Inwardness is the result of encountering and transcending dread, despair, and death in an act of faith. It is the courageous effort through which self-mastery is won. The inward man is above all an integral character. There is not the slightest discrepancy between his words and his actions. Integrity brings with it an acute perception of dissimulation in the environment and imposes the responsibility of undertaking a relentless critique of those practices and institutions that threaten the development of personal existence. His polemics and satires are not anti-intellectual but the employment of his considerable intelligence on behalf of a crusade against the pretentions of rationalism (and rationalization) gone wild. The inward man's philosophy is not speculative but lived truth. It manifests itself humorously as satirical exposure of hypocrisy and posturing. Humor is a possibility for the inward man not only because he is a Christian whose faith transcends tragedy but also because he finds the pretentions of the relative to absolute status are inherently humorous.

---

[77]Wir Freunde des Friedens und Kinder einer neuen Ethik, melden uns als Kriegsfreiwillige. Wir wollen toeten, wie die anderen, Wilhelm Herzog cited in Haecker, "Der Krieg", 142.

[78]Was man Frieden nennt, ist die Zustandsbenennung antagonal dem aeussersten Zustand, welcher der Krieg ist, Blei cited in Haecker, "Der Krieg", 147.

[79]Die Gewalt der Phrase hat sich ueber alle andere Gewalt gesetzt, Haecker, "Der Krieg", 132.

At this point we can raise the question, "What impact did Haecker's philosophy of inwardness, his depiction of Kierkegaard and his extension of the Dane's project in *Two Ages* have on his readers?" That is a difficult question to answer with any precision. However, the response to Haecker's presentation of Kierkegaard in *Der Brenner* itself can be ascertained; it can be taken as an index of the impact of Haecker's efforts on behalf of Kierkegaard before and during the first world war. After encountering Kierkegaard, Dallago expressed the idea that he was convinced he had left Christianity behind him only to find it was in fact placed directly in front of him by Kierkegaard.[80] Dallago had previously identified Christianity exclusively with legalism and casuistry of Catholic moral theology. Dallago was as uncompromising in his rejection of this rationalistic morality as the Church was in maintaining it. He found Catholicism implacably opposed to individual self-realization because it denied the fundamental sexual instincts nature implanted in us. By forcing us to deny our natural urges, the Church has produced the very immorality she claimed to oppose. Further, her elaborate theology resolved all questions into points of the most abstruse metaphysics. Her God was the *ens realissimum*, the most abstract and impersonal of concepts. Dallago would have none of it. He felt a moral obligation—despite the fact the very word moral was repugnant to him due to its legalistic overtones—to expose the inhumanity of Christian morality. Kierkegaard's notions of faith, sin, and truth enabled him to carry on his singular campaign against the Church in the very name of authentic Christianity.

Kierkegaard's disjunction between sin and faith enabled Dallago to unify the various strands of his world view to an extent that had not been possible previously. If faith is something totally inward and completely unjustifiable in terms of the canons of reason, and if sin is its opposite, then the two most pernicious sins would be conformism and intellectualism. Faith would be compatible with extreme individualism, which completely spurns convention and embraces danger. This appealed very much to the author of *The Book of Uncertainties*. The fact that Kierkegaard's concept of the

---

[80]Dallago, *Der Christ Kierkegaards*, 5.

Christian life fit Dallago's secular individualism is as revealing about Kierkegaard as it is about Dallago, for it indicates that it is at least conceivable that Kierkegaard's individualism was as appealing as his Christianity to his first twentieth-century public. While Dallago's readings are certainly heterodox, they do serve to illustrate such points well. As for Dallago himself, where Kierkegaard's texts seem to contradict his views he takes refuge in the notion that there is a residual Church-Christianity in the Dane's writings. Though Dallago may face difficulties, he wishes to maintain that he and Kierkegaard are in fundamental agreement on the basic notion that God is really man. Thus, Dallago, at least in his own mind, reconciled Kierkegaardian Christianity and naturalist humanism.

To Dallago, all genuine humanism proceeds from the insight that reason cannot penetrate ultimate reality, which can only be grasped in feeling: "More and more spiritual development has to yield the discovery of concealments and not a solution to the riddles of the universe in the sense of the deciphering of existence."[81] We attain such insight in abandoning ourselves to our feelings by eschewing the calculating and scheming intellect. Dallago's position involves several difficulties concerning which he had not the slightest inkling, such as the problem of whether we can indeed have any experiences that are immediate. His reading of this view into Kierkegaard is, at the very least, dubious. Yet, there is a certain plausibility to it. Does not Kierkegaard's account of the dialectic process through the stages on life's way proceed from sensuality and rise to the love of God in the celebrated "leap of faith?" Dallago and Kierkegaard certainly agree that love is a deeper mode of understanding than discursive ratiocination and that ultimate truth is a matter of becoming a person. The intimate connection between a person's individuality and ultimate truth is a riddle and paradox for both the Dane and the South Tyrolean; both view the zenith of wisdom as the act of embracing paradox. Further, the polemical side of the philosophy of inwardness struck a responsive chord in Dallago. His postwar writings are almost exclusively modeled upon *The*

---

[81]Die geistige Entwicklung immer mehr ein Auffinden von Verhangenheiten ergeben muesse und nicht eine Weltraetseloesung im Sinne einer Daseinsentraetselung, Dallago, "Ueber eine Schrift," B, 4:469.

Present Age and *The Instant*. Gone is the lyrical side so apparent in his early writings. Gone is the charm of the South Tyrolean landscape that meant so much to him and expressed itself in his poetry and his impressionistic short prose works of the early period. They are replaced by ever-lengthening harangues against the Church and Fascism in Italy and Austria. In short, Kierkegaard supplanted Nietzsche in his world view—and as a focal point for the postwar development of *Der Brenner*.[82]

Having traced the main lines of the story of Haecker's introduction of Kierkegaard into *Der Brenner*, it is necessary to return to the matter of Kierkegaard's impact upon twentieth-century German philosophers and to ask the question, "what role did Haecker's translation of *Two Ages*, and his other activities in *Der Brenner* on behalf of Kierkegaard, have in fixing the Dane's image?"

The present state of information concerning the intellectual biographies of the major figures in twentieth-century German thought is extremely sketchy; yet, we do know that all of the figures mentioned at the beginning of this essay, with the possible exception of Jaspers, read *Der Brenner*. Wittgenstein chose Ficker (due to Kraus's high opinion of him) to disburse part of his inheritance from his father in 1914. After the war he turned to Ficker when three publishers rejected the *Tractatus*. In the course of trying to convince Ficker that the point of seventy-five pages of dense aphorisms was related to the mission of *Der Brenner* Wittgenstein appears to have made reference to Kierkegaard's distinction in *Two Ages* between speaking, remaining silent and chattering. There can be no questions whatsoever that this is the single most important theme in Wittgenstein's philosophy both early and late; so a detailed investigation of the historical and systematic connections between Wittgenstein and Kierkegaard with special reference to *Two Ages* might well go a long way in answering at a profound level some very important questions about modern thought.[83]

---

[82]Stieg, *Brenner Studien*, 3:158-62.

[83]See Janik, "Wittgenstein, Ficker and Der Brenner," *Wittgentstein: Sources and Perspectives*, ed. C. Grant Luckhardt (Ithaca: Cornell, 1979) 161-89.

Heidegger subscribed to *Der Brenner* from 1911 until its last issue in 1954. He became the closest of friends with Ficker after their meeting in 1952 at Buehlerhoehe (where Heidegger had invited Ficker to hear the Trakl lecture, "Die Sprache im Gedicht") until Ficker's death in 1967.[84] There is little doubt that Heidegger's notion of "idle talk" in *Sein und Zeit* is drawn from *Two Ages*, which Heidegger would have read in Haecker's translation. Similarly, Heidegger's notion that silence itself is a mode of speech in the same work would appear to owe something to *Two Ages*—as well as to bear interesting and important links to Wittgenstein's views about the sayable and the unsayable. The exact nature of his debt to Kierkegaard's critique of society in *Two Ages* remains to be ascertained. (See John Hoberman's contribution to this volume). However, there is, once more, no question whatsoever that the topic is of the utmost philosophical importance.

Adorno, like Heidegger, became friendly with Ficker late in the latter's life. There is no question that part of Adorno's attraction to Ficker was related to their common concern for the poetry of Georg Trakl, but it is equally clear their respective criticisms of modern society had much in common with one another. There is no question that Ficker's views on these matters were profoundly influenced by Haecker's translation from *Two Ages*; it would be by no means outrageous to suggest that Adorno's was, as well.[85]

Neither Buber, Jaspers, nor Husserl knew Ficker personally but there is no question that Buber and Husserl read *Der Brenner* and good reason to suspect that Jaspers would have read Haecker's translation of *Two Ages*. In an autobiographical essay Buber mentions being astonished at the discovery that Ferdinand Ebner anticipated some of the central themes in *I and Thou* in the pages of *Der*

---

[84]See Janik, "Dallago und Heidegger: Ueber Anfang und Ende des Brenners," *Untersuchungen zum Brenner: Festschrift fuer Ignaz Zangerle*, ed. W. Methlagl, E. Sauermann, and S. P. Scheichl (Salzburg: Otto Mueller, forthcoming). Cf. Janik, "Style and Idea in the Later Heidegger: Rhetoric, Politics and Philosophy" (unpublished).

[85]On Adorno's relationship to *Der Brenner* see Methlagl, "Die Zeit und die Stunde der Zeit," *Studien zur Literatur des 19. und 20. Jahrhunderts in Oesterreich: Festschrift fuer Alfred Doppler*, ed. Holzner, Klein, and Wiesmueller (Innsbruck: University of Innsbruck, 1981) 153-78.

Brenner. Ebner's culturally pessimistic version of *I and Thou* was strongly influenced by Kierkegaard's *Two Ages*. If Buber came across Ebner by chance in *Der Brenner*, it is most unlikely that he would not have read Haecker's selection from *Two Ages*.[86]

Perhaps the strongest evidence for the widespread influence of Haecker's translation from *Two Ages* comes from Ficker's correspondence with a student of Husserl's, who reported that Husserl liked what he read in *Der Brenner* and particularly liked Haecker's "Afterword" to his selection from *Two Ages*.[87]

So, there is at least *prima facie* evidence that Husserl's concept of the crisis of western science is influenced by this encounter. Finally, Jaspers's critique of modernity is explicitly and unabashedly indebted to Kierkegaard's critique of society in *Two Ages*. Since there is little doubt that he would have read Haecker's translation, it is not outrageous to suggest that he was aware of Haecker's own publications.

The distinguishing characteristic of all of these philosophers is their commitment to a dramatic reconsideration of the nature and scope of philosophy as well as a reconsideration of the place of philosophy in human life. The substantive achievements of these figures, at least in their own eyes, are inconceivable in the absence of a radical critique of a decadent society, one which is condemned for precisely the reasons that Kierkegaard assaulted the present age. While the impact of *Der Brenner's* presentation of Kierkegaard on these thinkers cannot be determined with precision until we know a great deal more about their individual histories, there is no question that it was widely influential. Indeed, it is highly doubtful that a proper understanding of the Kierkegaard reception and/or the de-

---

[86]Martin Buber, "Autobiographical Fragments," *The Philosophy of Martin Buber*, ed., P. A. Schilpp and Maurice Friedman, "Library of Living Philosophers" (LaSalle: Open Court, 1967) 34. Cf. Rivka Horwitz, "Ferdinand Ebner als Quelle von Martin Buber's 'Ich und Du,'" *Unterscuhungen zum Brenner*.

[87]Hans Jaeger to Ludwig von Ficker December 16, 1923. This letter will be included in the collection of Ficker's correspondence that will be prepared for publication by the Brenner Archive under the direction of Walter Methlagl. I am indebted to Dr. Methlagl and Dr. Stieg for many informative discussions about *Der Brenner* and twentieth-century thought.

velopment of philosophy in the German-speaking world will be forthcoming until we are able to answer the philosophical and historical questions that Haecker's transmission of Kierkegaard in *Der Brenner* raise. What is beyond doubt, however, is that *Two Ages* is absolutely central to that story.

XI

Kierkegaard's *Two Ages* and Heidegger's Critique of Modernity

by John M. Hoberman

Kierkegaard and Heidegger

It was the best of times, it was the worst of times, it was the age of wisdom, it was the age of foolishness, it was the epoch of belief, it was the epoch of incredulity, it was the season of Light, it was the season of Darkness, it was the spring of hope, it was the winter of despair.[1]

"It is not readily apparent to the person beginning to read Heidegger's *Being and Time* that the book shows a heavy reliance

---

[1] Charles Dickens, *A Tale of Two Cities* (New York: New American Library, 1964) 13.

on the works of Kierkegaard."[2] This is a correct and important judgment whose documentation remains curiously incomplete, due in part to Heidegger's refusal to discuss Kierkegaard outside of a few footnotes to *Being and Time*. Heidegger's attitude toward his Danish predecessor may even be described as somewhat patronizing.[3] Why, on the other hand, historians of existentialism have failed to provide a more satisfactory explanation of this relationship is a separate and more complex matter that I will not attempt to explain beyond noting Heidegger's resistance and its undoubted effect upon later commentators. How these commentators have dealt with the Kierkegaard-Heidegger relationship is easier to describe. One approach simply includes Kierkegaard among other major figures who have influenced Heidegger, implying that the fact of influence is both well-established and difficult to describe in its specifics.[4]

A second interpretation acknowledges the importance of the relationship, emphasizing Kierkegaard's seminal position.[5] A third acknowledges the influence but emphasizes Heidegger's improvements on the Kierkegaardian original.[6] (The most satisfactory interpretations[7] combine the second and third viewpoints.) A fourth interpretation recognizes the relationship but interprets it as degeneration: "Heidegger, proceeding though he does from Kierkegaard, has, ironically enough, rationalized the Kierkegaardian

---

[2]Fernando Molina, *Existentialism as Philosophy* (Englewood Cliffs NJ: Prentice-Hall, 1962) 54.

[3]See Vincent Vycinas, *Earth and Gods: An Introduction to the Philosophy of Martin Heidegger* (The Hague: Martinus Nijhoff, 1961) 8; and M. Wyschogrod, *Kierkegaard and Heidegger* (London: Routledge & Kegan Paul Ltd., 1954) 128.

[4]Thomas Langan, *The Meaning of Heidegger* (New York: Columbia University Press, 1961) 8, 72fn.

[5]Calvin O. Schrag, *Existence and Freedom* (Evanston: Northwestern University Press, 1970) 13.

[6]Ibid., 11, 41, 45, 49; see also John Wild, *The Challenge of Existentialism* (Bloomington: Indiana University Press, 1970) 87.

[7]I am referring to the interpretations of Schrag and Wyschogrod.

theme into a rigid and almost scholastic system."[8] Finally, there is the Kierkegaard partisan for whom Heidegger is quite worthless.[9]

It is peculiar that the task of comparing existentialism's two major—and, presumably, related—figures should have resulted in this sort of cacophony. On the other hand, this is a genuinely difficult comparison for at least two reasons, the second of which may be traced to the first. The most general of Heidegger's brief commentaries on Kierkegaard at the end of *Being and Time* reads as follows: "In the nineteenth century, Søren Kierkegaard explicitly seized upon the problem of existence as an existentiell problem, and thought it through in a penetrating fashion. But the existential problematic was so alien to him that, as regards his ontology, he remained completely dominated by Hegel and by ancient philosophy as Hegel saw it. Thus, there is more to be learned philosophically from his 'edifying' writings than from his theoretical ones—with the exception of his treatise on the concept of anxiety."[10] The most detailed account of the differences that separate the ontologies of these thinkers has been provided by M. Wyschogrod. "Whereas Kierkegaard's concern with Being," he states, "basic as it is, is never made the object of explicit philosophical research, except in relation to more directly existential problems. Heidegger sets the problem of Being in the very center of his concern"; whereas "for Kierkegaard the ethicoreligious is primary and is above the ontological"; in Heidegger one finds "the supremacy of the ontological over the existential interest."[11] One need not accept Berdyaev's claim that Heidegger has put Kierkegaard's "genuinely existential experience into the straitjacket of rational categories" to recognize that he has developed a systematic ontology far beyond anything Kierkegaard imagined and that he probably would have found du-

---

[8]Nikolai Berdyaev, quoted in F. H. Heinemann, *Existentialism and the Human Predicament* (New York: Harper Torchbooks, 1958) 89.

[9]Kresten Nordentoft, *Kierkegaards psykologi* (Copenhagen: G. E. C. GAD, 1972) 40.

[10]Martin Heidegger, *Being and Time* (New York: Harper & Row, 1962) 494; see also 492, 497. For Heidegger's definitions of "existentiell" and "existential," see 33.

[11]*Kierkegaard and Heidegger*, 51, 143, 135.

bious at best. "Is being, then, a category?" he asks in 1842 or 1843. "The whole doctrine about being is a fatuous prelude to the doctrine of quality" (TA, 142; JP, 5: 1598).[12]

A second major difference between these thinkers, which appears to be one of temperament, can also be traced to the primary role assigned by Heidegger to Being. I am referring to Heidegger's fastidious disavowal of judgmental, not to mention polemical, intent, which contrasts sharply with Kierkegaard's natural tendency. "How fundamentally polemical I am by nature," the latter writes in a journal entry contemporary with *Two Ages* (*En literair Anmeldelse*, 1846), "I can best see in the fact that the only path by which the attacks of men can affect me is the sadness I feel on their behalf" (TA, 142; JP, 5: 5891). This is a most un-Heideggerian statement, both in its confessional tone and in the impulse that is confessed. "Any kind of polemics," Heidegger states in *What is Called Thinking?* (1954), "fails from the outset to assume the attitude of thinking. The opponent's role is not the thinking role. Thinking is thinking only when it pursues whatever speaks *for* a subject."[13] In *An Introduction to Metaphysics* (1935), Heidegger had already argued that polemics in the modern sense represents the degenerate use of an ancient concept:

> The *polemos* named here [in Heraclitus, Fragment 53] is a conflict that prevailed prior to everything divine and human, not a war in the human sense. This conflict, as Heraclitus thought it, first caused the realm of being to separate into opposites; it first gave rise to position and order and rank. In such separation, cleavages, intervals, distances, and joints opened. In the conflict a world comes into being. (Conflict does not split, much less destroy unity.

---

[12]The full quotation is as follows: "Is being, then, a category? It is by no means what quality is, namely, determinate being, determinate in itself; the accent lies on determinate, not on being. Being is neither presupposed nor predicated. In this sense Hegel is right—being is nothing; if, on the other hand, it were a quality, then one could wish enlightenment on how it becomes identical with nothing. The whole doctrine about being is a fatuous prelude to the doctrine of quality" (JP, 5: 1598).

[13]Martin Heidegger, *What is Called Thinking?* York: Harper Torchbooks, 1972) 13.

It constitutes unity, it is a binding-together, *logos*. *Polemos* and *logos* are the same.)[14]

Later in the same essay, Heidegger offers an account of how verbal polemics (unfortunately) became an authoritative kind of discourse: "logos, *phasis*, speech in the sense of statement, has become the arbiter over the being of the essent in so profound a sense that whenever one statement stands *against* another, when a contradiction, *antiphasis*, occurs, the contradictory cannot *be*. Conversely, what is not contradictory has at least the possibility of being."[15]

It is the fact of "unity" that renders mere polemics, such as arguments about the quality of modern culture, both futile and irrelevant. Heidegger's professions of moral and cultural neutrality, his disdain for *parti pris*, span his early and later phases and are both fascinating and dangerous. They fascinate because they are imperious in Heidegger's unique manner: anthropology, psychology, history, all of the "humane sciences," are devalued and in effect held hostage to "fundamental ontology." These claims are dangerous in the sense that they appear to promise more than they can actually offer. This potential discrepancy was identified by Gilbert Ryle in a review of *Being and Time* published in 1929: "The dangers lie in the undue extension of this method; if, for instance, our interpreter has, without realizing it, a theory of knowledge, or a metaphysical system, he may easily come to interpolate into the interpretations that he gives something that could never have been intuited in the exemplary instance he was examining. . . . Thus I suspect that certain theories of human nature have been interpolated into Heidegger's analysis of it; and on the other side the basic place of knowing and being-in-the-world or in any experiencing of a Meaning have been forgotten."[16]

---

[14]Martin Heidegger, *An Introduction to Metaphysics* (Garden City NY: Anchor Books, 1961) 51.

[15]Ibid., 157.

[16]Gilbert Ryle, "Heidegger's *Sein und Zeit*" [1929], in Michael Murray, ed., *Heidegger and Modern Philosophy* (New Haven: Yale University Press, 1978) 61.

More recently Karsten Harries has raised essentially the same objection: "But can *Being and Time* be considered a pure example of fundamental ontology? Do terms like 'authenticity' and 'inauthenticity' function in a purely descriptive manner? Rather, does Heidegger not choose them to call us, if not to a particular life, at least to a way of living? *Being and Time* can be read as an edifying discourse disguised as fundamental ontology. Heidegger may insist that 'inauthenticity' and 'idle talk' are not being used in a derogatory sense (SZ, 43, 167), but he himself acknowledges that finally we cannot divorce ontological inquiry from the concrete stance adopted by the inquirer."[17]

The idea that Heidegger, like Kierkegaard, summoned men through "edifying discourse" leads directly to the central question posed by this essay: How do their respective critiques of "modernity" resemble each other and how do they differ? Such critiques typically include "edifying" commentary, since few cultural critics have been able to resist offering their contemporaries the standard combination of bracing insults and improving suggestions, and I will argue that both Kierkegaard and Heidegger generally conform to this style. Both, in their respective eras, analyze "the present age" (*Nutidien, die Neuzeit*). The principal difficulty this comparison encounters is Heidegger's *sang froid*, his apparent refusal to *judge* in the traditional manner of cultural critics. Is he a cultural critic in the familiar (polemical) sense or is he really a fundamental ontologist? Can his claim to be nothing more than the latter be taken seriously?

A second problem is that of "influence." To assume that Kierkegaard and Heidegger are related in a chronological manner, to assume that the thinking of the former "precedes" that of the latter, is misleading, though I will argue below that there are important instances of apparent borrowings in *Being and Time* and perhaps in the later writings as well. It should be kept in mind that Heidegger's proclaimed point of departure—in effect, the pre-Socratics[18]—antedates both Kierkegaard and the Christology he

---

[17]Karsten Harries, "Heidegger as a Political Thinker," in *Heidegger and Modern Philosophy*, 307.

[18]See *An Introduction to Metaphysics*, 49.

embraced. Kierkegaard, too, has a theory of the ancients and the moderns,[19] but he, unlike Heidegger, does not map the decline of Western thought and experience using the Greeks as a norm.[20] (Despite its being ascribed to an "aesthetic" pseudonym, the "Ancient Tragical Motif" of *Either/Or*, vol. 1, develops a crypto-Christian theme.) He is too Hegelian to share Heidegger's awe of *the beginning*,[21] and he is too much of a Christian to view the Greeks as reverently as Heidegger did. It was Christianity, says Heidegger, that developed the doctrine that "the Greeks had reached the very gates of the absolute truth, namely the revealed truth of Christianity. . . . According to this widespread interpretation of history the Greeks are the classics of philosophy, because they were not yet full-grown Christian theologians."[22] This observation, and its acerbic humor, applies all too well to Kierkegaard: one need only think of the *Philosophical Fragments*, which present Socrates as the honored predecessor of Christ. Such diametrically opposed positions regarding Christian doctrine, as well as Heidegger's emphasis on pre-Christian thinkers, diminish the scope of "influence," but not to the degree that Heidegger would wish us to believe.

In the sections that follow we shall attempt to answer the following questions: How do these authors conceive of "the present age" and where do they find the origins of its cultural crisis? Does Kierkegaard's *Two Ages* constitute a basis for Heidegger's critique of modernity? What is the intellectual legacy of *Two Ages*?

"The Present Age"

Along with other important themes to which he gave his own imprint, Kierkegaard found the notion of the present age in He-

---

[19]See the "Ancient Tragical Motif" in *Either/Or*, vol. 1, which, although ascribed to an "aesthetic" pseudonym, may be assumed to represent in some respects Kierkegaard's own viewpoint.

[20]*What is Called Thinking?*, 19.

[21]*An Introduction to Metaphysics*, 32, 130.

[22]Ibid., 107.

gel.[23] One Hegelian text in which he found it is that section of Hegel's aesthetics that he had already plundered on behalf of "The Immediate Stages of the Erotic" in *Either/Or*, volume 1. What he found, however, is much more reminiscent of Heidegger's approach to cultural criticism than of what one finds in *Two Ages* or (in fragmentary form) throughout the pseudonymous authorship. Hegel's thesis is that "the spirit of our modern world, or, to come closer, of our religion and our intellectual culture, reveals itself as beyond the stage at which art is the highest mode assumed by man's consciousness of the absolute. The peculiar mode to which artistic production and works of art belong no longer satisfies our supreme need. We are above the level at which works of art can be venerated as divine, and actually worshiped." Hegel maintains that this development is not the disaster some would like to think: "Those who delight in grumbling and censure may set down this phenomenon for a corruption and ascribe it to the predominance of passion and selfish interests, which scare away at once the seriousness and cheerfulness of art. Or we may accuse the troubles of the present time and the complicated condition of civil and political life as hindering the feelings, entangled in minute preoccupations, from freeing themselves and rising to the higher aims of art."[24] Hegel's portrait of such cultural criticism is unflattering. His relative equanimity is understandable: he did not, after all, see the *Weltgeist* degenerating. Kierkegaard, as is well known, rejected Hegel's idea of historical development. Lacking Hegel's notion of progression in history, he viewed cultural crisis with less balance, and less confidence, than Hegel did.

Kierkegaard's critique of his age bears a much greater resemblance, in both tone and content, to Friedrich Schiller's *Letters on the Aesthetic Education of Man* (1795), addressed to a Danish prince (and Schiller's sponsor) that, on a political level, express a disillusionment with the French Revolution while preserving an allegiance to

---

[23]See Mark C. Taylor, *Journeys to Selfhood: Hegel & Kierkegaard* (Berkeley, Los Angeles, London: University of California Press, 1980) 50-51.

[24]G. W. F. Hegel, "On Art," in *On Art, Religion, Philosophy* (New York: Harper Torchbooks, 1970) 32, 32-33.

Enlightenment rationalism. Schiller's portrait of what he calls "the present age" (*das jetzige Zeitalter*) employs a Kierkegaardian rhetoric even as it calls for an eventual emancipation in terms Kierkegaard could not have accepted:

> It is true that deference to authority has declined, that its lawlessness is unmasked, and, although still armed with power, sneaks no dignity any more; men have awakened from their long lethargy (*Indolenz*) and self-deception, and by an impressive majority they are demanding the restitution of their inalienable rights. Nor are they merely demanding them: on every side they are bestirring themselves to seize by force what has, in their opinion, been wrongfully withheld from them. The fabric of the natural State is tottering, its rotten foundations are yielding, and there seems to be a *physical* possibility of setting law upon the throne, of honouring Man at last as an end in himself and making true freedom the basis of political association. Vain hope! The *moral* possibility is wanting, and the favourable moment finds an apathetic generation (*unempfängliches Geschlecht*).[25]

Schiller and Kierkegaard meet in their contempt for "an apathetic generation" that has achieved a perverse condition; indignation, in turn, breeds a rhetoric that finds contradiction everywhere: "Man portrays himself in his deeds, and what a form it is that is depicted in the drama of the present day! Here barbarity (*Verwilderung*), there enervation (*Erschlaffung*): the two extremes of human degeneracy, and both of them united in a single period of time!"[26] Schiller presents a spectacle meant to horrify. But coincident horrors that are opposed in principle (barbarity's energy *versus* enervation's apathy) are also the stuff of farce, as Kierkegaard realized. "The Unhappiest Man," of *Either/Or*, volume 1, employs this ironic device to make this hypothetical protagonist's distorted relationship to time both awful and yet somehow droll. *Two Ages* offers another combination of despair and the comic, though clearly subordinating the latter to the former. Schiller's polemic omits the comic element altogether:

---

[25]Friedrich Schiller, *On the Aesthetic Education of Man* (New York: Frederick Ungar Publishing Co., 1965) 34-35.

[26]Ibid.

> Selfishness has established its system in the very bosom of our exquisitely refined society, and we experience all the contagions and all the calamities of community without the accompaniment of a communal spirit.[27]

Community is present in its negative aspect, while the positive aspect is conspicuously absent; it is an ironic way for a community to exist.

> So we see the spirit of the time fluctuating between perverseness and brutality, between unnaturalness and mere Nature, between superstition and moral unbelief, and it is only the equilibrium of evil that still occasionally sets bounds to it.[28]

Schiller's irony is somber: community is present, but only as a phantom that is also a plague. "The equilibrium of evil" is assigned the ironic task of confining an unholy fluctuation between unwholesome extremes. All of this prefigures the rhetoric of *Two Ages*.[29]

Kierkegaard's short volume titled *En literair Anmeldelse* ("A Literary Review") is ostensibly a review of Thomasine Gyllembourg's novel *Two Ages* (1845). Its third and longest section, previously published in English as *The Present Age*, is a sustained polemic against a period of Danish history Kierkegaard was not alone in criticizing. The reign of Christian VIII, Kresten Nordentoft tells us, was "uninspiring in more than the usual degree." "The emancipation from the substance of morality and the revolt against traditional shared norms and institutions is, in Kierkegaard's opinion, the first and essential characteristic of the modern epoch. The second charac-

---

[27]Ibid., 36.

[28]Ibid., 37.

[29]Although Kierkegaard mentions Schiller on several occasions (EO, 1: 360; JP, 1: 123, 4: 4560, 5: 5982) I have found no evidence that he read the *Letters*. "For Hegel and his generation," Mark C. Taylor notes, "Schiller's *On the Aesthetic Education of Man* (1795) provided a definitive interpretation of the personal and social problems created by the industrialization and commercialization characteristic of modern society" (*Journeys to Selfhood*, 25). Taylor states that "Hegel and Kierkegaard attempt to follow Schiller's advice ['Live with your century; but do not be its creature']" (72) but he does not address the issue of whether Kierkegaard read *On the Aesthetic Education of Man*.

teristic is that this emancipation and revolt is being concealed."[30] It should be emphasized that *Two Ages*, for all its concern with ethics and "the specific gravity of the religious life," is much more than a moral tract. The quality that separates Kierkegaard's essay from Schiller's is an exasperation that has managed to preserve a rather grim sense for the absurd. It is, in addition, an exasperation that seems (ironically) to fault substance less than style, a fact that makes *Two Ages* less "edifying" than "aesthetic" in tone, even if ethics and "the religious life" are its real concerns. For Kierkegaard has chosen to render the collapse of public morality as a collapse of public style. The line that separates the ethicist's indignation from the aesthete's disappointment has been deliberately blurred.

"The present age," Kierkegaard asserts, "is essentially a *sensible, reflecting age, devoid of passion, flaring up in superficial, short-lived enthusiasm and prudentially relaxing in indolence*" (TA, 68). As the book's thesis-passage, this portrait has the formal simplicity of Schiller's conjoining of "barbarity" and "enervation." The author's basic tone of exasperation is better conveyed by a more representative passage:

> If we say of a revolutionary age that it *goes astray*, then we must say of the present age that it is *going badly*. The individual and the generation are continually contradicting themselves and each other, and therefore it would be impossible for a prosecuting attorney to establish any fact, because there is none. From the abundance of circumstantial evidence, one might conclude either that something extraordinary had happened or is about to happen. But that would be a wrong conclusion, for circumstantial evidence is the present age's only attempt at a show of strength, and its inventiveness and technical skill in contriving spellbinding mirages, and the rashness of its flares of enthusiasm employing the misleading shortcuts of proposed formal changes rate just as high in calculating shrewdness and the negative use of power as does the energetic and creative passion in the performance of the age of revolution. Exhausted by its chimerical exertions, the present age then relaxes temporarily in complete indolence. Its condition is like that of the stay-abed in the morning who has big dreams, then torpor, fol-

---

[30]Kresten Nordentoft, *Hvad siger Brand-Majoren?: Kierkegaards Opgør med sin Samtid* (Copenhagen: G. E. C. GAD, 1973) 35, 31.

lowed by a witty or ingenious inspiration to excuse staying in bed (TA, 69).

Two Ages alternates between serious analysis of a cultural crisis and a burlesque note Kierkegaard clearly felt was necessary to convey a sense of, and his active contempt for, "the present age." But the familiar quality of his humorous images stands in pointed contrast to the radical unfamiliarity of the epoch as he portrays it, an epoch whose existential structure, like that of "the unhappiest man," is depicted as radically perverse. The hallmarks of the age are meaninglessness, illusion, fraudulence, and exhaustion. It will be noted that each of these themes implies a dichotomy, and that each dichotomy suggests superior and inferior modes of experience.

Whereas "a passionate age *accelerates, raises up and overthrows, elevates and debases,* a reflective apathetic age does the opposite, it *stifles and impedes, it levels*"; whereas *"enthusiasm* is the unifying principle in a passionate age, so *envy* becomes the *negatively unifying principle* in a passionless and very reflective age." Stasis, "an enervating tension" replaces "will and energy"; "deep inward decency" is displaced by "crudeness," joy by "sniveling discontent," enthusiasm by "the garrulous common sense of experience," decision by "the fruitlessness of reflection," the "inspired venture" by the "acrobatic stunt" which dispenses with the element of real danger. The distinction between good and evil gives way to "a loose, supercilious, theoretical acquaintance with evil," "the originality of the ethical" becomes "fossilized formalism," "a narrowhearted custom and practice" (TA, 81, 80, 62, 66, 72, 78).

Not only does the existential condition of the age contradict all virtue and health, it further errs by suppressing contradiction itself. Kierkegaard introduces this idea in a discussion of the difference between character and characterlessness; it is "equivocation" (*Tvetydighed*) to be neither moral nor immoral; "equivocation" results when a "qualitative disjunction of the qualities is impaired by a gnawing reflection." This disjunction is, in effect, the principle of contradiction, which preserves not only the integrity of distinct (and opposite) experiences, but the integrity of the self as well:

The present age is essentially a sensible age, devoid of passion, and therefore it *has nullified the principle of contradiction*. . . . The existential expression of nullifying the principle of contradiction is to be in contradiction to oneself. The creative omnipotence implicit in the passion of absolute disjunction that leads the individual resolutely to make up his mind is transformed into the extensity of prudence and reflection—that is, by knowing and being everything possible to be in contradiction to oneself, that is, to be nothing at all. The principle of contradiction strengthens the individual in faithfulness to himself (TA, 97).

Kierkegaard anthropomorphizes the age because, as we shall see below, he will finally situate its fate within responsible individuals who are free to choose passion or indolence, ethics or ambiguity, action or anticipation. Kierkegaard anthropomorphizes the epoch by conceiving it as a (Hegelian) dynamic self, which progresses through self-dissatisfaction (the actual self *versus* the real self).[31] His portrait of the age is thus a portrait of man, an exercise in philosophical anthropology that is projected onto the stage of history.

Heidegger's approach to *die Neuzeit* is very different from what we find in *Two Ages*. We may begin by noting that Heidegger could never have accepted Kierkegaard's rhetorical device of personifying the age, since a rejection of anthropocentrism is a basic corollary of his doctrine of Being: "we must avoid singling out any special, particular essent, including man."[32]

A second point is that, while Kierkegaard tended to think of history as a Hegelian phantasm, Heidegger thought seriously about the problem of history in an original way, and it is within the context of this historical thinking that Heidegger's idea of "the present age" must be understood. As Nordentoft points out, Kierkegaard did situate his age within a historical context by seeing it, at least in part, as an epoch of sophistry that required the services of a new Socrates.[33] But this rather halfhearted parallel does not make Kier-

---

[31]See Mark C. Taylor, *Kierkegaard's Pseudonymous Authorship* (Princeton: Princeton University Press, 1975) 108ff.

[32]*An Introduction to Metaphysics*, 3.

[33]*Hvad siger Brand-Majoren?*, 32.

kegaard's idea of "the age" anything more than a specific segment of historical time in which a crisis has raised its threatening head. Heidegger's notion of history, however, includes the idea that "Being itself is, as self-destined, eschatological."[34] "The implications for an analysis of history of this eschatological notion of Geschichte," Thomas Langan writes, "are decisive. We are to read the historical destiny of the Eveningland [*Abendland*] much more in its beginning and in its end than in the epochs in between. . . . Consequently, the propositions of the pre-Socratics are no longer only objects of historical or philological interest, something past and dead; rather they are what is *most meaningful* for us plunged in the Evening of the Eveningland preparing itself 'for the Night of the World.'"[35] "Heidegger," W. D. Macomber has written, "finds reason to hope that history may have eschatological direction. Man may ultimately be driven—Heidegger's reading of history leads him to believe he *is* being driven—by the necessity of history to an inescapable encounter with the mystery."[36] The historical development of the West parallels the three stages of metaphysics: Greek antiquity, the Middle Ages, and the modern period that begins with Descartes and that now requires the surpassing of both metaphysics and technology. The present age is thus both "an age of maximum transition"[37] and an age of maximum peril. It is notable that Kierkegaard, on the other hand, does not use *Two Ages* to propound an eschatology of his own, if only because he does not have a conception of history that would permit him to do so. "When Heidegger asks: what is Being?" Karsten Harries points out, "he seeks to recover the Greek beginning of our historical existence, to recall us to that beginning, not to have us simply repeat it, but to transform it into a new beginning."[38] Kierkegaard has no corre-

---

[34]Martin Heidegger, *Holzwege* (Frankfurt am Main: Vittorio Klostermann, 1972) 302; quoted in *The Meaning of Heidegger*, 146.

[35]Ibid.

[36]W. B. Macomber, *The Anatomy of Disillusion: Martin Heidegger's Notion of Truth* (Evanston IL: Northwestern University Press, 1967) 112.

[37]*The Meaning of Heidegger*, 166.

[38]"Heidegger as a Political Thinker," 322.

sponding historical reality to which he could recall mankind; as a Christian polemicist, his function is to recall the Incarnation. The "historical" vision of *Two Ages* rather exemplifies a condition about which Heidegger was deeply concerned, "the historical nihilism of the modern era, in which man's fate is to be 'fateless.'"[39] One might argue, however, that to Kierkegaard the concept of fate was simply meaningless; his conception of "history" (for example, JP, 2: 1630, 1633, 1635, 1643, 1647, 1648; PF, 93-94) is nowhere deterministic. It is worth noting that, for all his denunciations of the age, Kierkegaard does not see individuals as doomed to succumb to that monstrous "public" that is "a kind of colossal something, an abstract void and vacuum that is all and nothing." For Kierkegaard, as for Heidegger, the present age is a challenge that man can, but may not, meet. The "public," he states, "is the cruel abstraction by which individuals will be religiously educated—or be destroyed" (TA, 93).

As early as *Being and Time* (1927), Heidegger had demonstrated an awareness of "the present age" as a concept: "authentic historiology becomes a way in which the 'today' gets deprived of its character as present; in other words, it becomes a way of painfully detaching oneself from the falling publicness of the 'today.' As authentic, the historiology that is both monumental and antiquarian is necessarily a critique of the 'Present.'"[40] In *An Introduction to Metaphysics* (1935) and "The Age of the World Picture" (1938), Heidegger makes his critique of the present quite specific. In the earlier work, he traces to America and Russia a leveling "demonism," one aspect of which is "the emasculation of the spirit through misinterpretation" which, in turn, has four related aspects: (1) the reinterpretation of the spirit as *intelligence*, or mere cleverness; (2) the fall of this spirit to the level of a manipulable tool; (3) the development of culture into autonomous and separate branches; and (4) "the spirit as utilitarian intelligence and the spirit as culture become holiday ornaments cultivated along with many other

---

[39]David Couzens Hoy, "History, Historicity, and Historiography" in *Being and Time*," in *Heidegger and Modern Philosophy*, 342.

[40]*Being and Time*, 449.

things."[41] In the later essay, Heidegger identifies "the essential phenomena of the modern age" as science, machine technology, art's movement "into the purview of aesthetics," the consummation of human activity as "culture," and a "loss of the gods" that leads to the substitution of mere "religious experience" for a more "decisive religiosity"[42]—a Kierkegaardian thesis indeed.

The difference between Heidegger and comparable cultural critics of the 1930s–Karl Jaspers, José Ortega y Gasset, and Johan Huizinga among others—is that he alone claims to eschew judgment. Ortega's ambivalence toward the revolt of the masses is not to be confused with the seigneurial, and somehow improbable, *hauteur* which Heidegger demonstrates as a cultural critic who is above offering cultural criticism implying some sort of committed judgment. In *What is Called Thinking?* Heidegger denounces that style of interpretation that "has in view only the adverse and somber traits of the age." "This tune," he continues, "is familiar to us all *ad nauseam*. A generation ago it was 'The Decline of the West.' Today we speak of 'loss of center.' People everywhere trace and record the decay, the destruction, the imminent annihilation of the world. We are surrounded by a special breed of reportorial novels that do nothing but wallow in such deterioration and depression."[43] In contrast, says Heidegger, "when our assertion speaks of the thought-provoking age and of what is most thought-provoking in it (*der bedenklichen Zeit und ihrem Bedenklichsten*), it is in no way tuned to a key of melancholy and despair (*auf den Ton des Trübsinns und der Verzweiflung gestimmt*). It is not drifting blindly toward the worst. It is not pessimistic. But neither is the assertion optimistic."[44] Heidegger rejects the categories of optimism and pessimism because they derive from "a peculiar relatedness of man to what we call his-

---

[41]*An Introduction to Metaphysics*, 40.

[42]Martin Heidegger, "The Age of the World Picture," in *The Question Concerning Technology* (New York: Harper Colophon Books, 1977) 116-17.

[43]*What is Called Thinking?*, 29.

[44]Ibid., 31.

tory" that "is by now habitual to us."[45] What Heidegger rejects is, in effect, a vulgar calculus of cultural value. The decisive thing about "judgments on the present" is "not that they evaluate everything negatively, but that they evaluate at all. They determine the value, so to speak the price range into which the age belongs."[46] "At issue here," as Dan Magurshak notes, "is more than a pretension not to be polemical; it is more a matter of a network of ways of thinking that sharply distinguishes the Heideggerian critique of modernity from SK's and that calls into question the nature and meaning of polemics."[47]

Two decades earlier, in *An Introduction to Metaphysics*, Heidegger had made the same point: "To speak of optimisim or pessimism is to look on being-there [*Dasein*] as a business proposition, successful or unsuccessful. This attitude is expressed in Schopenhauer's well-known words: 'Life is a business that doesn't cover its costs.' What makes this proposition untrue is not that 'life' does cover its costs in the end, but that life (as being-there) is simply not a business. True, for the last few centuries it has become one. And that is why Greek being-there is so mysterious to us."[48]

In the same volume Heidegger had delivered a peroration reminiscent of the Spenglerian style he disavows:

> The spiritual decline of the earth is so far advanced that the nations are in danger of losing the last bit of spiritual energy that makes it possible to see the decline (taken in relation to the history of "being"), and to appraise it as such. This simple observation has nothing to do with *Kulturpessimismus*, and of course it has nothing to do with any sort of optimism either; for the darkening of the world, the flight of the gods, the destruction of the earth, the transformation of man into a mass, the hatred and suspicion of everything free and creative, have assumed such proportions

[45]Ibid., 22.

[46]Ibid., 38.

[47]Personal communication to the author.

[48]*An Introduction to Metaphysics*, 149.

throughout the earth that such childish categories as pessimism and optimism have long since become absurd.[49]

This passage, and others like it, demonstrate that the rhetoric of cultural conservatism was by no means foreign to Heidegger's idiom, even as he dissociated himself from "judgments on the present." Heidegger's disdain for the "childish" emotionalism of optimistic and pessimistic assessments is at base a refusal to treat the "results" of history positivistically, as though they were products that could be weighed and measured; optimism and pessimism, Heidegger assumes, require calculations that he rejects as chimerical. The failure of this vulgar positivism may be seen in a wider context. "Heidegger," as Harries notes, "sees the history of the West as the working out of just one theme: our destiny is governed by the history of metaphysics, which conceals a finally futile search for security"—including, presumably, the illusory assessments of historical "results" described above. "Unless he learns to take a step beyond that history, man will lose his essence. Only this linear view of history leads Heidegger to his despairing analysis of the present age as so deeply fallen that all attempts to criticize and reform are already caught up in that fall."[50] We may note that Kierkegaard, too, rejects the spirit of calculation. In *Two Ages*, he remarks that "today we are everywhere lavishly regaled with pragmatic rules, a calculus of considerations (*Klogskabsregler, Hensyns-Beregninger*), etc" (TA, 70). But Kierkegaard does not interpret this as a temptation to think wrongly about history, but rather as a temptation to lose the self in a philistine sort of reflective activity.

The Question of Influence

It is very likely that Heidegger read Theodor Haecker's translation of the most important section of *Two Ages* ("The Present Age," (TA, 68-110) in an issue of the periodical *Der Brenner* published in Innsbruck in 1914; this material also appeared as a book in

---

[49]Ibid., 31.

[50]"Heidegger as a Political Thinker," 328.

1922.[51] It is less probable, if still conceivable, that Heidegger's treatment of such themes as "idle talk" (*Gerede*), "curiosity" (*Neugier*), and ambiguity (*Zweideutigkeit*) in *Being and Time* represents a series of independent discoveries. "Idle talk" and "ambiguity" appear in *Two Ages*, while "curiosity" is discussed in *The Concept of Anxiety* (CA 39, 57, 138), the value of which Heidegger acknowledges.[52] As for possible alternate sources, it may be noted that, in *The Protestant Ethic and the Spirit of Capitalism* (1904-1905), Max Weber uses the terms "faules Gerede" and the English "idle talk" (both in quotation marks).[53]

"Comparing" Kierkegaard and Heidegger is, at the very least, an intriguing exercise. Relevant to their respective critiques of modernity one finds two types of similarity. First, there are apparent similarities that upon closer examination turn out to be quite different interpretations of the same theme. And second, there are genuinely shared themes that constitute the real foundation of the comparative enterprise.

To the first category belong Christianity as a historical phenomenon and anti-Hegelianism. What, then, is Heidegger's relationship to Christianity?

Heidegger's early and formative interests were, as Pöggeler has shown, of an essentially Christian nature. The question of basic import for the early Heidegger was what type of human self-understanding is contained in the early Christian experience and way of life? It is this Christian experience of man's thrownness, his radical finitude, alienage, and his being a stranger in the world, as well as

---

[51]*Der Brenner* 4 (15 July 1914): 815-49, 869-86; *Kritik der Gegenwart* (Innsbruck: Brenner Verlag, 1922). I am deeply indebted to Habib C. Malik (Harvard University) and Allan Janik (Boston University Center for the Philosophy and History of Science) for bringing this information to my attention. Concerning the likelihood that Heidegger read this material, see Allan Janik, "Haecker, Kierkegaard, and *Der Brenner*: A Contribution to the Reception of Kierkegaard in the German-Speaking World," in this volume.

[52]*Being and Time*, 492, 494.

[53]Max Weber, "Die protestantische Ethik und der Geist des Kapitalismus," in *Gesammelte Aufsätze zur Religionssoziologie*, vol. 1 (Tübingen: Verlag von J. C. B. Mohr [Paul Siebeck], 1934) 167, 187.

the insignificance of the world itself (and all worldly science), which are articulated in Heidegger's "existentialism," and it is this interest in an experience alien to Greek rationalism that eventually provoked Heidegger's rupture with the tradition and, consequently, with Husserl.[54]

It would appear to be a long step from this rather general depiction of "the early Christian experience" to Kierkegaard's Christianity in particular, but this is not necessarily the case. "In essence," Thomas Langan comments, "the absence of the Living God and of his Saints from the destruction of the historical destiny of ontologies [in Heidegger's treatment of the Middle Ages] is an index of how Kierkegaardian Heidegger's concept of a Christianity would have to be if he were to believe in Christ. It is as though our author were reflecting the Protestant thinker's thought, when he tells us that the Christian is an isolated phenomenon, outside the current of history, voluntarily cut off from the realm of *Denken*, plunged into the night of nothingness, beyond all *Seiende*, alone in the depths of mystery where the singular encounter with the Singular God may take place."[55] It will be noted that Langan takes care to keep this connection between Heidegger and Kierkegaard a hypothetical one, which is probably more of a link than Heidegger would have conceded. "The new German philosophy [of the 1920s and 1930s]," one observer points out, "found a way of disposing of the Christian Kierkegaard by ignoring the Christian connotation of his philosophical concepts . . . and Heidegger makes himself doubly secure against any possible misreading by emphatic statements denying the relevance of any concept of God for an understanding of his philosophy."[56] In *Being and Time* Heidegger is critical of the "inadequate ontological foundations" of "the anthropology of Christianity" and "those residues of Christian theology within

---

[54]Gary B. Madison, "Phenomenology and Existentialism: Husserl and the End of Idealism," in Frederick Elliston and Peter McCormick, eds. *Husserl: Expositions and Appraisals* (South Bend IN: University of Notre Dame Press, 1977) 260.

[55]*The Meaning of Heidegger*, 163.

[56]Helen M. Mustard, "Søren Kierkegaard in German Literary Periodicals, 1860-1930," *Germanic Review* 26 (April 1951): 101.

philosophical problematics that have not as yet been radically extruded."[57] As we have already noted above, in *An Introduction to Metaphysics* Christianity is accused of disfiguring antiquity and misinterpreting Heraclitus' doctrine of the logos, a perverse influence to which Heidegger responds with impatient sarcasm:

> Heraclitus's doctrine of the logos was regarded as the forerunner of the logos which figures in the New Testament—in the prologue to the Gospel of St. John. The logos is Christ. But Heraclitus already spoke of the logos and this meant that the Greeks had reached the very gates of the absolute truth, namely the revealed truth of Christianity. . . . According to this widespread interpretation of history the Greeks are the classics of philosophy, because they were not yet full-grown Christian theologians.[58]

But this is exactly what Kierkegaard does in the *Philosophical Fragments*, which features a comparison of Socrates and Christ, pointedly treating the former as a kind of honorary Christian, a transformation that is amplified in the *Concluding Unscientific Postscript*. For the philohellenic Heidegger, such a rewriting of history amounts to a vulgar sacrilege: "But we shall first listen to Heraclitus himself before deciding what to think of him as a forerunner of Christianity."[59]

There is, in short, a great deal of evidence that suggests that the hypothetical "early Christian" tie between these two thinkers is balanced by their utterly different estimations of Christianity's historical significance. There is, however, at least one important point regarding Christianity on which they seem to agree. "Everyone with some capacity for observation," Kierkegaard writes in *The Point of View* [1848], "who seriously considers what is called Christendom [*Christenheden*], or the conditions in a so-called Christian country, must surely be assailed by profound misgivings. What does it mean that all these thousands call themselves Christians as a matter of course? These many, many men, of whom the greater part, so far as one can judge, live in categories quite foreign to

[57]*Being and Time*, 74, 272.

[58]*An Introduction to Metaphysics*, 107.

[59]Ibid.

Christianity [*Christendommen*]!" (PV, 22). This famous distinction is, of course, the basis of Kierkegaard's (eventually fanatical) campaign against the Danish church, and it reappears in Heidegger's essay "Nietzsches Wort 'Gott ist tot'":

> Christianism [*Christentum*] in this sense [in the sense of a *Weltanschauung*] and the Christianity [*Christlichkeit*] the New Testament faith are not the same thing. Even a non-Christian life can give its approval to Christianism and utilize it as a power factor; inversely, a Christian life does not necessarily need Christianity. . . . As long as these essential distinctions are despised, we shall never cease to evolve among inferior visions of the world and of the combats that are unleashed there.[60]

The irony of this apparent coincidence of views is that Heidegger has taken this distinction, not from Kierkegaard, but from Nietzsche: "Christianity [*Christentum*] is for Nietzsche the historical, world-political manifestation of the church and its claim to power within the conformation of Western man and his (*seiner neuzeitlichen Kultur*)."[61] Nietzsche and Heidegger make Kierkegaard's distinction between Christendom and Christianity, but they do not make it as Christians. It is Kierkegaard (in *Two Ages*) who recommends "the infinite liberation of the religious life" (TA, 85).

Do Kierkegaard and Heidegger share an anti-Hegelian doctrine? "Kierkegaard," Calvin O. Schrag has pointed out, "had already made us conscious of the comic predicament of the Hegelian, who in his preoccupation with the universal march of objective history and the mediation of logical categories forgets his personal existence. Similarly Heidegger cautions us against losing sight of the historical *Dasein* in our study of 'strange cultures' and world history."[62] Perhaps Schrag has in mind this passage from *Being and Time*: "Dasein has had its historicality so thoroughly uprooted by tradition that it confines its interest to the multiformity of possible types, directions, and standpoints of philosophical activity in the most exotic and alien of cultures; and by this very interest it seeks

---

[60]The translation is by Langan (164); see *Holzwege*, 203.

[61]*Holzwege*, 202-203.

[62]*Existence and Freedom*, 11-12.

to veil the fact that it has no ground of its own to stand on."[63] Elsewhere in the same volume Heidegger refers to "the most exotic and manifold cultures and forms of Dasein" as "merely a semblance. At bottom this plethora of information can seduce us into failing to recognize the real problem."[64] Kierkegaard has made essentially the same point—and certainly at Hegel's expense—in *Fear and Trembling*: "People commonly travel around the world to see rivers and mountains, new stars, birds of rare plumage, queerly deformed fishes, ridiculous breeds of men—they abandon themselves to the bestial stupor [*den dyriske Stupor*] which gapes at [*gloer paa*] existence, and they think they have seen something" (FT, 49).[65] Both writers warn of the seductive effects of sheer diversity, which can be a dangerous distraction from truth. But has Heidegger actually adopted a "Kierkegaardian" theme? Not necessarily: for Heidegger apparently found the idea of a promiscuous "sightless gaping" in Parmenides.[66]

Both Kierkegaard and Heidegger offer important arguments against Hegel. The pseudonymous authorship, for example, is filled with anti-Hegelian polemics of varying subtlety. In at least one respect, Heidegger's doctrine differs from that of Hegel for essentially Kierkegaardian reasons. Langan notes that "in positing the absolutized subject as temporal explanation for the presence of all things-that-are, Hegel constructed a philosophy that forms the absolute opposite pole to an existential doctrine of temporality based on a thinking of the truth of Dasein"; there is an "abyss separating the unconditioned will of the absolute in Hegel from the finite freedom of the Dasein in *Sein und Zeit*."[67] Heidegger's Dasein represents, as is well known, an innovation on what Kierkegaard calls in *Two Ages* "the category 'individuality'" (TA, 84); that Heidegger does not accept Kierkegaard's (Christian) notion of the self

---

[63]*Being and Time*, 43.

[64]Ibid., 76-77.

[65]See also *Being and Time*, 61.

[66]*An Introduction to Metaphysics*, 145.

[67]*The Meaning of Heidegger*, 176, 181.

is, in this context, less important than the fact that both "Dasein" and "the self" are accorded that "finite freedom" and autonomy that Hegel's individual, subject to the "claim of the World-Spirit," does not enjoy.[68] But do Kierkegaard and Heidegger share a *polemical* anti-Hegelianism? The answer is no, and to account for it we must look beyond Heidegger's principled aversion to the polemical mode. In *An Introduction to Metaphysics*, Heidegger makes it clear that he does not subscribe to "what is popularly and succinctly called the 'collapse of German idealism'"—a collapse in which Kierkegaard was only too happy to participate. "It was not German idealism that collapsed," Heidegger states; "rather, the age was no longer strong enough to stand up to the greatness, breadth, and originality of that spiritual world. . . ." The irony of Heidegger's argument is that it appears to lead directly to a Kierkegaardian text, namely *Two Ages*. "The lives of men," Heidegger writes, "began to slide into a world which lacked that depth from out of which the essential always comes to man and comes back to man, so compelling him to become superior and making him act in conformity to a rank. All things sank to the same level."[69] Kierkegaard's observations on "leveling" (*Nivelleringen*) in *Two Ages* are often accorded a prophetic status. In *Being and Time*, Heidegger uses the terms "level down" (*einebnen*) and "level off" (*nivellieren*) to denote analogous phenomena. "Distantiality, averageness, and leveling down [*Einebnung*], as ways of being for the 'they' [*das Man*], constitute what we know as 'publicness' [*die Öffentlichkeit*]." "The only time one knows is the public time which has been leveled off [*nivelliert*] and which belongs to everyone—and that means, to nobody."[70] In *An Introduction to Metaphysics* Heidegger finds the "demonic" results of levelling at work in America and Russia—a commonly heard theme in European right-wing circles during the 1930s. Is Heidegger's *Nivellierung* Kierkegaard's *Nivellering*? It is impossible to say. What *is* clear is that, even as they both take their points of departure in the "collapse of German idealism," one celebrates, and the other calls

---

[68]See G. W. F. Hegel, *The Philosophy of History* (New York: Dover, 1956) 37.

[69]*An Introduction to Metaphysics*, 37-38.

[70]*Being and Time*, 165, 477.

into question, the collapse itself. But for both this "collapse," whatever its real nature, has brought on "the present age."

Kierkegaard and Heidegger appear to differ radically with respect to another major Hegelian theme. As W. D. Macomber points
out, both Hegel and Heidegger posit "a total context of intelligibil-
ity from which all things and propositions draw their meaning and
significance." As the *discovering* form of being, Dasein discovers
other beings which belong to "a context or organized whole within
which [they are] accessible to discovery. This context or organized
whole Heidegger calls the world (*Welt*),"[71] while Hegel terms it "the
Absolute": "The truth is the whole."[72] Given Kierkegaard's hostility to this aspect of Hegelian philosophy, it is not surprising that he
abstains from offering an analogous concept of his own. (A. de
Waelhens's claim that "the *world* of *Sein und Zeit* is, in more than
one way, the God of Kierkegaard"[73] seems to me mistaken. Heidegger's preferred definition of *world* in *Being and Time* is "that
'*wherein*' a factical Dasein as such can be said to 'live.'")[74] This ab-
stention goes hand in hand with Kierkegaard's essentially negative
approach to the objective world and history, which he seems to
conceive of in other than Hegelian terms, as the following quotations from the *Journal* suggest: "The development of world history
is something like arguments—the discussion gets so involved with
parenthetical matters that finally it is almost impossible to recollect
the original issue" [1837]. Or: "With the help of history we want to
understand everything—and with the help of history we still only
understand everything inversely or backwards, or we understand
nothing. We constantly come to a wrong conclusion" [1848] (JP, 2:
1631, 1640). One can make too much of such statements, the "dialectical" formulation of which serves a polemical intent rather than
a disbelief in history itself. But the fact remains that Kierkegaard's

---

[71]*The Anatomy of Disillusion*, 23, 29.

[72]G. W. F. Hegel, *The Phenomenology of Mind* (New York: Harper Torchbooks,
1967) 81.

[73]A. de Waelhens, *La philosophie de Martin Heidegger* (Louvain: Publications
Universitaires de Louvain, 1955) 333.

[74]*Being and Time*, 93.

thinking in *Two Ages* is epochal rather than historical; its only concession to the idea of historical development is "the ultimate [*absolute*] difference between the modern era and antiquity" (TA, 92). As a cultural polemic, *Two Ages* scrutinizes a moment within history rather than the process of history. Such an approach to history has a basically rhetorical rationale.

Heidegger's famous discussion of the "fallen" character of "everyday Dasein" in *Being and Time* features three phenomena characteristic of Dasein in its inauthentic state: "idle talk" (*Gerede*), "curiosity" (*Neugier*), and "ambiguity" (*Zweideutigkeit*). One of the striking features of Heidegger scholarship is the apparent assumption that Heidegger pulled these terms out of a hat. Edward A. Tiryakian, one of a few (the first may have been Jean Wahl) to point out that Heidegger's concept of the "they" (*das Man*) corresponds to (he does not say: derives from) Kierkegaard's idea of the "public" (*Publikum*) in *Two Ages*, makes no mention of the fact that Heidegger's three inauthentic modes are found in Kierkegaard, two of them in *Two Ages*.[75] Even Schrag, who offers the most detail in this regard, does not suggest that Heidegger's terms may have come from *Two Ages*. "Heidegger, the ontologist," he points out, "has formulated Kierkegaard's fragmentary but illuminating descriptions of the unauthentic qualification of existence into a set of interrelated 'existentials' which delineate the universal structures of the concrete experience of unauthenticity."[76] In fact, Kierkegaard's contribution is less "fragmentary" than this author implies.

(1) Idle talk, Heidegger says, is constituted by "gossiping and passing the word along" (*Nach- und Weiterreden*), it "discourages any new inquiry and any disputation, and in a peculiar way suppresses them and holds them back."[77] *Two Ages* is filled with references to degenerate speech forms signifying the loss of passion and character: "gossip and rumor" (*Bysnak og Rygte*) (TA, 63), "talkativeness" (*Snaksomhed*) (TA, 64), "to chatter" (*at snakke*) (TA, 97),

---

[75]Edward A. Tiryakian, *Sociologism and Existentialism* (Englewood Cliffs NJ: Prentice-Hall, Inc., 1962) 128.

[76]*Existence and Freedom*, 45.

[77]*Being and Time*, 212, 213.

"pure drivel" (*Sladder*) (TA, 106), "to be loquacious" (*at raisonere*) (TA, 103). "By this chattering the distinction between what is private and what is public is nullified in a private-public garrulousness, which is just about what the public is. For the public [*Publikum*] is public opinion [*det Offentlige*] that is interested in what is utterly private" (TA, 100). Both authors address the phenomenon of "idle talk," conjoined with the idea of a public sphere, as a threat to the authentic self of the individual, but they stress different themes. Kierkegaard focuses on the incursion of the public into the private sphere, while Heidegger emphasizes the idea that "idle talk is a closing-off [*ein Verschliessen*], since to go back to the ground of what is talked about is something which it *leaves undone*."[78] Kierkegaard stresses the threatened status of the individual, Heidegger the threat posed to "any new inquiry and any disputation [*jedes neue Fragen und alle Auseinandersetzung*]."[79] It is a symptomatic difference.

(2) Curiosity, says Heidegger, "has become free . . . not in order to understand what is seen (that is, to come into a Being towards it) but *just* in order to see. It seeks novelty only in order to leap from it anew to another novelty."[80] Such a curiosity represents a modification of understanding (*Verstehen*) that Heidegger, for reasons to be discussed below, chooses not to call degenerate or "negative." Kierkegaard, too, conceives of a type of curiosity that functions, not as an instrument of the understanding, nor as an encouragement to faith, but as a distraction from the truth. In *The Concept of Anxiety*, the usefulness of which Heidegger acknowledges, Kierkegaard locates curiosity within the sphere of a (religiously) inadequate psychology: "If sin is dealt with in psychology, the mood becomes that of persistent observation, like the fearlessness of a secret agent, but not that of the victorious flight of earnestness out of sin. . . . The mood of psychology would be antipathetic curiosity [*Nysgjerrighed*], whereas the proper mood is earnestness expressed as courageous resistance" (CA, 15). This type of curiosity is degen-

---

[78]Ibid., 213.

[79]Ibid.

[80]Ibid., 216.

erate only in the sense that, when confronted with the phenomenon of sin, it is out of its depth. *Two Ages*, however, offers a type of
curiosity, even if the word itself is not used, which resembles Heidegger's interpretation. As a symptom of the "formlessness" of the
age Kierkegaard mentions "a frivolous philandering among great
diversities" (*den leflende Omgang mellem det Forskjelligste med det Forskjelligste*) (TA, 100). If he were to imagine the public as a person,
"more sluggish than he is evil," it would be one who "saunters
around looking for variety" (*slendrer da til Afvexling denne Person
omkring*) (TA, 94). Both Kierkegaard and Heidegger honor the ancient injunction against all that glitters, the temptation of the multifarious. In *Two Ages* it is "glittering illusion" (*glimrende Blendvaerk*)
(TA, 89); in *Being and Time* it is "the constant possibility of distraction [*Zerstreuung*]."[81] Curiosity in this sense is an essentially passive
perceptual promiscuity. Unlike Kierkegaard, however, Heidegger
does not associate this "existential characteristic" with a specific
epoch or type of epoch.

(3) "The present age is essentially a sensible age, devoid of passion, and therefore it *had nullified the principle of contradiction*" (TA,
97). This is Kierkegaard's preface to "ambiguity" (*Tvetydigheden*,
cognate to Heidegger's term and also translated as "equivocation")
in *Two Ages*. Both the individual and the age, if sufficiently vacuous,
can be characterized by ambiguity. "Morality is character; character
is something engraved χαρασσω but the sea has no character, nor
does sand, nor abstract common sense, either, for character is inwardness. As energy, immorality is also character. But it is equivocation to be neither one nor the other, and it is existential
equivocation [*Tvetydighed i Tilvaerelsen*] when the qualitative disjunction of the qualities is impaired by a gnawing reflection" (TA,
77-78; 80). The ambiguity of characterlessness is an essentially
"aesthetic" notion which criticizes a lack of passion, a criterion
Kierkegaard also applies to the present age: "The demoralization of
absolute monarchy and the decline of revolutionary periods have
frequently been described, but the decline of an age devoid of passion is just as degenerate, even though less striking because of its

---

[81]Ibid., 216.

ambiguity" (TA, 94). Here, as in the case of idle talk, Kierkegaard addresses the issue of "character." Heidegger's analysis of ambiquity addresses both the condition of the individual (he does not employ so judgmental a term as "character") and the problem of understanding that arose in conjunction with idle talk and curiosity. First, the ambiguity that results when it "becomes impossible to decide what is disclosed in a genuine understanding, and what is not" extends"even to Dasein's Being towards itself"[82]—presumably a reference to the problem of the individual's authenticity. Ambiguity can also subvert understanding by clouding the distinction between what is actually worth knowing and what is not; "Idle talk and curiosity take care in their ambiguity to ensure that what is genuinely and newly created [*das echt und neu Geschaffene*] is out of date as soon as it emerges before the public. . . . This ambiguity is always tossing to curiosity that which it seeks; and it gives idle talk the semblance of having everything decided in it."[83] Once again, Heidegger emphasizes the hazards encountered by Dasein as it engages in the discovery of other beings.

"The expression 'idle talk,'" Heidegger states, "is not to be used here in a 'disparanging' signification. Terminologically, it signifies a positive phenomenon which constitutes the kind of Being of everyday Dasein's understanding and interpreting."[84] This is, in effect, the claim Heidegger makes elsewhere regarding his cultural criticism, namely, that it is not judgmental. But how seriously can we take Heidegger's disclaimers of impartiality? Harries points out that: "If everyday language is idle talk, how can we claim that the guiding thread of the 'proximally and for the most part' leads us to anything like firm ground?" Given Heidegger's interpretation of idle talk, "how can we separate inauthenticity and community?"[85] Heidegger claims that idle talk, curiosity, and ambiguity are "def-

---

[82]Ibid., 217.

[83]Ibid., 218-19.

[84]Ibid., 211.

[85]Karsten Harries, "Fundamental Ontology and the Search for Man's Place," in *Heidegger and Modern Philosophy*, 74, 78.

inite existential characteristics" of Dasein in which" there is revealed a basic kind of Being which belongs to everydayness; we call this the 'falling' of Dasein." But "falling," itself a definite existential characteristic of Dasein, "does not express any negative evaluation," nor can we ascribe to it "the sense of a bad and deplorable ontical property of which, perhaps, more advanced stages of human culture might be able to rid themselves."[86]

Such passages express Heidegger's characteristic reserve and his rejection of polemics. It is to be noted that he rejects, with sardonic irony, the possibility that "more advanced stages of human culture" will do away with an aspect of man considered by some to be "bad and deplorable." Kierkegaard, by comparison, is both judgmental and polemical. In *Two Ages* a key term is "indolence" (*Indolents*), which derives in part from ambiguity: "In this state of indolent laxity, more and more individuals will aspire to be nobodies in order to become the public, . ." or, "Exhausted by its chimerical exertions, the present age then relaxes temporarily in complete indolence" (TA, 94, 69).

Kierkegaard's Christian anthropology, as it is presented in *The Sickness Unto Death* (1849), assumes that human nature harbors an inherent indolence, a spiritual passivity, for which the individual is ultimately responsible. "Very often a person in despair probably has a dim view of his own state, although here again the nuances are myriad" (SUD, 48). Most people tend to preserve, rather than abolish, the semi-obscurity (Kierkegaard ascribes to all obscurity "a dialectical interplay of knowledge and will") which permits them to remain in despair, with its illusory "security and tranquility" (*Tryghed og Beroligelse*) (SUD, 24). Heidegger, too, maintains that the "they" "brings Dasein a *tranquillity [Beruhigung]*, for which everything is 'in the best of order' and all doors are open. . . . When Dasein, tranquillized and 'understanding' everything, thus compares itself with everything, it drifts along towards an alienation in which its ownmost potentiality-for-Being is hidden from it. Falling Being-in-the-world is not only tempting and tranquillizing, it is at

---

[86]*Being and Time*, 219, 220.

the same time *alienating*."[87] But Heidegger waxes positively droll in his dissent from the Christian position: "It follows that our existential-ontological Interpretation makes no ontical assertion about the 'corruption of human Nature,' not because the necessary evidence is lacking [!], but because the problematic of this Interpretation is *prior* to any assertion about corruption or incorruption. . . . Ontically, we have not decided whether man is 'drunk with sin' and in the *status corruptionis*."[88]

Ultimately, in the later Heidegger, this difference between Christian and non-Christian existentialisms derives from different conceptions of freedom and responsibility. Kierkegaard knows that human freedom is not absolute, but his polemical approach to the theme of individual responsibility creates a rhetorical effect implying that it is. The difference between the two is, however, more than one of rhetorical emphasis. "Man," says Heidegger, "does not 'possess' freedom. At the best the contrary is true: freedom possesses man."[89] Heidegger's later concept of freedom, as Macomber points out, "is not a faculty or property of man: it is not the faculty of free choice or a property of the will."[90] It is for this reason that Heidegger rejects the "indolence" thesis, even as it is implicit in his notion of "fallenness." As late as *What is Called Thinking?*, he is still refusing to employ its implicit dichotomy between activity and passivity: "We would be making matters too easy for ourselves if we simply took the view that the dominion of one-track thinking has grown out of human laziness."[91]

It would be facile to claim that the comparative evidence presented above "speaks for itself". Given Heidegger's erudition, and the often bizarre channels through which intellectual influence flows, the question of influence cannot be finally resolved. What we can point to is a series of striking correspondences that seem to

---

[87]Ibid., 222.

[88]Ibid., 224.

[89]Quoted in *The Anatomy of Disillusion*, 99.

[90]Ibid., 98.

[91]*What is Called Thinking?*, 26.

link these two critiques of modernity. Is it simply fortuitous that Heidegger's existential characteristics have Kierkegaardian antecedents, that both thinkers criticize the press (TA, 90, 93),[92] that both comment on the futility of sheer speed as a human achievement? (TA, 64, 59)[93] It is probable that Kierkegaard's influence has been underestimated. It is, for example, characteristic that, in a recent monograph on Heidegger, one of the few that even attempts to find the origins of "Heidegger's diagnosis of individual alienation in modern society," George Steiner contents himself with those vague references to Kierkegaard that have become a standard feature of Heidegger commentary.[94] It is clear that, even today, the critique of modernity presented in *Two Ages* has not achieved the recognition it deserves.

The Legacy of Two Ages

Kierkegaard's critique of modernity has given rise to a legacy of undetermined origin. How else can one formulate the uncertainties this essay has attempted to diminish? "A century after his death," Tiryakian writes, "the same general thoughts are still being written about the crisis situation of the individual and its origin—the only major change that has occurred in the interim is that more and more persons have come to share the early diagnosis of Kierkegaard."[95] Is this in fact the case? And, if so, what has been the extent of Kierkegaard's influence?

In *Die geistige Situation der Zeit* (1931), Karl Jaspers assigns *Two Ages* a unique status:

---

[92]Martin Heidegger, "The Question Concerning Technology," in *The Question Concerning Technology*, 18.

[93]*Being and Time*, 140; "The Age of the World Picture," 135; *An Introduction to Metaphysics*, 31.

[94]George Steiner, *Martin Heidegger* (New York: Penguin Books, 1980) 108-109, 147-48.

[95]*Sociologism and Existentialism*, 125.

In the Hegelian dialectic an image of universal history was the mode in which the present became aware of itself; but there was an alternative possibility, that of ignoring the remote riches of concrete history, and of concentrating attention on the present. . . . Kierkegaard was the first to undertake a comprehensive critique of his time, one distinguished from all previous attempts by its earnestness. This critique of his was the first to be applicable to the age in which we are now living, and reads as if it had been written but yesterday.[96]

A half-century after Jaspers wrote these words, the critique of mass society has not only persisted, it has burgeoned into a dogma for which Marxist commentators hold both Kierkegaard and Heidegger responsible. One aspect of the Marxist critique of existentialism is a denigration of that critique of mass society which commences with *Two Ages*. An East German commentator labels the existentialist position a "pseudo-revolutionary, romantic critique of an abstract 'modern' society" that is conceived only in terms of "a 'negative' conception of industrial society."[97] In *The Destruction of Reason* (1962), Georg Lukács ridicules Karl Löwith's comparison[98] of *Two Ages* with *The Communist Manifesto* and calls Kierkegaard a "romantic anti-capitalist."[99]

There is, however, a more nuanced critique of Kierkegaard of Marxist derivation: that of Theodor W. Adorno, whose opinion of Kierkegaard's significance as a social thinker appears to have become more favorable over the years. Even in his early (1929-1930), and hostile, study of Kierkegaard, Adorno acknowledges that Kierkegaard has recognized "the misery of high-capitalist conditions." And in an appendix dating from the late 1930s he goes so far as to concede that: "In Kierkegaard's hostility to the masses, as conservative as it may present itself as being, there is still, as in the case of Nietzsche, a certain insight into the crippling dismemberment [*Verstümmeling*] of man through mechanisms of domination which turn

---

[96]Karl Jaspers, *Man in the Modern Age* (Garden City NY: Anchor Books, 1957) 10.

[97]Hans-Martin Gerlach, "Spätburgerliche Philosophie und Konservatismus," *Deutsche Zeitschrift für Philosophie* (Berlin) 24:5 (1976): 612.

[98]See Karl Löwith, *From Hegel to Nietzsche* (Garden City NY: Anchor Books, 1967).

[99]Georg Lukács, *Die Zerstörung der Vernunft* (Neuwied am Rhein: Luchterhand, 1962) 19, 254.

him into the mass."[100] It is also interesting to see that in the *Dialectic of Enlightenment* (1947), written with Max Horkheimer, Adorno specifically credits "the paradoxical Christians, the anti-official philosophers, from Pascal by way of Lessing and Kierkegaard to Barth"[101] with a religiosity specifically opposed to the spiritual demands exacted by anti-Semitism. It should also be noted that this important work of Frankfurt Marxism relies heavily on an idiom that must be regarded as at least partly of Kierkegaardian origin. When, for example, Horkheimer and Adorno write of "the leveling domination of abstraction" or "the total schematization of man,"[102] we would do well to recognize Kierkegaard's voice, even if Hegel is given the credit.

Adorno's critique of Heidegger, principally his *Jargon of Authenticity* (1964), is unsparing and even intemperate. It is untrue, Adorno states, "that, through Heidegger's admonitions about 'the They,' that social state reprimands grows better." Having referred to "the so-called mass society," Adorno notes that from "the ontological possibility of the inauthenticity of men" it is "only a step to the usual criticism of culture, which self-righteously picks on shallowness, superficiality, and the growth of mass culture."[103] In his *Negative Dialectics* (1966), Adorno grounds his dissatisfaction with this sort of criticism in a thesis that points back to a key term employed by Kierkegaard in *Two Ages*. Adorno points out

> an idea drafted by conservative culture critics in the nineteenth century and popularized since: that the world had become formless. The idea fed on art-historical theses like the one of an extinguished style-building force; originating in aesthetics, it spread as a view of the whole. The basic assumption of the art historians—that this loss is in fact a loss, and not indeed a powerful step toward

---

[100]Theodor W. Adorno, *Kierkegaard: Konstruktion des Ästhetischen* (Frankfurt am Main: Suhrkamp Verlag, 1962) 283.

[101]Max Horkheimer and Theodor W. Adorno, *Dialectic of Enlightenment* (New York: Seabury Press, n.d.) 179.

[102]Ibid., 13, 25.

[103]Theodor W. Adorno, *The Jargon of Authenticity* (Evanston: Northwestern University Press, 1973) 110, 44, 122.

unshackling the productive forces—is by no means established. Esthetically revolutionary theoreticians such as Adolf Loos still dared to say so at the beginning of the century; it has been forgotten only by the frightened culture critics, oathbound since to the existing culture. The lament about the loss of ordering forms increases with their very power.[104]

"What is *formlessness [Formløshed]*?" Kierkegaard asks in *Two Ages*. "It is the annulled passionate distinction between form and content; therefore in contrast to lunacy and stupidity it may contain truth, but the truth it contains can never be essentially true" (TA, 100). For Adorno, the "lament about a world-wide loss of forms" is dangerous because it constitutes a prologue to "the call for a binding order" which, in turn, will draw upon "the bad, coercive side of form." This is not, of course, the danger that preoccupies Kierkegaard; his concern is directed, not at the tyranny of form, but at its dissolution. In this dissolution Adorno sees, not chaos, but "a powerful step toward unshackling the productive forces."[105] He recognizes the reality of "the disintegration of culture and education," but he rejects the cultural conservative's static, undialectical interpretation of decline: "Where there is despair and meaningless misery, he sees only spiritual phenomena, the state of man's consciousness, the decline of norms. By insisting on this, criticism is tempted to forget the unutterable, instead of striving, however impotently, so that man may be spared."[106]

There is a crucial difference between a critique of a culture's aesthetics and a critique of culture from the standpoint of aesthetics. Adorno indicts the latter while practicing the former (for example, his scathing treatment of jazz). But *Two Ages* includes an "aesthetic" critique of culture, not as its foundation, but as a rhetorical instrument, as an accessory to an ethicoreligious argument. Nor is Kierkegaard's judgment of the age undialectical: "the public is the cruel abstraction by which individuals will be religiously educated—or

---

[104]Theodor W. Adorno, *Negative Dialectics* (New York: The Seabury Press, 1979) 94.

[105]Ibid., 94.

[106]Theodor W. Adorno, *Prisms* (London: Neville Spearman, 1967) 127, 19.

be destroyed" (TA, 93). This dialectic, which is presented in several variations in *Two Ages*, is easily drowned out by the (conservative) rhetoric of denunciation.

Like Heidegger, Adorno reacted to Kierkegaard with deep ambivalence. But this ambivalence, born of the difficulties Kierkegaard presents to his inheritors, is a part of the legacy of *Two Ages* and of his authorship as a whole.

Contributors

International Kierkegaard Commentary:
Two Ages
MEROLD WESTPHAL, Volume Consultant

LEE BARRETT is Assistant Professor of Theology at the Presbyterian School of Education.

PATRICIA G. CUTTING is Adjunct Associate Professor at the College of Santa Fe.

JOHN W. ELROD is Professor of Philosophy and Chairman of the Department of Philosophy at Iowa State University.

JOHN M. HOBERMAN is Assistant Professor of Germanic Languages at the University of Texas, Austin

ALAN JANIK is a Fellow of the Center for the Philosophy and History of Science, Boston University.

JACKIE KLEINMAN is a creative writer and Kierkegaard researcher who has taught at the Pontifical College Josephinum.

JAMES L. MARSH is Professor of Philosophy at St. Louis University.

ROBERT L. PERKINS is Professor of Philosophy at the University of South Alabama.

MICHAEL PLEKON is Assistant Professor of Sociology, Baruch College, City University of New York.

ROBERT C. ROBERTS is Associate Professor of Philosophy at Western Kentucky University.

MEROLD WESTPHAL is Professor of Philosophy and Chairman of the Department at Hope College.

Advisory Board

Editor
Robert L. Perkins
University of South Alabama

Advisory Board
John W. Elrod, Iowa State University
Paul Holmer, Yale University
Rex P. Stevens, Mercer University Press

Volume Consultant
Merold Westphal, Hope College

International Advisory Board
Niels Thulstrup, Denmark
Nelly Viallaneix, France
Wolfdietrich von Kloeden, Federal Republic of Germany
J. Heywood Thomas, Great Britain
Cornelio Fabro, Italy
Masaru Otani, Japan
Sixtus W. Scholtens, Netherlands

Index

International Kierkegaard Commentary: Two Ages

Designed by Margaret Jordan Brown

Composition by MUP Composition Department

Production Specifications:
>   text paper—60-pound Warren's Olde Style
>   endpapers—80-pound Warren's Olde Style printed PMS 422
>   cover—(on .088 boards) Kivar 9 Flannel Gray 6-338
>   Firenze finish
>   dust jacket—100-pound enamel, printed three colors
>   (PMS 427 gray, PMS 302 blue, and black), and varnished

Printing (offset lithography) by Omnipress of Macon, Inc.,
>   Macon, Georgia
Binding by John H. Dekker and Sons, Inc.,
>   Grand Rapids, Michigan